T0179212

Prediction and Analysis for Knowledge Representation and Machine Learning

Prediction and Analysis for Knowledge Representation and Machine Learning

Edited by

Avadhesh Kumar
Shrddha Sagar
T. Ganesh Kumar
K. Sampath Kumar
Galgotias University, Greater Noida, Uttar Pradesh

CRC Press
Taylor & Francis Group
Boca Raton London New York

CRC Press is an imprint of the
Taylor & Francis Group, an **informa** business

A CHAPMAN & HALL BOOK

First edition published 2022
by CRC Press
6000 Broken Sound Parkway NW, Suite 300, Boca Raton, FL 33487-2742

and by CRC Press
2 Park Square, Milton Park, Abingdon, Oxon, OX14 4RN

© 2022 selection and editorial matter, Avadhesh Kumar, Shrddha Sagar, T. Ganesh Kumar and K. Sampath Kumar; individual chapters, the contributors

CRC Press is an imprint of Taylor & Francis Group, LLC

Reasonable efforts have been made to publish reliable data and information, but the author and publisher cannot assume responsibility for the validity of all materials or the consequences of their use. The authors and publishers have attempted to trace the copyright holders of all material reproduced in this publication and apologize to copyright holders if permission to publish in this form has not been obtained. If any copyright material has not been acknowledged please write and let us know so we may rectify in any future reprint.

Except as permitted under U.S. Copyright Law, no part of this book may be reprinted, reproduced, transmitted, or utilized in any form by any electronic, mechanical, or other means, now known or hereafter invented, including photocopying, microfilming, and recording, or in any information storage or retrieval system, without written permission from the publishers.

For permission to photocopy or use material electronically from this work, access www.copyright.com or contact the Copyright Clearance Center, Inc. (CCC), 222 Rosewood Drive, Danvers, MA 01923, 978-750-8400. For works that are not available on CCC please contact mpkbookspermissions@tandf.co.uk

Trademark notice: Product or corporate names may be trademarks or registered trademarks and are used only for identification and explanation without intent to infringe.

ISBN: 978-0-367-64910-4 (hbk)
ISBN: 978-0-367-64911-1 (pbk)
ISBN: 978-1-003-12689-8 (ebk)

DOI: 10.1201/9781003126898

Typeset in Palatino
by KnowledgeWorks Global Ltd.

Contents

Preface

One of the domains of artificial intelligence is knowledge representation that focuses on the designing of the computer representation, which acquires information across the world for solving complex problems. Conventional procedural coding cannot justify knowledge representation for solving complex problems. By use of knowledge representation, we can make software more easily, and coding can be done sequentially and can be used in expert systems as well. Practically all languages of knowledge representation include a reasoning or inference engine as part of the system. There are a number of issues that might arise during the implementation of knowledge representation, including primitives, meta-representation, incompleteness, definitions and universals vs. facts and defaults, non-monotonic reasoning, expressive adequacy, reasoning efficiency, and so on. Knowledge representation and reasoning also include knowledge from psychology for solving human problems and helping in the formalization of complex problems for easy designing and building. This book will help researchers and practitioners to understand the structure of knowledge representation using machine learning techniques. As we know, machine learning is very important for precisely predicting future actions, as a number of architectures are designed by using static machine learning algorithms that constantly improve in the due course of time as a huge amount of data are captured and assimilated. This book has gathered some experts in knowledge representation and machine learning from across the world, who have contributed their knowledge in relation to different features of the domain. This book will stimulate the minds of the IT professionals, researchers, and academicians toward knowledge representation and machine learning.

Editor Biographies

Avadhesh Kumar is PVC at Galgotias University, Greater Noida, Uttar Pradesh, India. He has more than 21 years of academic and research experience. He was awarded his Ph.D. in Computer Science and Engineering in 2010 from Thapar University, Patiala, Punjab, India. He did his M.Tech. in Information Technology and B.Tech. in Computer Science and Engineering from Harcourt Butler Technological Institute (HBTI), Kanpur, UP, India. His research areas include software engineering, aspect-oriented software systems, component-based software development, soft computing, and artificial intelligence. He has published more than 30 research papers in reputed journals and conferences. He has authored three books and is a reviewer of many international journals and conferences. He has been a keynote speaker in many international conferences.

Shrddha Sagar is working as an Associate Professor in the School of Computing Science and Engineering, Galgotias University, Delhi-NCR, India. She has completed her Ph.D. in Computer Science from Banasthali University, Jaipur, India. Her main-thrust research areas are artificial intelligence, Internet of Things, machine learning, and big data. She is a pioneering researcher in the areas of artificial intelligence, Internet of Things, and machine learning, and has published more than 25 papers in various national/international journals. She has presented papers at national/international conferences and published book chapters for Taylor & Francis Group (CRC Press) and IGI Global.

Dr T. Ganesh Kumar works as an Associate Professor in the School of Computing Science and Engineering at Galgotias University, Delhi-NCR. He received his M.E. degree in Computer Science and Engineering from Manonmaniam Sundaranar University, Tamil Nadu, India. He completed his full-time Ph.D. degree in Computer Science and Engineering at Manonmaniam Sundaranar University. He was a co-investigator for two Government of India-sponsored projects. He has been published in many reputed international SCI- and Scopus-indexed journals and conferences. He is a reviewer of many reputed journals. He has published five patents in India.

Dr K. Sampath Kumar works as a Professor and the Research Coordinator in the School of Computing Science and Engineering, Galgotias University, Greater Noida, UP, Delhi-NCR, India. He has completed his Ph.D. in Data

Mining from Anna University-Chennai, Tamil Nadu, India and obtained his M.E. from Sathyabama University-Chennai, Tamil Nadu, India. He has over 20 years of teaching and industry experience. His expertise is in big data, cloud computing, IOT, artificial intelligence, and real-time systems. He has published more than 50 research articles in international journals and conferences and has also published five patents (IPR).

Contributors

Shruti Dambhare, Research Scholar, School of Computing Science and Engineering, Galgotias University, Greater Noida, Delhi-NCR, India.

K. Geetha, Former PG Scholar, PSN Engineering College, Tirunelveli, Tamil Nadu, India.

Anitha Julian, Professor, Saveetha Engineering College, Chennai, Tamil Nadu, India.

G. Karthick, Senior Associate, Pearson Educations, India.

Rathi Karuppasamy, Research Scholar, National Engineering College, Kovilpatti, Tamil Nadu, India.

Sandhya Katiyar, Department of Information Technology, Galgotias College of Engineering and Technology, Greater Noida, Delhi-NCR, India.

N. Krishnammal, Research Scholar, Manonmaniam Sundaranar University, Tirunelveli, Tamil Nadu, India.

C. Ramesh Kumar, School of Computing Science and Engineering, Galgotias University, Greater Noida, Delhi-NCR, India.

Sanjay Kumar, School of Computing Science and Engineering, Galgotias University, Greater Noida, Delhi-NCR, India.

G. Muthu Lakshmi, Manonmaniam Sundaranar University, Tirunelveli, Tamil Nadu, India.

R. Manimala, Research Scholar, Manonmaniam Sundaranar University, Tirunelveli, Tamil Nadu, India.

G. Muthulakshmi, Ph.D, Assistant Professor, Manonmaniam Sundaranar University, Tirunelveli, Tirunelveli, Tamil Nadu, India.

N. Partheeban, Professor, School of Computing Science and Engineering, Galgotias University, Greater Noida, Delhi-NCR, India.

R. Suchithra, Computer Science, Jain University (deemed to be university), Bengaluru, Karnataka, India.

Sudha Rajesh, Assistant Professor, B. S. Abdur Rahman Crescent Institute of Science and Technology, Chennai, India.

A. Ramya, Assistant Professor, B. S. Abdur Rahman Crescent Institute of Science and Technology, Chennai, India.

R. Ramyadevi, Assistant Professor, Saveetha Engineering College, Chennai, Tamil Nadu, India.

Priti Rishi, Associate Professor, SRM University, Sonepat, Delhi-NCR, India.

Dr Srinivasan Sriramulu, School of Computing Science and Engineering, Galgotias University, Greater Noida, Delhi-NCR, India.

Varun M. Tayur, Computer Science, Jain University (deemed to be university), Bengaluru, Karnataka, India.

Dr N. Thillaiarasu, ASP/SCIT, Reva University, Rukmini Knowledge Park, Yelehanka, Kattigenahalli, Bangalore, India.

1

Machine Learning

S. Sowmyayani

1.1 Introduction

With the tremendous increase in big data in the last decade, machine learning has become more important for solving problems in areas such as medical diagnosis, video surveillance, stock marketing, forecasting, etc. Machine learning algorithms find natural patterns in the given data that help to make better predictions. They are used for making critical decisions.

This chapter explores the definition of data, feature and its types in machine learning. The algorithms used to extract feature are discussed. The extracted features are then optimized using various filtering methods that are categorized as filter, wrapper, and embedded methods. Further, the performance metrics that are used for the machine learning algorithms are elaborated.

1.2 Data-Driven Models

1.2.1 Feature Space

In machine learning and pattern recognition, a *feature* is an individual measurable property being observed [1]. Choosing informative and independent features is an important task in all algorithms in pattern recognition, classification, and regression. Generally, features are numeric, but structural features are also available which are used in syntactic pattern recognition.

Examples:

- In character recognition, features may be histograms of black pixels counted along horizontal and vertical directions, number of internal holes, stroke detection, etc.
- In speech recognition, features may include noise ratios, length of sounds, relative power, filter matches, and many others.

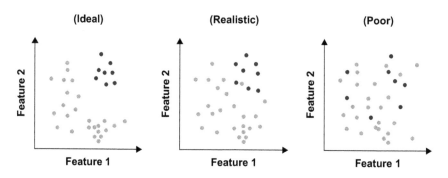

FIGURE 1.1
Feature space with two feature sets

- In computer vision, there are a large number of features such as edges and objects.

A *feature space* is the set of all possible values for a chosen set of features from the given data. The feature space can also be represented as a real space.

Given some labelled data on dogs and non-dogs, identify features and plot then in the feature space. If a perfect clustering of data-points is seen, then the features characterize dogs and non-dogs pretty well. It is conceivable to see some data-points representing cats appearing close to the dog cluster. But it is less conceivable to see data-points of any houses. In this ideal scenario where the data has good features, the ***spatial distance in the feature space is analogous to the conceptual distance*** for the target concept. Figure 1.1 shows three possible feature spaces of differing quality for a concept learning problem with two features.

The left-most feature space in Figure 1.1 depicts the feature space for concept learning. Black data-points belonging to the target concept are separable from the gray data-points which do not. Here, spatial distance corresponds to conceptual distance. This means there exists a perfect characteristic function based on these two features, and hence it is learnable. The middle one shows a more realistic feature space for concept learning. Spatial distance approximately corresponds to conceptual distance and a perfect characteristic function cannot be defined based on these features due to imperfect separation, but approximation to a characteristic function can be learnt with small error. In the rightmost image, it is difficult to approximate a characteristic function with any reasonable amount of error. In this case, the chosen features of the data do not associate spatial distance with conceptual distance.

1.2.2 Feature Extraction

Feature extraction refers to the process of transforming raw data into numerical features that can be processed for further prediction. Features are

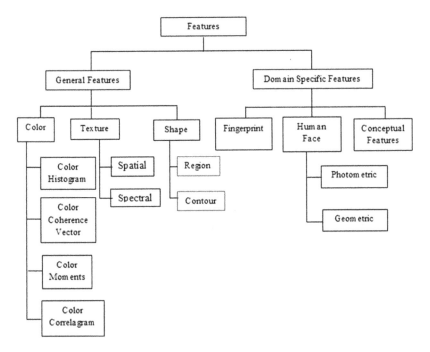

FIGURE 1.2
Feature classification

broadly classified as general features and domain-specific features as shown in Figure 1.2. The former include color, shape, and texture [2] while the latter include application oriented features. Both are broadly classified into 3 categories: Pixel-level features (features are evaluated for every pixel), local features (features are evaluated from the results of image sub-division), and global features (features are evaluated for an image). These features and their properties are shown in Table 1.1.

TABLE 1.1

Features and Their Properties

Feature type	Properties
Color features	RGB, LUV, HSV, HMMD
Texture features	Homogeneity, entropy, contrast, correlation, sum of square
Intensity features	Mean, median, standard deviation, intensity, skewness
Human features	Body shape, size, color, age, gender, height
Finger print features	Arches, loops, whorls
Conceptual features	Generic object knowledge, flexibility, attributes, mutability
Text features	Synonymy, polysemy, circularity, irregularity, area, perimeter, roundness
Shape features	Area, eccentricity, perimeter, diameter, Euler number, orientation, convex area, major axis, minor axis

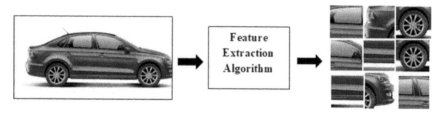

FIGURE 1.3
Features of a single image

Feature extraction can be done manually or automatically:

- In Manual feature extraction, relevant features are identified for a given problem and a method is described to extract those features. For this case, the domain knowledge can help to identify good features.
- Automated feature extraction uses algorithms or deep networks to extract features automatically from data without human intervention. This technique can be very useful when developing machine learning algorithms.

Figure 1.3 shows an example of features that are extracted from a car.

In Figure 1.3, the features of a single car are extracted using a feature extraction algorithm, which produces a vector of 1D array. In Figure 1.3, the features are extracted from just one car. A very important property of a feature is repeatability. Moreover, the feature should be able to detect a car in general not just this specific one. In practice, the feature will not be an exact copy of the piece in the input image. Figure 1.4 shows the difference between features extracted for a wheel from a single bike and multiple bikes.

The feature extraction algorithm should recognize patterns that define wheels in general regardless of where they appear in the image.

Machine learning models extract features as humans do. Extracting good features is a crucial step in building machine learning models. But it is difficult to identify a good feature. A good feature should recognize an object in all the ways it appears. The characteristics of a good feature are: identifiable,

Feature after looking   Feature after looking
at one image   at 1000s of images

FIGURE 1.4
Feature extracted from multiple images

trackable, consistent across various scales, illuminations, and viewing degrees, and finally visible even if the image is noisy or part of an object is not visible.

1.2.2.1 Extracting Features (Handcrafted vs Automated)

There are two types of features that can be extracted: Handcrafted and Automated. This subsection discusses some of the handcrafted features and automated features in detail.

Traditional Machine Learning Uses Handcrafted Features

In traditional machine learning problems, features are selected manually using the domain knowledge and are then fed to a classifier to predict the output. Some of the handcrafted feature sets are:

- Histogram of Oriented Gradients (HOG)
- Scale-Invariant Feature Transform (SIFT)
- Speeded Up Robust Feature (SURF)
- Local Binary Patterns (LBP)
- Local Ternary Patterns (LTP)
- Local Phase Quantization (LPQ)
- Completed Local Binary Patterns (CLBP)

Apart from these features, some objective features like visual texture [3], complexity [4, 5] and colorfulness are shown in Tables 1.2 and 1.3. For Texture features, GLCM (Gray Level Co-occurrence Matrix) is used which is a classic technique used for image texture analysis and classification [6].

Similarly, self-similarity and anisotropy are based on the Pyramid HOG (PHOG) image representation that was originally developed for object recognition and classification [11] and have been used to characterize the aesthetics and liking of images and artworks [8–10, 12]. The PHOG descriptors are global feature vectors based on a pyramidal subdivision of an image into sub-images, for which HOG [13] are computed.

Local colorfulness has been defined as a linear combination of the mean and standard deviation of the local chrominance values in color opponent space [19]. Colorfulness is not strictly related to the numbers of colors. An image can be more colorful even when it contains less different colors [20]. A global image colorfulness was computed as the mean value of the local colorfulness over a set of sub-windows covering the entire image support.

Deep Learning Automatically Extracts Features

In deep learning, the network extracts features automatically and learns the data by applying weights to its connections. The raw image is fed to the

TABLE 1.2

Texture Features

Type	Feature	Definition	Values
Texture (Grayscale)	Entropy	It characterizes the degree of randomness of the input image texture.	Entropy is 0 if all pixels have the same intensity value.
	Power	It is the average of the power spectral density over the image support, computed from the discrete 2D Fourier transform of the image.	It is measured in decibels.
	Contrast	It is the intensity contrast between a pixel and its neighbors averaged over the whole image.	It is equal to 0 for a constant valued image.
	Energy	It is sum of squared elements in the GLCM.	It is equal to 1 for a constant valued image.
	Homogeneity	It is the closeness of the distribution of elements in the GLCM with respect to the GLCM diagonal.	It is equal to 1 for a diagonal GLCM [7].
Texture (Color)	Self-similarity	It is computed using the Histogram Intersection Kernel (HIK) [8] to determine the similarity between HOG features at the individual levels of the PHOG [9–10].	Images of natural patterns typically have a highly self-similar structure, whereas artificial structures typically have a low self-similarity.
	Anisotropy	It describes how the gradient strength varies across the orientations in an image.	Low anisotropy means that the strengths of the orientations are uniform across orientations and high anisotropy means that orientations differ in their overall prominence [9].

network, which then passes it through several layers and identifies patterns within the image to create features. Neural networks can be thought of as combination of feature extractors and classifiers. Figure 1.5 illustrates extraction of features through deep learning.

Neural networks extract all the features and give them random weights. During training, these weights are adjusted to predict the output. The patterns would have higher weights with the highest appearance frequency, and more useful features are used further. The lowest weight features will have a very low impact on the output.

TABLE 1.3

Complexity and Colorfulness Features

Type	Feature	Definition	Values
Complexity	Compression Ratio	It is a measure that is positively correlated with image complexity [5]. The file size of a digitized image is a measure of its structural information [14].	As compression algorithms use image redundancy to reduce the file size, the more complex images need more elements.
	Feature Congestion (FC)	It is calculated as a weighted average of the local feature, contrast covariance over multiple spatial scales [15].	The larger the FC values, the higher the visual clutter.
	Subband Entropy	It encodes the image information. It is computed as a weighted sum of the entropies of the luminance and chrominance image subbands [15].	The larger the SE values, the higher the visual clutter.
	Number of Proto-Objects (NPO)	Number of image segments or super-pixels with similar intensity, color and gradient orientation features [16].	Larger NPO values correspond to higher levels of visual clutter.
	Mean Information Gain (MIG)	It is the difference between the spatial heterogeneity and the non-spatial heterogeneity of an image [17–18]. The MIG accounts for the inherent spatial correlations.	The MIG ranges over 0–1: MIG = 0 for uniform patterns and MIG = 1 for random patterns.
	Mean Gradient Strength	It is a subjectively perceived level of image complexity [9].	It increases with its number of edges.
Color	Number of Colors	Number of distinct colors in the RGB image.	
	Colorfulness	The sensation that an image appears to be more or less chromatic.	It varies from 0 (grayscale image) to 1 (most colorful image).

1.2.3 Feature Filtering

In machine learning, feature filtering is the process of selecting only relevant features for a particular application. This method is mainly used to simplify models, reduce training times, variance etc. [21, 22]. The feature selection technique removes features that are redundant or irrelevant without much loss of information [22]. A relevant feature may be redundant by another relevant feature [23]. Feature extraction is different from feature selection [24]. The former creates new features while the latter selects only subset of it.

A feature selection algorithm is used for selecting feature subsets using search technique. It gives scores for different feature subsets. One easy

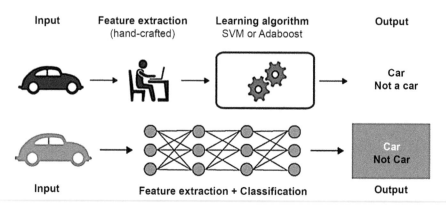

FIGURE 1.5
Handcrafted and deep feature extraction

method is to test all possible subset and find the one which has minimum error rate.

Subset Selection

The most popular subset selection algorithm is greedy hill climbing, which selects relevant features from the candidate set and modifies the old subset with the new. It uses a score for identifying the best subset. An exhaustive search defined with a stopping point is used for selecting the satisfactory feature subset. The stopping criterion is defined by a threshold or the program's maximum allowed run time or any other algorithms.

Some search algorithms find low-dimensional projections of the data that score highly. The features with largest projections in the lower-dimensional space are selected. Other search algorithms include: best fit, genetic algorithm [25], greedy forward selection [26–28], greedy backward elimination, particle swarm optimization [29], scatter search [30], and variable neighborhood search [31–32].

There are two filter measures for classification problems. They are correlation and mutual information. These metrics are considered as scores which are computed between a candidate set and the desired output. Other filter metrics are: class separability, consistency-based feature selection, and correlation-based feature selection. The class separability is further divided into error probability, inter-class distance, probabilistic distance, and entropy.

The optimality criteria are difficult to choose as there may be multiple objectives. The most common criteria include accuracy which is corrected by the number of features selected. Examples include Bonferroni/RIC, maximum dependency feature selection, Akaike information criterion (AIC) [33–34], Bayesian information criterion (BIC), minimum description length (MDL), Mallows's Cp, false discovery rate (FDR), and maximum entropy rate [35].

1.2.3.1 Feature Selection Method Based on Mutual Information

There are many feature selection algorithms that use mutual information as scores for selecting features [36]. One such algorithm is minimum-redundancy-maximum-relevance (mRMR) algorithm which is discussed here.

The mRMR Algorithm

This method uses either mutual information, correlation or similarity scores to select features [37]. It is defined by relevance and redundancy. For a feature set S, the relevance is defined by the average of all mutual information between the individual feature f_i and the class c. The redundancy of all features in the set S is the average value of all mutual information values between the feature f_i and the feature f_j:

The mRMR criterion is a combination of two measures given above and is defined as follows:

$$\text{mRMR} = \max_S \left[\frac{1}{|S|} \sum_{f_i \in S} I(f_i;c) - \frac{1}{|S|^2} \sum_{f_i,f_j \in S} I(f_i;f_j) \right] \quad (1.1)$$

It underestimates the utility of features in some cases, as it has no way to quantify interactions between features that can increase relevance. Sometimes individual features are useless but are useful when combined. This algorithm balances between relevancy and redundancy in different ways [36–38].

Another drawback is that once a feature is selected, it cannot be deselected later.

The next score derived for the mutual information is based on the conditional relevancy. It is given as

$$\text{SPEC}_{\text{CMI}} : \max_{\mathbf{x}} \{\mathbf{x}^T Q\mathbf{x}\} \quad \text{s.t.} \ \|\mathbf{x}\| = 1, x_i \geq 0 \quad (1.2)$$

where $Q_{ii} = I(f_i;c)$ and $Q_{ij} = I(f_i;c \mid f_j), i \neq j$. The SPEC$_{\text{CMI}}$ can be solved using the dominant eigenvector of Q, and hence is very scalable. It also handles second-order feature interaction.

Brown et al. [36] uses joint mutual information [39] as a score for feature selection. This score finds the feature and adds to the already selected features, in order to avoid redundancy. The score is formulated as follows:

$$\text{JMI}(f_i) = \sum_{f_j \in S} \left(I(f_i;c) + I(f_i;c \mid f_j) \right) = \sum_{f_j \in S} \left[I(f_i;c) + I(f_i;c) - \left(I(f_i;f_j) - I(f_i;f_j \mid c) \right) \right]$$

$$(1.3)$$

The score uses the conditional mutual information and the mutual information to find the redundancy between the selected features $(f_j \in S)$ and the feature under investigation f_i.

1.2.3.2 Hilbert-Schmidt Independence Criterion (HSIC) Feature Selection

If the data is high-dimensional and it has small samples, the HSIC lasso can be used [40]. HSIC lasso optimization problem is given as

$$\text{HSIC}_{\text{Lasoo}} : \min_x \frac{1}{2} \sum_{k,i=1}^{n} x_k x_l \text{HSIC}(f_k, f_l) - \sum_{k=1}^{n} x_k \text{HSIC}(f_k, c) + \lambda \|\mathbf{x}\|_1, \quad \text{s.t. } x_1, \ldots, x_n \geq 0$$

(1.4)

where $\text{HSIC}(f_k, c) = \text{tr}\left(\overline{\mathbf{K}}^{(k)} \overline{\mathbf{L}}\right)$ is a kernel-based independence measure, $\text{tr}(\cdot)$ denotes the trace, λ is the regularization parameter, $\overline{\mathbf{K}}^{(k)} = \mathbf{\Gamma} \mathbf{K}^{(k)} \mathbf{\Gamma}$ and $\overline{\mathbf{L}} = \mathbf{\Gamma} \mathbf{L} \mathbf{\Gamma}$ are input and output centered Gram matrices, $K_{i,j}^{(k)} = K\left(u_{k,i}, u_{k,j}\right)$ and $L_{i,j} = L\left(c_i, c_j\right)$ are Gram matrices, $K(u, u')$ and $L(c, c')$ are kernel functions, $\mathbf{\Gamma} = \mathbf{I}_m - \frac{1}{m} \mathbf{1}_m \mathbf{1}_m^T$ is the centering matrix, $\mathbf{I}_m$ is the m-dimensional identity matrix (m is the number of samples), $\mathbf{1}_m$ is the m-dimensional vector with all ones, and $\|\cdot\|_1$ is the ℓ_1-norm.

The HSIC lasso can be written as

$$\text{HSIC}_{\text{Lasso}} : \min_x \frac{1}{2} \left\| \overline{\mathbf{L}} - \sum_{k=1}^{n} x_k \overline{\mathbf{K}}^{(k)} \right\|_F^2 + \lambda \|\mathbf{x}\|_1, \quad \text{s.t. } x_1, \ldots, x_n \geq 0 \qquad (1.5)$$

where $\|\cdot\|_F$ is the Frobenius norm.

1.2.3.3 Feature Selection Based on Correlation

The correlation feature selection (CFS) measure selects features that are highly correlated with the classification [41–42]. It is calculated using merit. The merit of a feature subset S consisting of k features is given as:

$$\text{Merit}_{S_k} = \frac{k \overline{r_{cf}}}{\sqrt{k + k(k-1)\overline{r_{ff}}}} \qquad (1.6)$$

where, $\overline{r_{cf}}$ is the average of all feature-classification correlations, and $\overline{r_{ff}}$ is the average of all feature-feature correlations. Then the CFS is defined as:

$$\text{CFS} = \max_{S_k} \left[\frac{r_{cf_1} + r_{cf_2} + \cdots + \tau_{cf_k}}{\sqrt{k + 2\left(r_{f_1 f_2} + \cdots + r_{f_i f_j} + \cdots + r_{f_k f_{k-1}}\right)}} \right] \qquad (1.7)$$

The r_{cf_i} and $r_{f_i f_j}$ variables are referred to as correlations.

FIGURE 1.6
Filter method

1.2.3.4 *Feature Selection Methods Based on Combination of Models*

The feature selection methods are classified as: wrappers, filters, and embedded methods based on how they combine the feature selection method and the model.

Filter Method

Filter methods select features regardless of what model is used. They are based on the correlation among features and suppress the non-relevant features. The remaining features are used to classify the data for classification or regression model. These methods are extensive to computation and are robust to overfitting [43]. Some features remove variables highly correlated to each other. Figure 1.6 shows this method. The filter methods use mutual information, pointwise mutual information [44], relief-based algorithms [45], and Pearson product-moment correlation coefficient as a measure.

Wrapper Method

Wrapper methods use a predictive model for scoring. Each subset is trained using a model, which is tested on a hold-out set. The number of errors made on that hold-out set is the score for that subset. Figure 1.7 illustrates the wrapper method.

Wrapper methods evaluate subsets of variables that detect the possible interactions between variables [46].

Embedded Method

The embedded method is a combination of both filter and wrapper methods. This method uses its own variable selection process and performs feature selection and classification simultaneously. The most popular embedded method is the LASSO method. Bolasso is one of the variations of the LASSO method which bootstraps samples [47]. Elastic net regularization is one of the

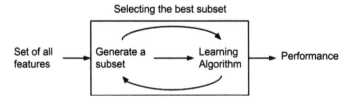

FIGURE 1.7
Wrapper method

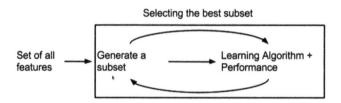

FIGURE 1.8
Embedded method

embedded LASSO methods which combines the L1 penalty of the LASSO method and the L2 penalty of the ridge regression method. FeaLect is another embedded LASSO method that gives scores to all the features based on combinatorial analysis of regression coefficients [48]. The auto-encoders feature selection (AEFS) method is also an embedded LASSO method that further extends LASSO to nonlinear scenario with auto-encoders [49]. Figure 1.8 shows the embedded method for feature selection. Table 1.4 shows the differences and examples between these methods.

1.3 Generalization Performance

1.3.1 Computational Complexity

In this section, the computational power of deep learning is discussed in various domains such as image classification, object detection, question answering, named entity recognition and machine translation. The computational requirements have increased rapidly in each of these domains which automatically increase its performance. If this progress continues,

TABLE 1.4

Filter, Wrapper, and Embedded Methods

Method	Computational Complexity	Drawback	Examples
Filter	Less computationally expensive than wrappers	Produces a feature set that is not fitted to a specific model [50]	Information gain, chi-square test, fisher score, correlation coefficient, variance threshold
Wrapper	High computation time if the number of variables increases	Increases overfitting risk when the number of observations is insufficient	Sequential feature selection, genetic algorithms, recursive feature elimination algorithm [51]
Embedded	Lies between filters and wrappers		LASSO, stepwise regression

the computational requirements will rapidly increase both technically and economically. Thus, this analysis suggests that deep learning progress will either be conditionally stopped by its computational requirements or it can increase the efficiency of deep learning.

It is found that the computational complexity of deep learning models is increasing. The relationship between performance, model complexity, and computational requirements of deep learning is still unclear. But still deep learning is more reliant on computing power than other techniques. The growing computational requirement of deep learning is discussed further.

Early Days

In 1960, Frank Rosenblatt found that a three-layer neural network ran a long way toward the feasibility of a perceptron as a pattern-recognizing device. But, Rosenblatt already recognized if the number of connections in the network increases, the burden on a conventional digital computer increases [52]. Later in 1969, Minsky and Papert solved this problem by introducing deeper neural networks [53].

In the next decade, neural networks grew their computational requirements proportionally, as shown in Figure 1.9(a). Hence, deep learning models in 2009 remained too slow for large-scale applications, which made researchers use small-scale models or use fewer samples [54].

The sudden change appears when deep learning began to use GPUs, which yielded a 5 – 15 times speed-up. In 2012, this had grown to more than 35 times speed up [55] which led to the inventory of AlexNet model [56–57]. The implementation of GPU-based deep learning has contributed to these systems being widely adopted. But from 2012 to 2019, the amount of computing power grew much faster, at around 10 times per year [58]. This rate is faster than the 35 times total improvement from moving to GPUs.

The increase arises from a less economically attractive source, i.e., when running models for more time on more machines. For example, in 2012 AlexNet was trained using 2 GPUs for 5 to 6 days [59], in 2017 ResNeXt-101 [60] was trained with 8 GPUs for over 10 days, and in 2019 NoisyStudent was trained with ≈1,000 TPUs for 6 days [59]. Another extreme example is the machine translation system, "Evolved Transformer," which used more than 2 million GPU hours and cost millions of dollars to execute [61].

Present Day

To examine the computation time of deep learning, research domains such as image classification (ImageNet benchmark), object detection, question answering, named-entity recognition, and machine translation are examined.

Two separate analyses of computational requirements are discussed reflecting the two types of information: (1) Computation per network pass (the number of floating point operations required for a single pass in the network, also measurable using multiply-adds or the number of parameters in the model) and (2) Hardware burden (the computational capability of the hardware used

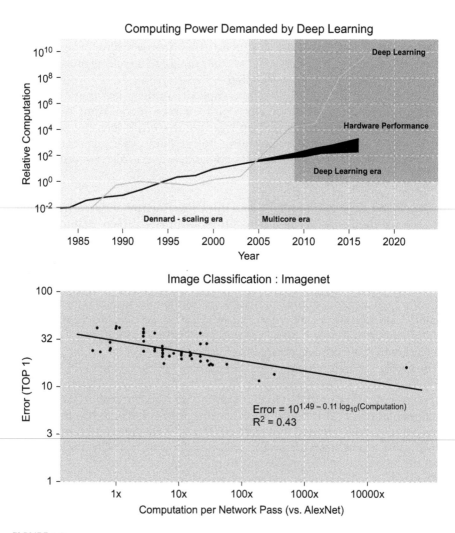

FIGURE 1.9
Computing power used in: (a) deep learning models of all types (b) image classification models
tested on the ImageNet benchmark (normalized to the 2012 AlexNet model)

to train the model, calculated as #processors × ComputationRate × time). The
analysis is done in image classification as it contains more data and history
using the performance metric classification error rate.

Figure 1.9 (b) shows the fall in error rate in image recognition on the
ImageNet dataset and its correlation with the computational requirements
of those models. Each data-point indicates a state-of-the-art deep learning
model. As it is plotted on a log-log scale, a straight line indicates a polynomial growth in computing per unit of performance. Computational power
is not only a highly statistically important output indicator, but it also has

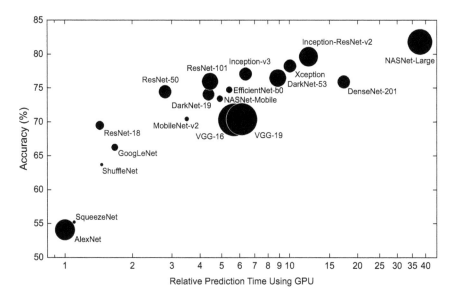

FIGURE 1.10
Performance of Various Deep Learning Models

strong explanatory strength, explaining 43 percent of the ImageNet output variance. Figure 1.10 shows the performance graph of various deep learning models.

Development in training models depends on a significant increase in the amount of computational power being used in deep learning. A dependency on computational power to boost efficiency is not exclusive to deep learning, but has also been seen in other fields, such as weather prediction and oil exploration [61]. But in those areas, as may be a problem for deep learning, the cost of systems has increased tremendously, with many cutting-edge models now being run on some of the world's largest computer systems.

Future

In this section, to understand the estimated computational power required to hit various benchmarks, projections from each domain are extrapolated. In order to make these goals concrete, they are described not only in terms of the necessary computational capacity, but also in terms of the economic and environmental costs of training such models on current hardware. Because the polynomial and exponential functional forms have roughly equivalent statistical fits, both are reported in Table 1.5.

Table 1.5 shows that the hardware, environmental, and economic costs are very high. To improve the performance and to achieve the target, some efforts have been made, but this still increases other costs. From Table 1.5, it is clear that additional 10^5 times more computing is needed to get an error rate of 5% for ImageNet. To improve this further, additional hardware, more

TABLE 1.5

Performance Benchmarks on the Computation from Deep Learning Based on Projections from Polynomial and Exponential Models

Benchmark	Error Rate (%)	Polynomial			Exponential		
		Computation Required (Gflops)	Environment Cost (CO_2)	Economic Cost ($)	Computation Required (Gflops)	Environment Cost (CO_2)	Economic Cost ($)
ImageNet*	Today 11.5	10^{14}	10^6	10^6	10^{14}	10^6	10^6
	Target 1:5	10^{19}	10^{10}	10^{11}	10^{27}	10^{19}	10^{19}
	Target 2:1	10^{28}	10^{20}	10^{20}	10^{120}	10^{112}	10^{112}
MS COCO*	Today 11.5	10^{14}	10^6	10^6	10^{15}	10^7	10^7
	Target 1:5	10^{23}	10^{14}	10^{15}	10^{29}	10^{21}	10^{21}
	Target 2:1	10^{44}	10^{36}	10^{36}	10^{107}	10^{99}	10^{99}
SQuAD 1.1*	Today 11.5	10^{13}	10^4	10^5	10^{13}	10^5	10^5
	Target 1:5	10^{15}	10^7	10^7	10^{23}	10^{15}	10^{15}
	Target 2:1	10^{18}	10^{10}	10^{10}	10^{40}	10^{32}	10^{32}
CoLLN 2003*	Today 11.5	10^{13}	10^5	10^5	10^{13}	10^5	10^5
	Target 1:5	10^{43}	10^{35}	10^{35}	10^{82}	10^{73}	10^{74}
	Target 2:1	10^{61}	10^{53}	10^{53}	10^{181}	10^{173}	10^{173}
WMT 2014 (EN – FR)*	Today 11.5	10^{12}	10^4	10^{14}	10^{12}	10^4	10^4
	Target 1:5	10^{23}	10^{15}	10^{15}	10^{30}	10^{22}	10^{22}
	Target 2:1	10^{43}	10^{35}	10^{35}	10^{107}	10^{99}	10^{100}

*ImageNet – Image Classification, MS COCO – Object Detection, SQuAD – Question Answering, CoLLN – Named Entity Recognition, WMT – Machine Translation

efficient algorithms, or other improvements are required. The rapid growth in computing requirements in Table 1.5 shows that deep learning will not achieve performance targets. Hence, fundamental rearchitecting is necessary to reduce this computational burden. But this could be a challenging task. The lower computational burden of flexible models is $O(\text{Performance}^4)$, which is much better than current deep learning methods.

1.3.2 Vapnik-Chervonenkis (VC) Dimension

The classifier classifies the data according to the algorithm given. The algorithm efficiency depends on the kind and size of the data used for it. It differs between classifiers. So, before using a classifier, it is necessary to know what kind of data the classifier classifies. This can be answered using a classifier's VC dimension, which formally quantifies the power of a classification algorithm.

The VC dimension of a classifier is defined as the size of the largest set of points that the classification algorithm can shatter [62].

In a plane with N points, the classifier must be able to shatter a *single* configuration of N points. For every possible assignment of classes, the classifier must be able to perfectly partition the plane such that the classes are separated exactly. For example if there are N points, there are 2^N possible assignments of 2 classes, so the classifier must be able to properly separate the points in each of these.

In Figure 1.11 (a), the VC dimension for this classifier is *at least* 3, as it can shatter 3 points. In each of the $2^3 = 8$ possible assignment of positive and negative classes, the classifier is able to perfectly separate the two classes.

If linear classifier is lower than 4, it is unable to segment the positive and negative classes in at least one assignment. Two lines would be necessary to separate the two classes in this situation (see Figure 1.11 (b)).

It is proved that the linear classifier's VC dimension is *at least* 3, and *lower than* 4. Hence it is concluded that its VC dimension is *exactly* 3. If the VC dimension is N, then the classifier shatter *a single* configuration of N points.

1.3.3 No-Free-Lunch Theorem

The "No Free Lunch" theorem states that for every problem there is no one model that fits best. Also, a good model for one problem often does not hold for another problem, so trying different models and finding one that works better for a specific problem is common in machine learning. This is called as unsupervised learning.

In order to find the best model, validation or cross-validation is widely used to determine the predictive performance of several models of varying complexity. Multiple algorithms may also train a model that works well. For example, linear regression could be trained by normal equations or gradient descent.

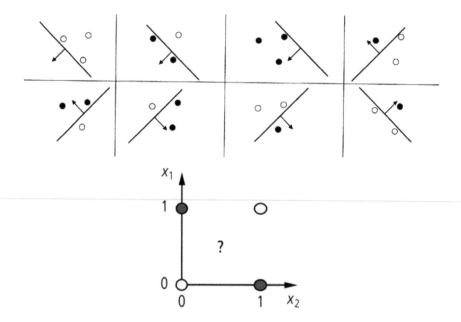

FIGURE 1.11
(a) VC dimension of a linear classifier with 3 points of 2 classes (b) VC dimension of a linear classifier with 4 points of 2 classes

Depending on the problem, it is important to analyze the trade-offs between speed, accuracy and complexity of different models and algorithms and find a model that works best for that particular problem. The computational cost of finding a solution, averaged over all problems in the class, is the same for any method.

1.3.4 Ensembles Learning

Ensemble learning combines multiple weak models to solve the same problem to obtain better results. When weak learners are combined correctly, it may increase performance.

Single Weak Learner

Choosing good model is very important in machine learning to obtain better results for classification or regression. The model is selected based on quantity of data, application specific features, dimensionality of the data and distribution hypothesis. It is proved that a low bias and a low variance are the most important factors for selecting a model. Both differ in opposite directions. Also, the model should have enough degrees of freedom. But, more degrees of freedom results in high variance and low bias. This is called as bias-variance tradeoff which is shown in Figure 1.12.

In ensemble learning, weak learners (or base models) are the basic building blocks for designing any model. These models do not perform well

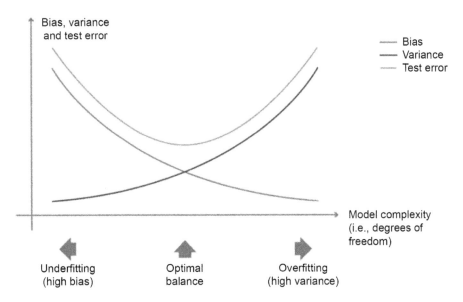

FIGURE 1.12
Bias vs. variance

individually due to high bias or high variance. The ensemble methods combine weak learners by reducing bias and/or variance of and create a strong learner that improves performances.

Combining Weak Learners

As discussed earlier, the ensemble learning combines weak models or base models. There are two types of ensemble models based on combinations of base models: homogeneous ensembles and heterogeneous ensembles. If a single base model trained in different ways is combined, it is a homogeneous ensembles model. If different types of base models are combined, this is called a heterogeneous ensembles model.

If the base models are chosen with low bias and high variance, then the aggregated model should reduce variance. Similarly, if base models with low variance and high bias are selected, it should reduce bias.

There are three kinds of algorithms that aim at combining weak learners: bagging, boosting, and stacking. The first two algorithms use homogeneous weak learners while the third uses heterogeneous weak learners. Bagging and boosting differs in the way they combine the weak learners. The former combines sequentially while the latter combines them parallel. The stacking method combines the weak learners parallel by training a meta-model to output a prediction. The bagging method tries to reduce variance whereas boosting and stacking will try to reduce bias.

In the subsections, bagging, bootstrapping, bagging and random forests, two most popular variants of boosting such as adaptive boosting (adaboost) and gradient boosting are discussed. Finally in the last subsection, an overview of stacking is focused.

1.3.4.1 Bagging

The most popular method of bagging is bootstrapping, which is discussed in this subsection.

Bootstrapping

This method creates an ensemble model that is more robust than the basic models. It generates observations (also called bootstrap samples) of size B from the input dataset of size N by replacing B observations which is shown in Figure 1.13.

This method has good statistical properties. It acts as a representative and independent sample of the true distribution of data. There are two things to be considered. First, the size of the initial dataset should be large enough to make sampling from the dataset a good approximation of the entire dataset, which is known as representativity. Second, relative to the size of the bootstrap samples, the size of the selected samples should be large enough so that the samples do not overlap too much, which is called independence.

Bootstrap samples are also used to evaluate the statistical estimator, which is a function of some observations. So, a random variable is used with variance coming from these observations. It is important to test on several samples taken from the data to estimate the variance of such an estimator. If only truly independent samples are considered, it would require too much data compared to the amount actually available. Then bootstrapping generates several almost-representative and almost-independent bootstrap samples, which allow the variance of the estimator to be approximated by evaluating its value for each of them.

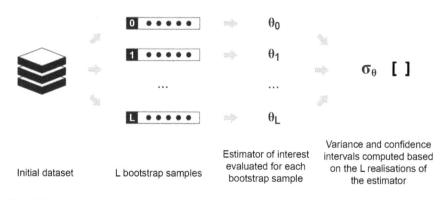

| Initial dataset | L bootstrap samples | Estimator of interest evaluated for each bootstrap sample | Variance and confidence intervals computed based on the L realisations of the estimator |

FIGURE 1.13
Bootstrapping process

Explanation on Bagging

When training a model, it returns an output based on the training dataset for the given input. Even when the model is designed, it is subject to variability, i.e., if another dataset is used, the model should be designed again.

The bagging method combines several independent models by averaging their predictions to reduce variance. If fully independent models are used, it would require too much data. Hence, a good approximation of bootstrap samples is used to fit models that are almost independent.

First, several bootstrap samples are generated such that each new bootstrap sample functions as a separate dataset derived from the true distribution. For each of these samples, a weak learner is then fit and eventually aggregates them and averages their outputs. Thus, an ensemble model is obtained with less variance. So, L bootstrap samples of size B are denoted as

$$\left\{z_1^1, z_2^1, \ldots, z_B^1\right\}, \left\{z_1^2, z_2^2, \ldots, z_B^2\right\}, \ldots, \left\{z_1^L, z_2^L, \ldots, z_B^L\right\}$$

$$z_b^l \equiv b - \text{th observation of the } l \text{-th bootstrap sample}$$

(1.8)

Here, all independent weak learners are fitted.

$$w_1(.), w_2(.), \ldots, w_L(.)$$

(1.9)

Then those are aggregated using averaging process to obtain an ensemble model with a lower variance. For example, a strong model can be defined as

$$s_L(.) = \frac{1}{L} \sum_{l=1}^{L} w_l(.) \qquad (\textit{simple average, for regression problem})$$

$$s_L(.) = \arg\max_k \left[\text{card}\left(l \mid w_l(.) = k\right) \right] \quad (\textit{simple majority vote, for classification problem})$$

(1.10)

For regression, the outputs of individual models are averaged to obtain the output of the ensemble model. In classification, the class predicted by each model is given a vote and the class that has the majority of the votes is selected. This is called hard-voting. In soft voting, the probabilities of each class returned by all the models are obtained which is averaged and then the class with the highest average probability is selected. Both types can be either simple or weighted. It is illustrated in Figure 1.14.

Random Forests

Random forest is one of the bagging methods. Learning trees are the base models of ensemble methods. Strong learners are composed of multiple trees which are called "forests." A forest can be shallow (few depths) or deep (many depths). The former have less variance and high bias while the latter have low bias and high variance.

Knowledge Representation and Machine Learning

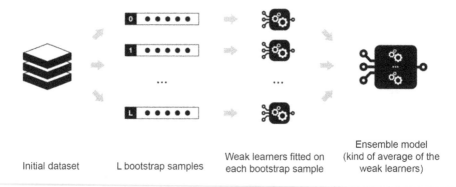

Initial dataset   L bootstrap samples   Weak learners fitted on   Ensemble model
                                                      each bootstrap sample   (kind of average of the
                                                                                     weak learners)

FIGURE 1.14
Bagging process

The random forest method reduces variance by combining deep trees to produce an output. It also makes the multiple fitted trees a bit less correlated with each other. Features are sampled when growing each tree to produce a bootstrap sample and then a subset is selected randomly to create the tree. The random forest method is shown in Figure 1.15.

The advantages of this method are:

- Not all trees have the same data to make their decision which decreases the similarity between the different outputs.
- It makes missing data more robust in the decision-making process.

It is still possible to regress or classify observations with missing data based on trees, using features where data is not missing. Thus, to construct more robust models, the random forest algorithm uses the bagging method and random feature subspace selection.

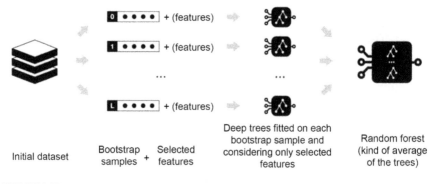

Initial dataset   Bootstrap   Selected   Deep trees fitted on each   Random forest
                         samples +   features   bootstrap sample and   (kind of average
                                                        considering only selected   of the trees)
                                                        features

FIGURE 1.15
Random forest method

1.3.4.2 Focus on Boosting

The weak models are no longer combined separately from one another in sequential methods. They are iteratively fitted by the seeing the previously fitted models. Boosting is an ensemble model which produces a model with less bias than the weak learners that compose it. The boosting method is shown in Figure 1.16.

Boosting methods work similarly to bagging methods, but it reduces variance. Boosting combines multiple weak learners sequentially. Each new model is fitted by observing difficulties in the previous models in the sequence. Finally, a strong learner with lower bias is obtained.

As the weak learners are less computationally expensive, these are combined. As computations to fit the different models can't be done in parallel, they are ideally fitted sequentially. But this is too expensive. So after choosing weak learners, they are fitted sequentially and aggregated using two important boosting algorithms: adaboost and gradient boosting.

Adaptive boosting or adaboost updates the weights attached to each of the training dataset whereas gradient boosting updates the value of these observations. The way both methods try to solve the optimization problem differentiates both of them.

Adaptive Boosting

In adaptive boosting (often called "adaboost"), the ensemble models are defined as a weighted sum of L weak learners

$$s_L(.) = \sum_{l=1}^{L} c_l \times w_l(.) \tag{1.11}$$

where c_l's are coefficients and w_l's are weak learners.

It is difficult to find the best ensemble model with this form. An iterative optimization process is used to solve this problem which leads to a

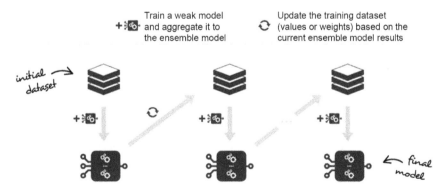

FIGURE 1.16
Boosting method

sub-optimal solution. In adaptive boosting, the weak learners are added sequentially by looking each iteration for the best possible pair to add to the current ensemble model. The $(s_l)'$ is defined such that

$$s_l(.) = s_{l-1}(.) + c_l \times w_l(.) \tag{1.12}$$

where c_l and w_l are chosen pair such that s_l is the model that fits the best. Hence, the best possible improvement over s_{l-1} can be written as

$$(c_l, w_l(.)) = \arg\min_{c,w(.)} E\left(s_{l-1}(.) + c \times w(.)\right) = \arg\min_{c,w(.)} \sum_{n=1}^{N} e\left(y_n, s_{l-1}(x_n) + c \times w(x_n)\right)$$
$$\tag{1.13}$$

where E is the fitting error and e is the error. The optimum is approximated by optimizing and adding the weak learners locally to the strong model instead of optimizing globally over all the L models in the sum.

The performance of a weak learner depends on the contribution to the strong learner. The adaptive boosting is shown in Figure 1.17.

Gradient Boosting

In gradient boosting, the ensemble model is built by the weighted sum of weak learners

$$s_l(.) = s_{l-1}(.) + c_l \times w_l(.) \tag{1.14}$$

where c_l's are coefficients and w_l's are weak learners.

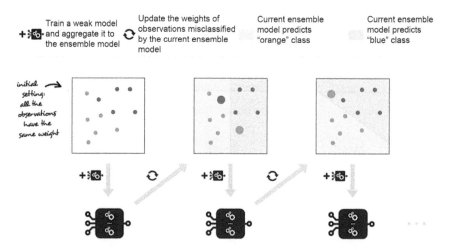

FIGURE 1.17
Adaptive boosting

Like adaboost, finding the optimal model is too difficult and an iterative approach is used to solve it. This method uses sequential optimization process. It casts the problem into a gradient descent one. At each iteration, a weak learner is fitted to the opposite of the gradient of the current fitting error with respect to the current ensemble model. The gradient descent process over the ensemble model can be written as

$$s_l(.) = s_{l-1}(.) - c_l \times \nabla_{s_{l-1}} E(s_{l-1})(.) \qquad (1.15)$$

where E is the fitting error of the given model, c_l is a coefficient corresponding to the step size and

$$-\nabla_{s_{l-1}} E(s_{l-1})(.) \qquad (1.16)$$

is the inverse of the gradient of the fitting error. The opposite of the gradient is tested in the training dataset for observations. These evaluations are called pseudo-residuals which are attached to each observation. A new instance of the weak model is added even if the values of these pseudo-residuals are already known. So, the weak learners are fitted to the pseudo-residuals computed for each observation. Finally, the coefficient c_l is computed following a one dimensional optimization process. The gradient boosting is shown in Figure 1.18.

Initially, the pseudo-residuals are set to observation values. Then the following steps are repeated for L times (L models of the sequence):

- Fit the best possible weak learner to pseudo-residuals.
- Compute the optimal step size for updating the ensemble model in the direction of the new weak learner.
- Update the model by adding the step size obtained in the previous step.
- Compute new pseudo-residuals.

By repeating these steps, the L models are built sequentially and aggregated using gradient descent approach. While adaptive boosting uses local optimization problem, gradient boosting uses a gradient descent approach. Thus, gradient boosting is a general form of adaboost method.

1.3.4.3 Stacking

Stacking combines different types of weak learners using a meta-model, whereas bagging and boosting combine weak learners. There are two things to build the stacking model: the L learners to be fit and the meta-model that combines them.

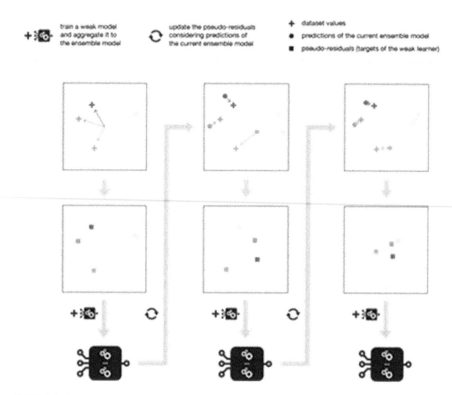

FIGURE 1.18
Gradient boosting

The stacking ensemble model is designed based on the following steps:

- Initially, the training data is split into two folds
- The weak learners are chosen and fitted to data in the first fold
- For each weak learner, the output is predicted for data in the second fold
- Meta-model is fitted for the second fold using predictions made by the weak learners

The purpose of splitting the dataset in two parts is that the first part is used for the training of the weak learners and the second part is used for the training of the meta-model. The drawback of this split is that only half of the data is used to train the base models and the remaining half is used to train the meta-model. This is solved using the "k-fold cross-training" approach such that all the observations can be used to train the meta-model. For k^{th} fold observation, the prediction is done with weak learners trained on the k-1 folds that do not contain the kth fold observation. The stacking method is shown in Figure 1.19.

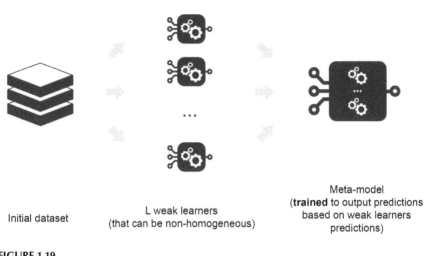

Initial dataset

L weak learners
(that can be non-homogeneous)

Meta-model
(**trained** to output predictions
based on weak learners
predictions)

FIGURE 1.19
Stacking method.

1.4 Conclusion

This chapter gives a study of recent techniques that are used in many researches. More specifically, analysis of big data is studied from scratch. The workflow of many algorithms starts with identifying features, followed by feature extraction, feature filtering, and finally performance evaluation. All the above methods are discussed elaborately with their types.

References

[1] Bishop, Christopher M. *Pattern recognition and machine learning*. Springer, 2006.
[2] Shih, Timothy K., Jiung-Yao Huang, Ching-Sheng Wang, Jason C. Hung, and Chuan-Ho Kao. "An intelligent content-based image retrieval system based on color, shape and spatial relations." Proceedings-National Science Council Republic of China, Part A Physical Science and Engineering 25, no. 4 (2001): 232–243.
[3] Lucassen, Marcel P., Theo Gevers, and Arjan Gijsenij. "Texture affects color emotion." Color Research & Application 36, no. 6 (2011): 426–436.
[4] Forsythe, Alex, Marcos Nadal, Noel Sheehy, Camilo J. Cela-Conde, and Martin Sawey. "Predicting beauty: fractal dimension and visual complexity in art." British Journal of Psychology 102, no. 1 (2011): 49–70.
[5] Marin, Manuela M., and Helmut Leder. "Examining complexity across domains: relating subjective and objective measures of affective environmental scenes, paintings and music." PloS One 8, no. 8 (2013): e72412.

[6] Haralick, Robert M., Karthikeyan Shanmugam, and Its' Hak Dinstein. "Textural features for image classification." IEEE Transactions on Systems, Man, and Cybernetics 6 (1973): 610–621.

[7] Corchs, Silvia Elena, Gianluigi Ciocca, Emanuela Bricolo, and Francesca Gasparini. "Predicting complexity perception of real world images." PloS One 11, no. 6 (2016): e0157986.

[8] Barla, Annalisa, Emanuele Franceschi, Francesca Odone, and Alessandro Verri. "Image kernels." In International Workshop on Support Vector Machines, pp. 83–96. 2002. Springer, Berlin, Heidelberg.

[9] Redies, Christoph, Seyed Ali Amirshahi, Michael Koch, and Joachim Denzler. "PHOG-derived aesthetic measures applied to color photographs of artworks, natural scenes and objects." In European Conference on Computer Vision, pp. 522–531. 2012. Springer, Berlin, Heidelberg.

[10] Braun, Julia, Seyed Ali Amirshahi, Joachim Denzler, and Christoph Redies. "Statistical image properties of print advertisements, visual artworks and images of architecture." Frontiers in Psychology 4 (2013): 808.

[11] Bosch, Anna, Andrew Zisserman, and Xavier Munoz. "Representing shape with a spatial pyramid kernel." In Proceedings of the 6th ACM international conference on Image and video retrieval, pp. 401–408. 2007.

[12] Hayn-Leichsenring, Gregor U., Thomas Lehmann, and Christoph Redies. "Subjective ratings of beauty and aesthetics: correlations with statistical image properties in western oil paintings." i-Perception 8, no. 3 (2017): 2041669517715474.

[13] Dalal, Navneet, and Bill Triggs. "Histograms of oriented gradients for human detection." In 2005 IEEE computer society conference on computer vision and pattern recognition (CVPR'05), vol. 1, pp. 886–893. 2005. IEEE.

[14] Donderi, Don C. "An information theory analysis of visual complexity and dissimilarity." Perception 35, no. 6 (2006): 823–835.

[15] Rosenholtz, Ruth, Yuanzhen Li, and Lisa Nakano. "Measuring visual clutter." Journal of Vision 7, no. 2 (2007): 17.

[16] Yu, Chen-Ping, Dimitris Samaras, and Gregory J. Zelinsky. "Modeling visual clutter perception using proto-object segmentation." Journal of Vision 14, no. 7 (2014): 4.

[17] Lindgren, Kristian, Cristopher Moore, and Mats Nordahl. "Complexity of two-dimensional patterns." Journal of Statistical Physics 91, no. 5–6 (1998): 909–951.

[18] Proulx, Raphaël, and Lael Parrott. "Measures of structural complexity in digital images for monitoring the ecological signature of an old-growth forest ecosystem." Ecological Indicators 8, no. 3 (2008): 270–284.

[19] Hasler, David, and Sabine E. Suesstrunk. "Measuring colorfulness in natural images." In International Society for Optics and Photonics 5007, Human Vision and Electronic Imaging VIII, pp. 87–95. 2003.

[20] Palus, Henryk. "Colourfulness of the image and its application in image filtering." In Proceedings of the Fifth IEEE International Symposium on Signal Processing and Information Technology, 2005. pp. 884–889. IEEE, 2005.

[21] James, Gareth, Daniela Witten, Trevor Hastie, and Robert Tibshirani. *An introduction to statistical learning.* Vol. 112. Springer, New York. 2013.

[22] Bermingham, Mairead L., Ricardo Pong-Wong, Athina Spiliopoulou, Caroline Hayward, Igor Rudan, Harry Campbell, Alan F. Wright et al. "Application of

high-dimensional feature selection: evaluation for genomic prediction in man." Scientific Reports 5 (2015): 10312.

[23] Guyon, Isabelle, and André Elisseeff. "An introduction to variable and feature selection." Journal of Machine Learning Research 3, (2003): 1157–1182.

[24] Sarangi, Susanta, Md Sahidullah, and Goutam Saha. "Optimization of data-driven filterbank for automatic speaker verification." Digital Signal Processing (2020): 102795.

[25] Soufan, Othman, Dimitrios Kleftogiannis, Panos Kalnis, and Vladimir B. Bajic. "DWFS: a wrapper feature selection tool based on a parallel genetic algorithm." PloS One 10, no. 2 (2015): e0117988.

[26] Figueroa, Alejandro. "Exploring effective features for recognizing the user intent behind web queries." Computers in Industry 68 (2015): 162–169.

[27] Figueroa, Alejandro, and Günter Neumann. "Learning to rank effective para-phrases from query logs for community question answering." In AAAI 13, (2013): 1099–1105.

[28] Figueroa, Alejandro, and Günter Neumann. "Category-specific models for ranking effective paraphrases in community question answering." Expert Systems with Applications 41, no. 10 (2014): 4730–4742.

[29] Zhang, Yudong, Shuihua Wang, Preetha Phillips, and Genlin Ji. "Binary PSO with mutation operator for feature selection using decision tree applied to spam detection." Knowledge-Based Systems 64 (2014): 22–31.

[30] López, Félix García, Miguel García Torres, Belén Melián Batista, José A. Moreno Pérez, and J. Marcos Moreno-Vega. "Solving feature subset selection problem by a parallel scatter search." European Journal of Operational Research 169, no. 2 (2006): 477–489.

[31] García-Torres, Miguel, Félix García-López, Belén Melián-Batista, José A. Moreno-Pérez, and J. Marcos Moreno-Vega. "Solving feature subset selection problem by a hybrid metaheuristic." Hybrid Metaheuristics (2004): 59–68.

[32] García-Torres, Miguel, Francisco Gómez-Vela, Belén Melián-Batista, and J. Marcos Moreno-Vega. "High-dimensional feature selection via feature group-ing: a variable neighborhood search approach." Information Sciences 326 (2016): 102–118.

[33] Akaike, Hirotugu. "Prediction and entropy." In *Selected Papers of Hirotugu Akaike*, pp. 387–410. Springer, New York, NY, 1985.

[34] Burnham, Kenneth P., and David R. Anderson. *Model selection and multimodel inference: A practical information-theoretic approach*, 2nd ed. Springer, New York, 2002.

[35] Einicke, Garry Allan, Haider A. Sabti, David V. Thiel, and Marta Fernandez. "Maximum-entropy-rate selection of features for classifying changes in knee and ankle dynamics during running." IEEE Journal of Biomedical and Health Informatics 22, no. 4 (2017): 1097–1103.

[36] Brown, Gavin, Adam Pocock, Ming-Jie Zhao, and Mikel Luján. "Conditional likelihood maximisation: a unifying framework for information theoretic fea-ture selection." Journal of Machine Learning Research 13, no. 1 (2012): 27–66.

[37] Peng, Hanchuan, Fuhui Long, and Chris Ding. "Feature selection based on mutual information criteria of max-dependency, max-relevance, and min-redundancy." IEEE Transactions on pattern analysis and machine intelligence 27, no. 8 (2005): 1226–1238.

[38] Nguyen, Hai Thanh, Katrin Franke, and Slobodan Petrovic. "Towards a generic feature-selection measure for intrusion detection." In 2010 20th International Conference on Pattern Recognition, pp. 1529–1532. 2010. IEEE.

[39] Yang, Howard Hua, John Moody. "Data visualization and feature selection: new algorithms for nongaussian data" *(PDF)*. Advances in Neural Information Processing Systems (2000): 687–693.

[40] Yamada, Makoto, Wittawat Jitkrittum, Leonid Sigal, Eric P. Xing, and Masashi Sugiyama. "High-dimensional feature selection by feature-wise kernelized lasso." Neural Computation 26, no. 1 (2014): 185–207.

[41] Hall, Mark Andrew. "Correlation-based feature selection for machine learning." 1999.

[42] Senliol, Baris, Gokhan Gulgezen, Lei Yu, and Zehra Cataltepe. "Fast Correlation Based Filter (FCBF) with a different search strategy." In 2008 23rd International Symposium on Computer and Information Sciences, pp. 1–4. 2008. IEEE.

[43] Hamon, Julie. "Optimisation combinatoire pour la sélection de variables en régression en grande dimension: Application en génétique animale." PhD diss., 2013.

[44] Yang, Yiming, and Jan O. Pedersen. "A comparative study on feature selection in text categorization." In Icml 97, no. 412–420 (1997): 35.

[45] Urbanowicz, Ryan J., Melissa Meeker, William La Cava, Randal S. Olson, and Jason H. Moore. "Relief-based feature selection: Introduction and review." Journal of Biomedical Informatics 85 (2018): 189–203.

[46] Phuong, Tu Minh, Zhen Lin, and Russ B. Altman. "Choosing SNPs using feature selection." In 2005 IEEE Computational Systems Bioinformatics Conference (CSB'05), pp. 301–309. 2005. IEEE.

[47] Bach, Francis R. "Bolasso: model consistent lasso estimation through the bootstrap." In Proceedings of the 25th International Conference on Machine Learning, pp. 33–40. 2008.

[48] Zare, Habil, Gholamreza Haffari, Arvind Gupta, and Ryan R. Brinkman. "Scoring relevancy of features based on combinatorial analysis of lasso with application to lymphoma diagnosis." BMC Genomics 14, no. S1 (2013): S14.

[49] Han, Kai, Yunhe Wang, Chao Zhang, Chao Li, and Chao Xu. "Autoencoder inspired unsupervised feature selection." In 2018 IEEE International Conference on Acoustics, Speech and Signal Processing (ICASSP), pp. 2941–2945. 2018. IEEE.

[50] Zhang, Yishi, Shujuan Li, Teng Wang, and Zigang Zhang. "Divergence-based feature selection for separate classes." Neurocomputing 101 (2013): 32–42.

[51] Guyon, Isabelle, Jason Weston, Stephen Barnhill, and Vladimir Vapnik. "Gene selection for cancer classification using support vector machines." Machine Learning 46, no. 1–3 (2002): 389–422.

[52] Rosenblatt, Frank. "Perceptron simulation experiments." In Proceedings of the IRE 48, no. 3 (1960): 301–309.

[53] Minsky, Marvin, and Seymour A. Papert. *Perceptrons: An introduction to computational geometry.* MIT press, 2017.

[54] Raina, Rajat, Anand Madhavan, and Andrew Y. Ng. "Large-scale deep unsupervised learning using graphics processors." In Proceedings of the 26th Annual International Conference on Machine Learning, pp. 873–880. 2009.

[55] NVIDIA Corporation. Tesla P100 Performance Guide - HPC and Deep Learning Applications. NVIDIA Corporation, 2017.

[56] Krizhevsky, Alex, Ilya Sutskever, and Geoffrey E. Hinton. "ImageNet classification with deep convolutional neural networks." Advances in Neural Information Processing Systems, (2012): 1097–1105.
[57] Belkin, Mikhail, Daniel Hsu, Siyuan Ma, and Soumik Mandal. "Reconciling modern machine-learning practice and the classical bias–variance trade-off." Proceedings of the National Academy of Sciences 116, no. 32 (2019): 15849–15854.
[58] Amodei, Dario, and Danny Hernandez. "AI and Compute." Heruntergeladen von https://blog. openai. com/aiand-compute. 2018.
[59] Xie, Qizhe, Minh-Thang Luong, Eduard Hovy, and Quoc V. Le. "Self-training with noisy student improves ImageNet classification." In Proceedings of the IEEE/CVF Conference on Computer Vision and Pattern Recognition, pp. 10687–10698. 2020.
[60] Xie, Saining, Ross Girshick, Piotr Dollár, Zhuowen Tu, and Kaiming He. "Aggregated residual transformations for deep neural networks." In Proceedings of the IEEE conference on computer vision and pattern recognition, pp. 1492–1500. 2017.
[61] So, David R., Chen Liang, and Quoc V. Le. "The evolved transformer." arXiv preprint arXiv:1901.11117. 2019.
[62] Vapnik, Vladimir N., and A. Ya Chervonenkis. "On the uniform convergence of relative frequencies of events to their probabilities." In *Measures of complexity*, pp. 11–30. Springer, Cham, 2015.

2

Design of a Knowledge Representation and Indexing: Background and Future

N. Thillaiarasu, N. Partheeban, and Srinivasan Sriramulu

2.1 Introduction

The previous few years have seen enormous upsurge in information accessibility in the electronic structure, ascribed to the steadily mounting utilization of the World Wide Web (WWW). For some individuals, the WWW has become a fundamental method for giving and looking to data prompting huge measure of information collection. Looking web in its current structure is anyway a goading experience since the information accessible is excess and in different structures. Web clients wind up finding enormous number of answers to their basic inquiries, considerably putting additional time in breaking down the yield results because of its immenseness. However, numerous outcomes here end up being unessential and one can discover a portion of the additional intriguing connections forgot about from the outcome set.

One of the foremost clarifications for such inadmissible condition is the explanation that majority of the current information assets in its current structure are intended for human cognizance. When utilizing this information with machines, it turns out to be profoundly infeasible to get great outcomes without human intercessions at normal levels. In this way, one of the significant difficulties looked by the clients as suppliers and shoppers of web time is to envision astute instruments and speculations in information portrayal and handling for making the current information machine reasonable. A few investigations have been completed toward this path and some of the most intriguing arrangements proposed are the semantic online metaphysics to consolidate information understanding by machines. The goal here is to insightfully speak to information, empowering machines to better comprehend and upgrade catch of existing data. Here the principal accentuation is given to the idea for building importance-related idea networks [1] for information portrayal. At last, the thought is to coordinate machines in furnishing yield aftereffects of high caliber with least or no human mediation.

DOI: 10.1201/9781003126898-2

33

Lately, the advancement of metaphysics [2] is acquiring consideration from different examination bunches across the globe. There are a few meanings of metaphysics simply dependent upon the application or undertaking it is expected for. Philosophy is one of the grounded information portrayal techniques; on a conventional ground, cosmology characterizes the basic jargon for researchers who need to share data on a field or area. One has found in the previous years that different exploration bunches have been devotedly testing semantic-related [3] metaphysics pointed toward making web dialects machine reasonable.

2.2 Related Work

Perhaps the most essential explanations behind philosophy development [1] are to encourage sharing of normal information about the underlying data of information among people or electronic specialists. This property of cosmology in turn empowers reuse and sharing of data over the web by different specialists for various purposes. Cosmology [3] can likewise be viewed as one of the principal methods for information portrayal through its capacity to speak to information regarding semantic connection it imparts to the next information. There are a few created instruments for cosmology development and portrayal like protege-2000 [4], a graphical device for philosophy altering furthermore, information securing that can be adjusted to empower reasonable displaying with new and developing semantic web dialects. Protege-2000 has been utilized for a long time now in the field of medication and producing. This is a profoundly customizable apparatus as a metaphysics editorial manager credited to its critical highlights like an extensible information model, a customizable record design for a book portrayal in any conventional language, a customizable UI and an extensible engineering that empowers coordination with different applications, which makes it effectively uniquely customized with a few web dialects. Regardless of whether it licenses simpler philosophy development, the drawback is its prerequisite of mediation at normal levels for organizing the ideas of its metaphysics. The WWW Consortium (W3C) has built a language for encoding information on web to make it machine reasonable, called the Resource Description Framework (RDF) [5]. Here, it helps electronic media accumulate data on the information and makes it machine reasonable. In any case, anyway RDF itself doesn't characterize any natives for creating ontologies. Related to the W3C, the Defense Advanced Research Projects Agency (DARPA) has created DARF, a specialist markup language (DAML) [6], by broadening RDF with additional expressive developments pointed toward encouraging specialist collaboration on the web. This is vigorously roused by research in portrayal rationales (DL) and permits a few kinds of idea definitions in ontologies.

There are a few different applications like the semantic internet searcher called the SHOE Search, and The Unified Medical Language System is utilized in the clinical space to grow enormous semantic organization. In the following area, we acquaint our methodology with this issue of information portrayal, the executives and data recovery [7] also, ultimately talking about the conceivable solution.

2.2.1 Crossover Approach-Extended Semantic Network

2.2.1.1 General View

The concept of a semantic network is information speaking to organize coming about from the cooperation including two organizations, one naturally developed proximal organization and the second annually built semantic organization. Here, the essential thought is to build up a cutting-edge approach joining the highlights of human and machine hypothesis of idea [8], which can be of colossal use in the most recent information portrayal, characterization, design coordinating and philosophy improvement fields. We propose to imagine a novel technique for information portrayal [9] incompletely dependent on brain demonstrating and halfway on the numerical technique.

In ESN, we attempt to build up an organization of ideas dependent on human developed semantic organization projected as the primary focal piece of the organization which is later exposed to elaboration using the measurable information got by our numerical models dependent on the information bunching and mining calculations. This produces another methodology for information portrayal, which can later be utilized for enhancing data search and characterization techniques and empowering simple and quick data recovery. The ESN structures a half construction by acquiring the highlights of both the source organizations, registered in an unexpected way also, autonomously, making it a powerful and an ideal methodology. Our proposition is to build an organization of ideas like cosmology, however utilizing a technique where minima! Human mediation is required. We call this a semi-administered organization of ideas communicating to certain characteristics of a philosophy which later is elaborated by adding the data acquired from the numerically expounded proximal work. Our suspicion here is that this strategy will create the equivalent yield as any conventional cosmology yet will incredibly diminish the development time, credited to its numerical displayed expansion. A portion of the significant focuses we desire to accomplish through this strategy for information portrayal network are to make development of semantic-based idea organizations practical by crusading least human mediation to limit time put resources into development by presenting numerical models without losing on quality [10]. It aims to distinguish a decent harmony among minds and numerical models to grow better information communicating to networks with great accuracy and high review.

Semantic organization semantic network [11] is fundamentally a named, coordinated chart allowing the utilization of nonexclusive principles, legacy and article situated programming [8]. It is regularly utilized as a type of information portrayal. It is a coordinated diagram comprising vertices, which speak to ideas and edges, I presenting semantic relations between the ideas. The most ongoing language to communicate semantic organizations is KL-ONE [12]. Named hubs and a solitary marked edge relationship can exist between semantic hubs. Furthermore, there can be multiple connections between a solitary pair of associated words: for example the relationship isn't really even and connection between the hubs can exist through other aberrant patlis. The following is a piece of a customary semantic net, demonstrating four named hubs and three marked edges between them. In fact, a semantic organization is a hub and edge-named coordinated diagram, and it is often portrayed that way. The extent of the semantic network is expansive, considering the semantic arrangement of a wide scope of phrasing in various areas. K-major groupings of semantic types incorporate creatures, anatomical designs, biologic function, chemicals, occasions, actual articles and ideas or thoughts. The connections between the semantic kinds give the construction to the organization and speak to significant connections. In our semantic organization model, all idea relations are built in light of the importance every idea pair shares, with a chance of something else than one connection between a solitary pair of associated hubs. All the joins utilized in interfacing the hub depend on the IJML [13] joins, consisting of four distinct sorts of cooperative lines as demonstrated later. They have, as of now, picked up an exploratory premise [14], after considering and investigating the necessities of our methodology. We start with our area name communicating to the super class in our methodology. The super class is associated with its subclasses dependent on the classification of the connection they share, which can be browse the four connections we give. The four connections speak to the straightforward UML connections of affiliation, structure, launch and legacy.

Knowledge Representation Essentials

The following are the types of data that should be spoken to in AI frameworks:

Object: Objects are all current realities about items in our reality space. E.g., guitars contain strings, trumpets are metal instruments.

Events: Events are the activities that happen in our reality.

Performance: It portrays conduct that incorporates information about the way to get things done.

Meta-information: It's information about what we all know.

Facts: Facts are the certainties about this present reality and what we speak to.

Knowledge base: The focal part of the knowledge-based specialists is the information base. It's termed KB. The knowledge base may be a gathering of the sentences (here, sentences are utilized as a specialized term and not indistinguishable with English language) [15].

Information: Knowledge is mindfulness or commonality picked up by encounters of realities, information and circumstances. Following are the kinds of data in human-made reasoning:

Following are the sorts of information in human-made reasoning:

Types of Knowledge

Following are various types of knowledge:

1. Declarative knowledge: Declarative information is to believe something. It incorporates ideas, realities and items. It's additionally called spellbinding information and communicated in declarative sentences. It's easier than procedural language.

2. Procedural knowledge: It is otherwise called basic information. Procedural information may be a kind of information which is responsible for realizing the way to accomplish something. It is often straightforwardly applied to any. It incorporates rules, systems, techniques, plans, then on procedural information relies upon the assignment on which it alright could also be applied.

3. Meta-knowledge: Information about different sorts of information is called meta-information (Figure 2.1).

FIGURE 2.1
Types of knowledge

4. Heuristic knowledge: Heuristic information is communicating information on certain specialists during a recorded or subject. Heuristic information are general guidelines hooked in to past encounters, attention to approaches, which are acceptable to figure yet not ensured.

5. Primary information: The underlying data is significant to basic reasoning. It depicts associations between various thoughts, for example, kind of, part of and get-together of something. It depicts the association that exists between thoughts or articles. The connection among information and knowledge: information on genuine universes assumes a significant part in knowledge and same for making AI. Information assumes a vital part in showing insightful conduct in AI specialists. A specialist is just prepared to precisely follow up on some info when he has some information or experience that input. Let's assume on the off chance that you met somebody that is communicating in during a language which you don't have a clue, at that point how you'll prepared to act subsequently. Something identical applies to the canny conduct of the specialists. As we will see in beneath graph, there's one executive that acts by detecting the climate and utilizing information. However, in the event that the information part won't present, at that point, it can't show clever conduct.

AI Knowledge Cycle

The following components are the intelligent behavior model (Figure 2.2):

Perception

Learning

Knowledge representation and reasoning

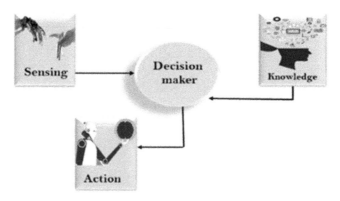

FIGURE 2.2
AI knowledge cycle

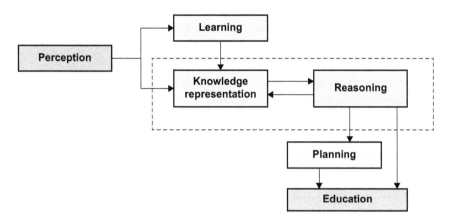

FIGURE 2.3
AI framework for knowledge representation

Planning

Execution

The preceding outline is demonstrating how an AI framework can connect with this present reality and which segments assist it with indicating knowledge. Computer-based intelligence framework has perception part by which it recovers data from its current circumstance. It tends to be visual, sound or another type of tangible information. The learning segment is answerable for gaining from information caught by perception comportment. In the total cycle, the primary segments are information portrayal and reasoning [16]. These two parts are associated with indicating the insight in machine-like people. These two parts are free with one another, yet in addition coupled together. The arranging and execution rely upon examination of knowledge portrayal and thinking (Figure 2.3).

Ways to Deal with Information Portrayal

There are for the most part four ways to deal with information portrayal, which are given as follows:

1. Straightforward social information:
   It is the least complex method of putting away realities that utilize the social technique, and every reality about a bunch of the article is set out efficiently in segments.
   This methodology of information portrayal is acclaimed in data set frameworks where the connection between various substances is addressed.
   This methodology has little chance for induction.
   Model: Coming up next is the basic social information portrayal in Table 2.1

TABLE 2.1

Straightforward Social Information

Player	Weight	Age
Player 1	66	24
Player 2	56	30
Player 3	74	33
Player 4	52	26

2. Inheritable knowledge:

In the inheritable information approach, all information should be put away into a progressive system of classes.

All classes ought to be masterminded in a summed up structure or a hierarchal way.

In this methodology, we apply legacy property.

Components acquire values from different individuals from a class.

This methodology contains inheritable information that shows a connection among occasion and class, and it is called occurrence connection.

Each individual edge can address the assortment of characteristics and its worth.

In this methodology, articles and qualities are addressed in boxed hubs.

We use arrows that point from objects to their qualities (Figure 2.4).

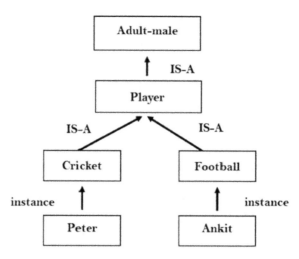

FIGURE 2.4
Inheritable knowledge

3. Inferential knowledge:
   Inferential information approach addresses information as formal rationales.
   This methodology can be utilized to infer more realities.
   It ensured rightness.
   Model: Let's assume there are two explanations:

   Marcus is a man

   All men are mortal

   At that point, it can address as,

   man (Marcus)

   $$\forall x = man\ (x) - > mortal\ (x)s$$

4. Procedural information:
   Procedural information approach utilizes little projects and codes, which portrays how to do explicit things and how to continue. In this methodology, one significant guideline is utilized, which is If-Then standard. In this information, we can utilize different coding dialects, for example, LISP and Prolog languages. We can undoubtedly address heuristic or space explicit information utilizing this methodology. Yet, it isn't essential that we can address all cases in this methodology [17].

Requirements for Information Representation Framework

A decent information portrayal framework should have the accompanying properties.

1. Authentic accuracy: KR framework ought to can address all sort of required information.
2. Inferential adequacy: KR situation ought to have capacity to control the illustrative constructions to deliver new information relating to existing design.
3. Inferential efficiency: The capacity to coordinate the inferential information system into the most beneficial headings by putting away fitting aides.
4. Acquisitional proficiency: The capacity to gain the new information effectively utilizing programmed techniques.

Procedures of Information Portrayal

There are mostly four different ways of information portrayal which are given as follows:

Consistent representation

Semantic network representation

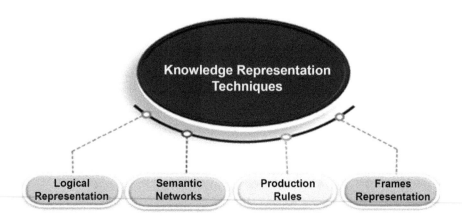

FIGURE 2.5
Knowledge representation techniques

Casing representation
Creation rules

1. Intelligent representation
   Consistent portrayal is a language for certain solid standards that manage recommendations and has no vagueness in portrayal. Coherent portrayal implies making an inference dependent on different conditions. This portrayal sets out some significant correspondence rules. It comprises absolutely characterized grammar and semantics, which bolsters the sound deduction. Each sentence can be converted into rationales utilizing linguistic structure and semantics (Figure 2.5).
   Punctuation:

   Linguistic uses are the standards that choose how we can develop legitimate sentences in the rationale.
   It figures out which image we can use in information portrayal.
   Instructions to compose those images.

   Semantics:

   Semantics are the principles by which we can decipher the sentence in the rationale.
   Semantic likewise includes doling out a significance to each sentence.
   Legitimate portrayal can be ordered into primarily two rationales:
   Propositional logics (PLs)
   Predicate rationales

2. Semantic Network Representation

Semantic organizations are option of predicate rationale for information portrayal. In semantic organizations, we can address our insight as graphical organizations. This organization comprises hubs addressing items and circular segments which portray the connection between those articles. Semantic organizations can order the item in various structures and can likewise connect those articles. Semantic organizations are straightforward and can be handily expanded.

This portrayal comprises the most part two kinds of relations:

IS-A connection (Inheritance) kind of connection

Model: Following are a few explanations which we need to address as hubs and circular segments.

Explanations:

Jerry is a feline.

Jerry is a vertebrate

Jerry is claimed by Priya.

Jerry is earthy colored shaded.

All mammals are creature.

In the preceding graph, we have addressed the diverse kind of information as hubs and curves. Each article is associated with another item by some connection (Figure 2.6).

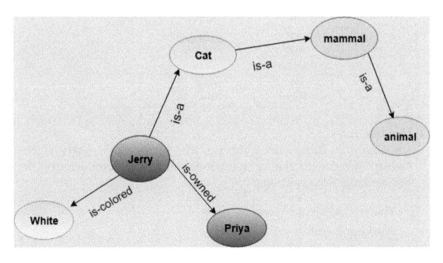

FIGURE 2.6
Information graph

3. Edge representation

A casing is a record-like design that comprises an assortment of qualities and its qualities to portray a substance on the planet. Edges are the AI information structure what partitions information into foundations by addressing generalizations circumstances. It comprises an assortment of openings and space esteems. These openings might be of any sort and sizes. Spaces have names and qualities that are called features [18].

Features: The different parts of a space are known as facets. Aspects are highlights of edges, which empowers us to put requirements on the edges. Model: IF-NEEDED realities are called when information of a specific space is required. An edge may comprise quite a few openings, and a space may incorporate quite a few features, and aspects may have quite a few qualities. An edge is otherwise called opening channel information portrayal in human-made consciousness.

Casings are obtained from semantic organizations and later advanced into our cutting-edge classes and articles. A solitary casing isn't a lot of helpful. Casings framework comprises an assortment of edges which are associated. In the edge, information about an article or occasion can be put away together in the information base [19]. The edge is a kind of innovation which is generally utilized in different applications including natural language preparing and machine dreams.

Model: 1

We should take an illustration of a casing for a book:

S. No	Streams
Title	Software Engineering
Genre	Engineering
Author	Dr. Raja
Edition	Edition
Year	2021
Page	560

4. Creation rules

Creation rules framework comprises (condition, activity) sets which signify, "On the off chance that condition, at that point activity". It has basically three sections:

The arrangement of creation rules

Working memory

The perceive demonstration cycle.

Underway principles specialist checks for the condition and on the off chance that the condition exists, at that point creation rule fires and comparing activity is completed. The condition is applied to some portion of the standard figures out which rule might be applied to an issue. Also, the activity part does the related critical thinking steps. This total cycle is known as a perceive demonstration cycle. The working memory contains the depiction of the present status of issues addressing and rule can compose information to the working memory. This information coordinate and may fire other rules. If there is another circumstance (state), at that point, numerous creation rules will be terminated together, and this is called struggle set. In the present circumstance, the specialist needs to choose a standard from these sets, and it is known as a compromise [20].

Model:

On the off chance that (at transport stop AND transport shows up) THEN activity (get into the transport).

On the off chance that (on the transport AND paid AND void seat) THEN activity (plunk down).

On the off chance that (on transport AND unpaid) THEN activity (pay charges).

On the off chance that (transport shows up at objective) THEN activity (get down from the transport).

Information representation and NLP in AI.

Issues in information portrayal.

The fundamental target of information portrayal is to make the inferences from the information, yet there are numerous issues related with the utilization of information portrayal strategies.

Some of them are recorded beneath:
Allude to the preceding chart to allude to the accompanying issues.

1. Significant credits
   There are two credits appeared in the graph. Since these credits uphold property of legacy, they are of prime significance.

2. Connections among credits
   Essentially, the ascriptions used to depict objects are only the substances. Notwithstanding, the ascriptions of an article don't rely upon the encoded explicit information.

3. Picking the granularity of portrayal
   While choosing the granularity of portrayal, it is important to know the accompanying factors:
   a. What are the natives and at what level should the information be addressed?
   b. What ought to be the number (little or enormous) of low-level natives or significant level realities?

Significant-level realities might be inadequate to reach the inference while low-level natives may require a ton of capacity.

For instance: Suppose that we are keen for later realities:

John spotted Alex.

Presently, this could be addressed as "Spotted (agent(John), object (Alex))"

Such a portrayal can make it simple to respond to questions, for example, Who spotted Alex?

Assume we need to know: "Did John see Sue?"

Given just a single reality, client can't find that answer.

Henceforth, the client can add different realities, for example, "Spotted (x, y) → saw (x, y)"

4. Addressing sets of items
   There are a few properties of items which fulfill the state of a set together, however not as person.
   Model: Consider the affirmation made in the sentences:
   "There are more sheep than individuals in Australia", and "English speakers can be discovered everywhere on the world".
   These realities can be depicted by including a statement to the sets addressing individuals, sheep and English.

5. Finding the correct design varying
   To portray a specific circumstance, it is consistently imperative to discover the entrance of right design. This should be possible by choosing an underlying design and afterward changing the decision.
   While choosing and turning around the correct design, it is important to take care of following issue proclamations. They remember the cycle for how to:

   Select an underlying proper design.

   Fill the essential subtleties from the current circumstances.

   Decide a superior design if the at first chose structure isn't suitable to satisfy different conditions.

   Discover the arrangement if none of the accessible designs is proper.

   Make and recall another design for the given condition.

   There is no particular method to take care of these issues, yet a portion of the viable information portrayal procedures can possibly settle them.

   Rationale representation.

Realities are the overall explanations that might be either True or False. In this manner, rationale can be utilized to address such straightforward realities.

To construct a logic-based portrayal:

Client needs to characterize a bunch of crude images alongside the necessary semantics.

The images are relegated together to characterize legitimate sentences in the language for addressing TRUE realities.

New coherent proclamations are shaped from the current ones. The explanations which can be either TRUE or bogus yet not both are called recommendations. A revelatory sentence communicates an assertion with a recommendation as substance.

Model: The definitive "cotton is white" communicates that cotton is white. Thus, the sentence "cotton is white" is a genuine assertion.

What is PL?

Propositional rationale is an investigation of recommendations.

Each suggestion has either a valid or a bogus worth, yet not both at a time.

Suggestions is addressed by factors.

For instance: Symbols "p" and "q" can be utilized to address recommendations.

There are two sorts of suggestions:

1. Straightforward preposition
2. Compound prepositions.
   1. A basic relational word: It doesn't contain some other relational word.
      For instance: Rocky is a canine.
   2. A compound relational word: It contains more than one relational words.
      For instance: Surendra is a kid and he prefers chocolate.

Six Mostly Used Types of Semantic Networks

Definitional networks – These organizations accentuate and manage just the subtype or are a connection between an idea type and a recently characterized subtype (Figure 2.7). A delivering network is alluded to as speculation chain of command. It bolsters the legacy rule for copying credits (Figure 2.8).

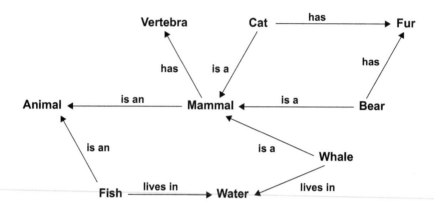

FIGURE 2.7
Rule for copying credits

Affirmation networks – Design to attest suggestions is planned to state proposals [21]. Generally, information in an attestation network is authentic except if it is set apart with a modular chairman. Some affirmation frameworks are even considered the model of the sensible constructions hidden the trademark semantic regular dialects (Figure 2.8).

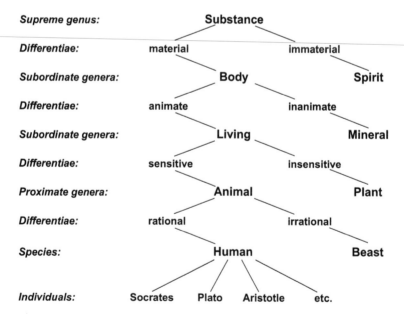

FIGURE 2.8
Trademark semantic regular dialect

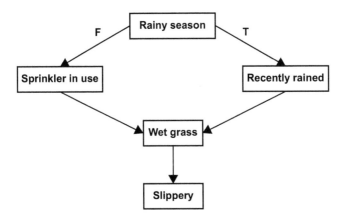

FIGURE 2.9
Sample for implicational network

Implicational networks – It uses implication as the essential association for interfacing hubs. These organizations are likewise used to clarify examples of feelings, causality and even allowances (Figure 2.9).

Executable network-containing components that can make a few changes in the actual organization by consolidating a few methods, for instance, for example, appended methodology or marker passing, which can perform two-way messages, or affiliations, and look for designs (Figure 2.10).

Learning networks – These are the organizations that form and expand their portrayals by securing information through models. They contain components in such organizations bring changes inside the actual organization through portrayal by making sure about data. An exemplary model could resemble the changing of new data from the old framework by including and barring hubs and curves or by changing mathematical characteristics called loads and associated with the bends and hubs (Figure 2.11).

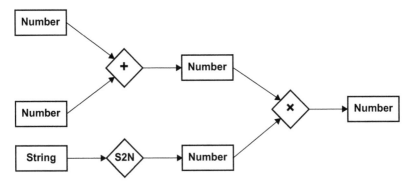

FIGURE 2.10
Executable network-containing components

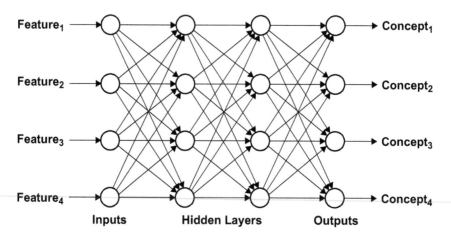

FIGURE 2.11
Learning networks

Crossover networks – These are the networks that join at least two of the past strategies, either in a solitary organization or in a different, yet intently communicating network hybrid organization has been obviously made to execute thoughts with respect to human psychological instruments, while some are made by and large for PC execution (Figure 2.12).

Since semantic organizations in human-made brainpower likewise come in numerous other changed structures, we referenced a couple of significant ones; there are a lot more, almost 40. While these devices have more prominent potential for supporting machines as well as human clients as they continue looking for handling thoughts and languages, they can't supplant the psychological abilities of a human mind.

2.3 Conclusion

The request on data depiction, the heads, sharing and recuperation are both fascinating and complex, fundamentally with the co-rise among man and machine. This investigation chapter presents a novel local area–situated working strategy, unequivocally concerning data depiction and recuperation. The suggestion tries to present a cross-variety data depiction approach exactly as ontologies that are snappier and easy to create. The potential gains of our methodology concerning the previous work is our inventive strategy of joining machine assessments with human reasoning limits. We use the specific, nonevaluated results given by human capacity if there ought to emerge an event of semantic sort out and subsequently consolidate it with the machine decided data from proximal results. The way that we endeavor

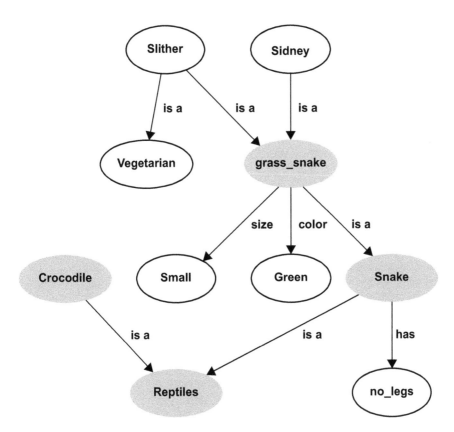

FIGURE 2.12
Crossover networks

to merge results from two exceptional perspectives structures potentially the most captivating features of our energy research. We consider it to be as coordinated by mind and controlled by machines. One of the significant drawbacks of this system is finding the right harmony for joining the thought associations of semantic association with the word network got from the proximal association. Our impending go to work is recognize this accurate mix between the two colossal procedures and setting up a benchmark to measure our model profitability.

References

[1] N.F. Noy and D.L. McGuinness, Ontology Development 101: A Guide to Creating Your First Ontology, Stanford University, Stanford, CA.
[2] R. Gruber, "Toward principle for the design of ontologies used for knowledge sharing", in Proc. of International Workshop on Formal Ontology, March 1993.

[3] N. Thillaiarasu and S. Chenthur Pandian, "Enforcing security and privacy over multi-cloud framework using assessment techniques," in 2016 10th International Conference on Intelligent Systems and Control (ISCO), Coimbatore, 2016, pp. 1–5, DOI: 10.1109/ISCO.2016.7727001.

[4] N.F. Noy, M. Sintek, S. Decker, M. Crubezy, R.W. Fergerson and M.A. Musen, Creating Semantic Web Contents with Protégé 2000, Stanford University, IEEE Intelligent Systems, 2001.

[5] D. Brickley and R.V. Guha, Resource Description Framework (RDF) Schema Specification, Proposed Recommendation: World Wide Web Consortium, 1999.

[6] J. Helder and D.L. McGuinness, The DARPA Agent Markup Language. IEEE Intelligent Systems, 2000.

[7] N. Thillaiarasu, M. Susmitha, D. Devadharshini and T. Anantharaj, "Solar powered fire extirpation robot with night vision camera," in 2019 5th International Conference on Advanced Computing & Communication Systems (ICACCS), Coimbatore, India, 2019, pp. 741–744, DOI: 10.1109/ICACCS.2019.8728438.

[8] J.F. Sowa, Conceptual Structures: Information Processing in Mind and Machine, Addison-Wesley Longman Publishing Co., Inc., Boston, MA, 1984.

[9] J.F. Sowa, Knowledge Representation: Logical, Philosophical, and Computational Foundations, Brooks Cole Publishing Co, Pacific Grove, CA, 2000.

[10] E. Reingold and J. Nightingale. "Artificial intelligence tutorial review." PSY371 (1999).

[11] M.R. Quillian, Semantic memory, in M. Minsky (ed.), Semantic Information Processing, pp. 227–270, MIT Press, Cambridge, MA, 1968.

[12] R.J. Brachman, D.L. McGuinncss, P.F. Patel-Schneider, L.A. Resnick, et al., Living with CLASSIC: when and how to use a KL-ONE-Like language, in Principles of Semantic Networks, Morgan Kaufmann, 1991.

[13] S. Ranjithkumar and N. Thillaiarasu, A survey of secure routing protocols of the mobile ad-hoc network, SSRG International Journal of Computer Science and Engineering (SSRG-IJCSE), 2: (2015).

[14] M.E. Winston, R. Chaffin and D. Herrmann, A taxonomy of part-whole relations, Cognitive Science, 11: 417–444 (1987).

[15] N. Thillaiarasu, S. Chenthur Pandian, G. Naveen Balaji, R.M. Benitha Shierly, A. Divya and G. Divya Prabha, Enforcing confidentiality and authentication over public cloud using hybrid cryptosystems, in J. Hemanth, X. Fernando, P. Lafata, Z. Baig (eds.), International Conference on Intelligent Data Communication Technologies and Internet of Things (ICICI) 2018. ICICI 2018. Lecture Notes on Data Engineering and Communications Technologies, vol. 26, Springer, Cham, 2019. https://doi.org/10.1007/978-3-030-03146-6_175.

[16] S.A. Mahe, P.M. Riccio et S. Vaillies: des elements pour un modele: la lutte des classes! Revue Genie Logicicl, n°58, Paris, septembre 2001.

[17] M. Ménager, Programme Toxicologie Nucléaire Environnmentale: Comment fédérer et créer une communauté scientifique autour d'un enjeu de société, Intelligence Collective Partage et Redistribution des Savoirs, Nimes, France, septembre 2004.

[18] N. Shyamambika and N. Thillaiarasu, "A survey on acquiring integrity of shared data with effective user termination in the cloud," in 2016 10th International Conference on Intelligent Systems and Control (ISCO), Coimbatore, 2016, pp. 1–5, DOI: 10.1109/ISCO.2016.7726893.

[19] J. Aberg and N. Shahmehri, User Modelling as an Aid for Human Web Assistants, User Modeling 2001: 8th International Conference, UM 2001, Southaven, Germany, July 13–17, 2001.

[20] N. Thillaiarasu and S. Chenthur Pandian, A novel scheme for safeguarding confidentiality in public clouds for service users of cloud computing, Cluster Computing, 22: 1179–1188 (2019). https://doi.org/10.1007/s10586-017-1178-8.

[21] N. Thillaiarasu, S.C. Pandian, V. Vijayakumar, et al., Designing trivial information relaying scheme for assuring safety in a mobile cloud computing environment, Wireless Networks (2019). https://doi.org/10.1007/s11276-019-02113-4.

3

Prediction Analysis of Noise Component Using Median-Based Filters Cascaded with Evolutionary Algorithms

A. Ramya, Sudha Rajesh, G. Karthick, Sudha Rajesh, and G. Karthick

3.1 Introduction

Approximately 100 years ago, several representation learning methods were planned to study the fundamental structure of data, whether linear or non-linear, supervised or unsupervised, some "shallow" otherwise "deep". Deep architectures are primarily used for representation learning and have shown excellent results in a variety of applications, including speech recognition, object detection and image classification. In this chapter, we look at how data representation learning methods have progressed. Specifically, we look at both conventional feature learning algorithms and cutting-edge deep learning models.

It begins with a history of data representation learning strategies before introducing additional online tools such as books, tutorials, and courses. Finally, in this section, we offer some explanations about the evolution of data representation learning and suggest a few intriguing research directions.

Representation learning has developed as a technique to abstract features from unlabeled data by working out a neural network on a secondary supervised learning task. At a present time, various organization's personal huge amounts of data were completely kept as unstructured and unlabeled. Nowadays, the amount of data used for the business requirement is comparatively small and locating new labels are very slow and classy. Due to these reasons, the methodologies that are abstracted from unlabeled data to rise the performance growth of data-limited tasks are temperately valued.

While traditional unsupervised learning techniques will permanently be staples of machine learning (ML) pipelines, representation learning has developed as a different approach to feature extraction with the continued

DOI: 10.1201/9781003126898-3

success of deep learning. Features of representation learning are abstracted from unlabeled data by working out a neural network on a secondary, supervised learning task.

3.2 A New Perception – Object Recognition

In reality, they equally mentioned and recognized the technologies, targeted subjects and some exact algorithms similar to deep learning. Both recognitions are severely connected to computer vision, in which the image is understood by computers.

Visual data processing occurs in the ventral visual stream. It is a main part of the computer brain which helps in object recognition. We can easily recognize different size objects and set them in the similar group [1]. This occurs and develops due to in variances. Object recognition involves of recognizing, identifying and locating objects within an image with a specified degree of confidence. This process is classified into four main tasks they are:

1. Classification
2. Tagging
3. Detection
4. Segmentation

The significant task in object recognition is to detect what is in the image and with what level of confidence. The procedure of this task is comparatively uncomplicated. It leads with the description of the ontology, specifically the class of object to detect. Subsequently, equally classification and tagging recognize what is in the image and the related level of confidence.

Although classification identifies only one class of objects, tagging can identify multiple ones for a given picture. In addition, in classification, the algorithm will only recall that there is a dog, disregarding all other classes. On the other hand, in tagging, it will try to return all the best classes matching to the picture. After recognize what is in the image, we need to detect the objects. There are two behaviours such as detection and segmentation.

Detection shows outputs like a rectangle, also called bounding box, where the objects remain. It is an identical robust technology, liable to negligible errors and inaccuracies. Otherwise, segmentation recognizes the objects for each pixel in the picture, succeeding in a very accurate map. Although the accuracy of segmentation rests on a general and frequently time-intense training of the neural network, adequate performance of the operation is high can show and bring very remarkable results in practice cases similar to cancer detection.

3.3 Object Recognition in Image Processing

The term "object recognition" refers to a set of interconnected computer vision tasks that include recognizing objects in digital images [2]. Image classification includes imagining the class of a single object in an image. Object localization is the process of recognizing the location of one or more objects in an image and drawing a bounding box around their length. Object detection bridges the gap between the two tasks by detecting and classifying one or more objects in an image. It can differentiate between the three computer vision tasks mentioned next:

- **Image classification:** Consider an object's class or type in a picture. Consider the class or type of an object in an image as input. The result is a grade for a class (maybe one or more integers that are mapped to class labels).
- **Localization of object**: Detect the presence of objects in an image and show their position with a bounding box. An image with one or more additional elements, such as a photograph, is referred to as an input. There may be one or more bounding boxes as an output (e.g. well defined by a point, width and height).
- **Detection of object**: Using a bounding box and the groups or types of the placed objects, detect the presence of objects in an image. An image with one or more additional elements, such as a photograph, is called an input. One or more bounding boxes, as well as a class mark for each bounding box separately (e.g., specified by a point, width, and height) [3].

Another postponement of this breakdown of computer vision tasks is object segmentation. "Object instance segmentation" or "semantic segmentation" is when instances of recognized objects are designated by highlighting the individual pixels of the object rather than a coarse bounding box. Object recognition is a type of challenging computer vision activities, as we can see from this collapse [4].

Participation in the ILSVRC tasks has resulted in the bulk of recent advances in image recognition complications. This is an annual academic competition with different competitions for each of these three problem categories, with the aim of encouraging discrete and distinct progress at each level that can be leveraged more widely.

- **Localization of a single object:** Algorithms produce a list of object groupings that exist in the image, which is shown sideways with an axis-aligned bounding box that represents the position and scale of a single instance of each object category.

- **Detection of objects**: Algorithms generate a list of object groupings found in the image, which is shown sideways with an axis-aligned bounding box representing the location and scale of a single instance of each object category.

"Single-object localization", we can deduce, is a condensed version of the more specifically defined "Object Localization" limiting the localization tasks to artefacts of a single kind inside a picture, which we would do as a casual activity. An example from the ILSVRC paper relating single-object localization and object detection is shown next. Keep track of how each situation's ground reality expectations have changed [5].

3.3.1 Single-Object Localization and Object Detection are Compared

To test the output of a model for image classification, the mean classification error across the predicted class labels is used. To test the concert of a model for single-object localization, the distance between the expected and predicted bounding boxes for the expected class is used, while the precision and recall for each of the best matching bounding boxes for the recognized objects in the image are used to assess a model's object recognition efficiency [6].

3.4 Multitask and Transfer Learning

Multitasking by learning several tasks at the same time aims to improve generalization. It can be seen as emulating human learning habits because the environment we live in requires us to know a wide range of skills. We move information from one activity to another, and these tasks are linked to make it more casual for us.

Any or all of the tasks in the Multi-Task Learning (MTL) model can be used to spread knowledge. It may be important to selectively share information across tasks, depending on the structure of task comprehension. Tasks, for example, can be grouped or organized in a hierarchy, or they can be connected based on a metric [7]. Assume that the parameter vector modelling task is a linear grouping of some fundamental sources, as detailed later. The task affiliation can be seen when the tasks are compared in terms of this source. For example, the intersection of nonzero coefficients transversely tasks indicates thinness commonality. Tasks in dissimilar groups that disjoint or overlap arbitrarily in terms of their bases result in a task grouping that agrees on some tasks lying in a subspace formed by some subset of basic elements. It's possible that a priori knowledge of the task is needed, or that knowledge can be gained from data. Indirectly, graded task relatedness may be demoralized without presumptive a priori knowledge or specific learning ties. Explicit learning of sample meaning across tasks, for example, can be performed to agree on the feasibility of mutual learning across different domains. In ML science, storing knowledge acquired while solving one problem and applying it to a separate but related problem is a difficult problem. When learning to recognize vehicles, for example, the information acquired can be applied when attempting to recognize trucks [8].

Theoretically, transfer learning can be explained in terms of domain and assignment. The domain D is made up of a feature space X and a marginal probability distribution $P(X)$, where $X = \{x_1, x_2...x_n\}$ ε X. Assume a particular domain, $D = \{X,P9X0\}$, a task consists of two components: A mark space Y and an objective predictive function $f(.)$ (designated by $T = Y,f(.))$, which is derived from a collection of pairs of training data $\{x_i, y_i\}$, where x_i ε X and y_i ε Y. The function $f()$ can be used to create a new instance of x with the label $f(x)$.

Assume a learning assignment and a root domain D_s. T_s, a learning assignment T_T, and a goal domain D_T transfer learning objectives to aid progress in the learning of the target predictive feature $f_T(.)$ in D_T using D_s and T_s information, wherever $D_s \neq D_T$, or else $T_s \neq T_T$. By manipulating a group of auxiliary tasks that are not the same as the principal ones, one may attempt to learn a group of principal tasks using dissimilar tasks. In a number of contexts, joint learning of various tasks that use the same input data may be helpful. Prior task comprehension experience can contribute to more lightweight and useful representations for each task grouping, according to the target, by eliminating idiosyncrasies in data delivery. Novel techniques are being developed that build on a previous multitask technique by encouraging each task grouping to share a low-dimensional representation. The computer programmer can exploit an error in different classes of assignments, rendering the two representations useless. Experiments on synthetic and real data have shown that combining unrelated tasks can produce substantial gains over conventional multitask learning methods.

The principle of knowledge transfer as it applies to multitask learning is known as knowledge transfer. A shared representation is established concurrently across tasks in traditional multitask learning, while a shared representation is established sequentially across tasks in transfer of knowledge. An image-based object classifier can modify a robust representation, which could be useful for other algorithm's learning similar tasks. For example, a feature extractor can be used to perform preprocessing for another learning algorithm using the pretrained model. Alternatively, the pretrained model can be used to construct a model with a similar architecture that can then be fine-tuned to learn a new classification mission. Learning in a flexible online community, stationary learning environments have traditionally benefited from multitask learning and knowledge sharing. The name given to their allowance to non-stationary settings is group online adaptive learning (GOAL). Sharing knowledge can be particularly beneficial for newcomers who work in rapidly evolving environments, as they can benefit from another learner's previous experience to quickly become acquainted with their new surroundings. Group-adaptive learning has a broad variety of applications, from financial time-series prediction to content recommendation systems to visual thoughtfulness for adaptive autonomous agents [9].

3.5 Domain Adaptation

Domain adaptation is the capability to spread over an algorithm skilled in one or more "source domains" to a dissimilar (but associated) "target domain". Domain adaptation is a subsection of transfer learning. Deep domain adaptation allows one to migrate the information gained by a particular deep neural network (DNN) on a base task to a new target task that is connected to it. It has proven to be effective in tasks like image classification and style transfer [10].

Domain adaptation can be done in a variety of ways. Two methods are commonly used in "shallow" (not deep) domain adaptation: Reweighing the source samples and working out on the reweighed samples, and learning a shared space to balance the distributions of the source and target datasets. Although these strategies may be true in the sense of deep learning, the deep structures learned by DNNs regularly give rise to more transferable representations, with the transferability suddenly decreasing in higher layers [11]. We attempt to use this property of DNNs in deep domain adaptation. Domain adaptation may also be categorized as supervised, semi-supervised or unsupervised depending on the data you have from the target domain.

In supervised domain adaptation, you have very rare labelled amounts of data. Occasionally, you do take few labels of the target dataset for training that's weakly supervised training. Generally, in domain adaptation, it's unsupervised individual. It's not only labelling data.

Semi-supervised domain adaptation with subspace learning (SDASL) is to link the domain gap by together creating good subspace feature representations to lessen domain discrepancy and leveraging un-labelled target data in unification with labelled data.

Unsupervised domain adaptation (UDA) is the process of training a statistical model on marked data from a source domain to perform better on data from a target domain, with only unlabeled data in the target domain as input.

For a variety of tasks, deep learning has generated cutting-edge results [6]. While supervised learning methods have been shown to be effective, they require that training and testing data come from the same distribution, which is not always the case. As an alternative to this experiment, single-source UDA will carry situations where a network is skilled on marked data from a source domain and unlabeled data from a similar but different target domain, with the target domain's goal line of accomplishment well at test time. As a result, a slew of single-source, characteristically homogeneous unsupervised deep domain adaptation methods have emerged, joining the controlling factors. To minimize dependency on potentially expensive target data labels, deep learning hierarchical representations with domain adaptation are used. Alternative methods, special and communal elements, effects and theoretical understandings will all be compared and contrasted in this study. We keep track of this by looking at currently open application areas and research directions.

Only if the training and test data follow the same distribution, all well-known ML algorithms, for both supervised and unsupervised learning, perform well. Most mathematical models must be replicated from recently collected data when the distribution deviates, which can be expensive or impossible in certain situations. As a result, developing methods that minimize the time and effort needed to acquire new labelled samples by adjusting data provided in similar areas and using these additional diagonally comparable fields have become crucial. This has led to the creation of a modern ML method known as transfer learning, which is a learning environment assisted by a human's ability to deduce knowledge from tasks to learn more effectively [12].

Despite a wide variety of transfer learning scenarios, the primary aim of this survey is to provide an overview of current theoretical rankings in domain adaptation, a subfield of transfer learning that is perhaps the most common. In this subfield, the data distribution between training and test data is presumed to vary diagonally, while the learning task remains the same [2].

We provide the first comprehensive overview of the remaining findings related to the domain adaptation problem, including learning bounds based on various statistical learning frameworks [13].

Artificial intelligence (AI) and ML are no longer science fiction; they're here to stay. Although it took us a long time to get here, recent heavy investment in this area appears to have accelerated growth.

Although ML is making tremendous strides in cyber security and autonomous vehicles, there is still a long way to go in this field as a whole. This is due to ML's inability to tackle a number of roadblocks that continue to impede progress.

3.6 Challenges

3.6.1 Networks of Memory

Memory networks, also known as memory augmented neural networks, use a lot of working memory to store data. This type of neural network requires a memory block that can both be written to and delivered by the network, this is a significant challenge that ML must overcome. We need to find a better way for networks to determine facts, store them and access them quickly when required to achieve truly well-organized and real AI [14].

3.6.2 Natural Language Processing (NLP)

We still have a long way to go before we can reach natural language processing (NLP) and comprehension, despite a lot of money and time invested. Also for deep networks, this remains a significant obstacle. We currently use computers to represent languages and act as if logic were constructed on top of them. This, on the other hand, has always been a flop.

3.6.3 Pay Close Attention

To assimilate a vast number of features, human visual systems employ a highly accurate method of consideration. In contrast, ML is currently based on small amounts of input stimuli, one at a time, and only assimilates the effects at the end. For ML to reach its full potential, we need instruments that mimic the human visual system and are built into neural networks.

3.6.4 Learning in a Single Sitting

While neural network applications have advanced, we still lack the ability to perform one-shot learning. Traditional gradient-based networks, on the other hand, require a significant amount of data to be collected, which is often in the form of rigorous iterative training. As a substitute, we need to figure out how to teach neural networks from only one or two examples [11].

3.6.5 Video Training Information

We've been using video training data so far, but we're still relying on static images as a backup. To improve the performance of ML systems, we must allow them to learn by hearing and detecting. As a result, we have been taking advantage of learning by detecting our energetic environment using video datasets, which are much more relaxed than static images [15].

3.6.6 Object Recognition

Object recognition is difficult for algorithms to accurately classify since imagine classification and localization in computer vision and ML are still missing. The only way to keep going is to put more time and energy into resolving this problem [16].

3.6.7 Decentralization of AI

AI hasn't yet been completely democratized thanks to big data and computing resources. If we can do this, we can have the wisdom to face the world's problems head-on.

3.7 Distributed Representation

The term "distributed representation" refers to a many-to-many relationship between two different forms of representation (such as concepts and neurons). Each concept is characterized by many neurons – individually neuron contributes in the representation of many perceptions.

Distributed representation defines the same data features transversely multiple scalable and interdependent layers. Separately layer describes the information with the similar level of accuracy, but familiar for the level of scale. These layers are learned simultaneously but in a non-linear fashion. This imitator human logic in a neural network, since each idea can be accessed by more than one neuron firing and each neuron can signify more than one perception [17].

In non-distributed or local representation, individually likely value has a unique representation slot, which involves a lot of memory to method a large database than the distributed method.

3.8 Disentangling Factors of Variation

A conditional generative model for learning to separate the hidden factors of variation in a set of labelled observations and distinguish them into complementary codes. One code reviews the specified factors of variation connected with the labels [18]. The other reviews the remaining unspecified variability. Through training, the only available source of supervision originates from our ability to separate among different observations belonging to the same class [19]. Illustrations of such explanations include pictures of a set of labelled objects captured at different lookouts, or recordings of a set of speakers uttering multiple phrases. In both instances, the intra-class diversity is the basis of the unspecified factors of variation: Individually object is observed at multiple viewpoints, and each speaker commands multiple phrases. Learning to disentangle the specified factors from the unspecified ones develops relaxed when strong supervision is imaginable [20]. Undertaking that through training, we have access to pairs of images, where individually pair shows two different objects taken from the same viewpoint. This basis of alignment permits us to resolve our task using current methods. Though, labels for the unspecified features are generally unavailable in accurate scenarios where data acquisition is not severely measured. We address the problematic of disentanglement in this further general setting by merging deep convolutional autoencoders with a form of adversarial training [21]. Both factors of variation are indirectly captured in the organization of the learned embedding space and can be used for explaining single-image analogies. Trial results on synthetic and real datasets display that the planned technique is skilled of generalizing to hidden classes and intra-class variability (Unproblematic representation learning is calculated by learning disentangled representations. The unsupervised disentanglement learning without inductive biases is technically impossible, and that current inductive biases and unsupervised approaches do not agree to reliably learn disentangled representations. While one capability has restricted access to supervision in many real-world environments, for example, by manual labelling of approximately factors of variance in a few training samples, we investigated the impact of such supervision on high-tech disentanglement approaches and achieved large-scale learning by testing over 52,000 models under controlled and repeatable conditions. We believe that a limited number of labelled examples (0.01–0.5% of the data set) are sufficient to complete model collection on high-tech unsupervised models, even if the labels are potentially misleading and incomplete [22].

3.9 Experimental Proof for Prediction Analysis Using Medical Images

Noise can be occurred during the acquisition, transformation and also by human error. These noises seriously affect the important features in an image, which may lead to false diagnosis of the diseases [23]. By using the low radiation system for scanning the dense tissues, the detection of region of interest (ROI) will become less reliable. Therefore, before handling the detection and classification phases, the source image has to undergo the pre-processing stage [24].

Generally, the occurrence of noise in an image is a known factor; therefore, the sufficient measures have to be taken to eradicate the noise without losing the feature information [25]. For detecting the breast cancer and calcification, mammography is the defined type of device [4]. Usually, noise-free pixel supplies more adequate detail in an image which may sometimes subject to the replacement process which causes the loss in image quality [26]. Non-local averaging filter compares the grey-scale image with the geometrical configuration in a whole neighbourhood window with smoothing filter. In [27] discussed the noise removal methodology where the impulse noise density ratio moves from low to high in the polluted images [28].

In this paper, we proposed the denoising system for mammogram and ultrasound images. At first, input images are debased with an impulse noise density which varies from 10% to 90%. The denoising channels utilized in this work have detection and modifying stage for expelling the noise candidate from an image [29, 30]. This type of two-stage filter does not change the originality of an image and also preserves the internal edges efficiently. After the filtration stage, the resultant is cascaded with an optimization algorithm to minimize error rate by using the appropriate parameters. The different denoising filter is used with the artificial bee colony (ABC) and bacterial foraging optimization (BFO) algorithm separately. The optimization algorithm ABC and BFO are used in with the denoising filter to get the optimized denoising result, where it minimizes the mean square error of the resultant medical image. From the comparative analysis, it has been found that the proposed framework scheme such as Adaptive Switching Median Filter (ASWMF) [31] with BFO fabricate the better outcome which enhancement in visual quality [32].

3.9.1 Overview of Optimization Algorithms

Evolutionary algorithm has the behaviour of biological species [23] that can be inherited for the optimizing the application.

3.9.1.1 Artificial Bee Colony Algorithm

The ABC algorithm uses the mannerism of biological species such as fish, birds, ants, bees, etc. [33]. The ABC optimization uses the mannerism of bees which are categorized into employed bees, onlooker bees and scout bees. Each and every bee has their individual jobs like searching for food, its source and best location to store it. The below-mentioned pseudocode briefly describes the functionality of ABC [34]. In Figure 3.1 ABC algorithm is shown [33].

INITIALIZE the source of food for all the bees
REPEAT
Employed Bees Stage (concludes the food source and assess the nectar (fitness value)
Onlooker Bees Stage (select the best food source based on employee bee behaviour)
Scout Bees Stage (abandon food is found and replaced with newer food source)
Register the track of newer food source
UNTIL (Maximum CPU utilization time)

FIGURE 3.1
ABC algorithm code

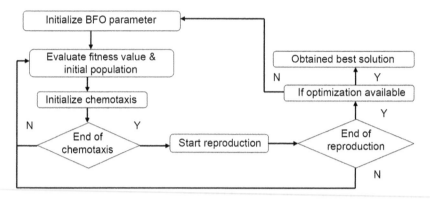

FIGURE 3.2
BFO algorithm flow chart

3.9.1.2 Bacterial Foraging Optimization Algorithm

The BFO technique inherits the idea of *Escherichia coli* bacteria for optimizing the system (Figure 3.2) [26]. The main stages of this algorithm have four steps such as chemotaxis, swarming, reproduction and elimination and dispersal. From the moment of bacteria, chemotaxis is responsible. Usually, bacteria have the flagellum, which is used to travel from one place to another by swimming [35]. Bacteria generally group themselves in concentric patterns with the help of swarming. The unhealthy bacteria expire in the reproductive process and the healthy one divides into two [36]. With the change of climatic condition, elimination and dispersal happen [16]. The BFO algorithm adjusts the run-length parameter dynamically during execution to balance the exploration swapping [37].

3.9.2 Design of the Proposed Framework

In this work, we proposed the impulse noise reduction filter for medical images. The filter presented in this work is cascaded with the efficient optimization algorithm such as ABC and BFO.

The idea behind denoising the medical image using the spatial domain is to prevent the loss of important features in an image [38]. The spatial domains can be modified suitably according to the threshold functions. The thresholding function determines the quality of the image and amount of noise pixel detected. Detection and modification of pixels are the two phases of these denoising filters (Figure 3.3). In the detection phase, each filter has its own different ways of estimating the threshold for detecting the noisy pixel from an image, but the filtration process holds with the basis of the standard median filter with some edge-preserving techniques. The noise removal stage in the proposed work starts by finding the noise pixels in an image by implementing the traditional filtering concept called local averaging and

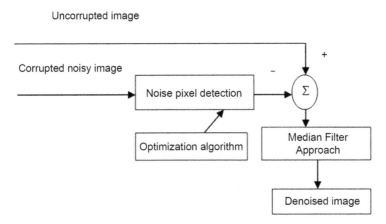

FIGURE 3.3
Block representation of the denoised filter with optimization algorithm

replaces the polluted pixel with the median value. The above-mentioned denoising techniques are cascaded with the ABC and BFO algorithm separately to curtail the MSE between the target image and the corrupted image. The BFO algorithm with ASWMF gives the better result when it compares with the other filters with ABC and BFO algorithm.

The cascading optimization strategies utilized in this work have various factors and it is picked by the quantity of pixel in an information picture. For the ABC calculation, we have discovered the colony size must be 60 and the number of cycles is picked as 120 tentatively. Here various cycles are equivalent to the halting criteria. The parameter picked for BFO calculation is the total number of bacteria population picked for looking through the region which is equivalent to the size of the selected window size. The number of the cycle in the chemotaxis step is set up to 5. For the swimming, reproduction and dispersal 5 are made as a default value. The likelihood of the elimination and dispersal is 0.5. We have estimated the parameter for controlling the optimization algorithm by various experimental studies.

3.9.3 Evaluation Metrics and Simulation Results

The performance of the median-based denoising filters with evolutionary algorithms is applied to mammogram and ultrasound images of 512×256 size. The efficiency of the cascaded filter is analysed with the help of PSNR (peak signal-to-noise ratio) and SSIM (structural similarity index), MSE for the varying noise densities 10, 30, 50, 70, 90. The PSNR factors deal with the noise ratio in an image, while the SSIM [39] has three different components such as luminance, contrast and structural information. The tabulated data from Tables 3.1 to 3.4 depict the performance of noise removal filter for medical image.

TABLE 3.1

PSNR and SSIM Value Obtained for Denoising Filters with ABC Algorithm – Mammogram Image

Metrics	Noise Density (%)	Median	ASMF	MDBUTMF	DAWSMF	RAMF	ADTMF	ASWMF
PSNR	10	28.0164	31.8491	35.2672	33.1214	34.4890	36.6428	37.1204
	30	24.6120	27.9470	31.4276	30.7862	30.0112	34.4601	35.0469
	50	19.6700	23.0176	27.1619	26.0416	25.1102	28.4691	30.6494
	70	13.0017	19.0679	20.3741	21.7691	21.2616	25.6412	26.0091
	90	10.9100	15.0567	18.9472	18.9916	17.8687	22.1801	21.1246
SSIM	10	0.5084	0.6002	0.6793	0.6913	0.7322	0.7625	0.8001
	30	0.4065	0.5120	0.5525	0.5543	0.6078	0.6300	0.6860
	50	0.3011	0.4930	0.4011	0.4108	0.4391	0.4031	0.5103
	70	0.2957	0.3769	0.3410	0.3001	0.3741	0.3994	0.4936
	90	0.2695	0.2761	0.2843	0.2812	0.2760	0.2994	0.3234
MSE	10	78.4135	72.7468	70.5139	63.4610	54.6512	51.3018	44.0221
	30	86.5214	86.0017	82.3741	69.7709	60.3210	68.0164	59.7510
	50	90.3641	89.3657	89.3954	77.0317	72.0395	73.3684	67.4201
	70	112.1496	99.1450	97.3217	91.0031	89.0174	86.4513	83.6514
	90	120.3017	108.0139	106.0103	98.1369	103.0369	97.0398	91.0198

TABLE 3.2

PSNR and SSIM Value Obtained for Denoising Filters with ABC Algorithm –Ultrasound Image

Metrics	Noise Density (%)	Median	ASMF	MDBUTMF	DAWSMF	RAMF	ADTMF	ASWMF
PSNR	10	25.5462	29.6914	32.1524	30.8601	31.1432	32.6011	35.1446
	30	21.7409	24.2744	26.1777	27.0069	27.3570	30.7281	33.9400
	50	17.0001	20.7606	21.0174	24.2708	23.6472	27.2470	27.8709
	70	13.6409	16.8809	19.0197	20.0911	20.7714	22.8611	23.9907
	90	8.9071	13.8601	17.1426	18.0108	16.1280	20.0011	19.0813
SSIM	10	0.4012	0.4071	0.5351	0.5748	0.6056	0.6331	0.6401
	30	0.3540	0.3924	0.4661	0.4852	0.5218	0.5678	0.5912
	50	0.2883	0.3071	0.3236	0.3905	0.4020	0.4012	0.4548
	70	0.2567	0.2900	0.2945	0.3067	0.3605	0.3600	0.3694
	90	0.2307	0.2414	0.2738	0.2851	0.2606	0.2812	0.2900
MSE	10	80.5612	77.5623	76.2145	70.0215	64.4587	60.0659	51.1278
	30	87.9401	81.1780	85.1456	79.4986	77.4523	68.9854	57.4236
	50	93.4101	98.3568	94.7856	87.1458	82.6325	79.7856	77.1256
	70	104.0398	109.7856	103.6598	93.4563	94.4869	92.3259	86.4512
	90	129.5410	113.6521	110.4523	104.8563	103.4523	98.2546	95.1456

TABLE 3.3

PSNR and SSIM Value Obtained for Denoising Filters with BFO Algorithm – Mammogram Image

Metrics	Noise Density (%)	Median	ASMF	MDBUTMF	DAWSMF	RAMF	ADTMF	ASWMF
PSNR	10	29.9469	33.7601	36.0010	35.6127	34.9901	37.9201	38.2487
	30	25.4674	29.5030	32.0018	29.1223	30.4489	34.0219	35.0146
	50	19.1301	24.0707	28.2019	25.7600	26.0761	28.1401	29.3290
	70	13.8012	21.9460	23.0000	21.6492	23.6421	25.7408	25.5061
	90	11.0176	18.8112	20.0176	19.1202	20.1670	22.7691	23.2001
SSIM	10	0.5914	0.6817	0.6940	0.7044	0.7840	0.7949	0.8017
	30	0.4402	0.5321	0.5675	0.6477	0.6733	0.6934	0.6917
	50	0.3959	0.4876	0.4994	0.4912	0.5011	0.5130	0.5946
	70	0.3027	0.3517	0.4031	0.4011	0.4058	0.4019	0.4812
	90	0.2957	0.2944	0.3019	0.3009	0.3115	0.3219	0.3443
MSE	10	80.1269	75.2369	69.5896	62.3265	55.4789	59.3658	46.8563
	30	89.2349	81.6523	75.2589	77.2145	62.9856	66.4532	57.1259
	50	94.7856	96.2659	81.8652	83.8563	76.6327	78.9547	71.6352
	70	109.2356	106.3269	98.5974	95.8563	93.1862	91.2648	83.9856
	90	116.2659	113.1753	107.4596	101.7436	97.5296	98.4265	92.6532

TABLE 3.4

PSNR and SSIM Value Obtained for Denoising Filters with BFO Algorithm – Ultrasound Image

Metrics	Noise Density (%)	Median	ASMF	MDBUTMF	DAWSMF	RAMF	ADTMF	ASWMF
PSNR	10	27.0164	32.1214	34.0641	32.9400	34.0012	33.2613	36.0818
	30	23.1701	29.1611	30.8924	29.6742	30.1019	30.3471	34.1492
	50	19.4690	25.7069	23.7489	24.4200	27.0019	26.5469	29.8607
	70	15.7701	19.2310	20.5619	20.2000	22.5600	23.8400	25.6419
	90	10.9146	16.5677	18.1489	18.9409	19.0700	21.2709	21.9944
SSIM	10	0.4985	0.5369	0.5952	0.6367	0.6914	0.7024	0.7610
	30	0.3548	0.4982	0.5019	0.5418	0.5916	0.6352	0.6811
	50	0.3057	0.3747	0.4077	0.4122	0.4012	0.5493	0.5622
	70	0.2962	0.3011	0.3760	0.3467	0.3633	0.4044	0.4237
	90	0.2714	0.2793	0.2876	0.2948	0.2997	0.3041	0.3070
MSE	10	87.853	80.4586	74.1452	66.3657	67.4783	58.1963	53.3259
	30	93.2358	88.8452	85.6593	79.3756	78.6519	65.1637	66.9834
	50	102.32	94.6412	96.9614	90.1367	84.9641	76.5627	74.9364
	70	115.1358	109.8236	101.0397	103.3947	93.0657	84.9614	83.5297
	90	123.7436	118.9527	109.4637	111.9127	104.7369	99.8264	94.4628

TABLE 3.5

Average Computational Complexity of Speed Obtained for Denoising Filters with ABC Algorithm

Image	Median	ASMF	MDBUTMF	DAWSMF	RAMF	ADTMF	ASWMF
Mammogram	42.60	37.85	36.44	27.41	15.30	17.72	8.65
Ultrasound	48.34	45.61	34.07	30.96	23.47	19.98	10.52

The comparison and performance analysis is made with the seven different filters such as standard median filter, ASMF, MDBUTMF [40], DAWSMF, RAMF, ADTMF, ASWMF with ABC and BFO algorithm separately in terms of PSNR and SSIM. From Tables 3.1 to 3.4, the performance factor is tabulated for median-based denoising filter combined with the ABC and BFO optimization algorithm. Tables 3.3 and 3.4 show the tabulated results of various denoising filters with BFO algorithm for mammogram and ultrasound images. Here 85 mammogram image's and 72 ultrasound image's average results were tabulated. From the above-mentioned tables, it is observed that PSNR and SSIM measures keep decreases when noise percentage goes to the higher level. It is observed from the above tables that ADTMF and ASWMF produce the fair result for ABC and BFO algorithm under very high noise density.

Tables 3.5 and 3.6 depict the result of computational complexity of speed of denoising algorithm with ABC and BFO separately. The computation speed analysis from Tables 3.5 and 3.6 shows that the ASWMF with ABC and BFO results the better complexity when it is compared with the other denoising algorithm worked in this paper.

Figure 3.4 (a) and (b) represents the impulse noise candidate 70% applied to an image. Figure 3.4 (a) is the mammogram breast (mdb265) image taken from Mammographic Image Analysis Society (MIAS) dataset which is available publically. Figure 3.4 (b) represents the original and corrupted ultrasound normal prostate image. The ultrasound image is taken from socially available dataset repository signal processing laboratory.

The visual observation is also made for a mammogram and ultrasound image for the impulse noise corrupted image of noise density 10%–90%.

TABLE 3.6

Average Computational Complexity of Speed Obtained for Denoising Filters with BFO Algorithm

Image	Median	ASMF	MDBUTMF	DAWSMF	RAMF	ADTMF	ASWMF
Mammogram	40.85	37.95	30.51	28.37	21.73	19.72	10.78
Ultrasound	53.17	44.74	37.39	29.61	24.04	17.69	13.42

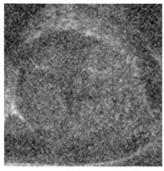

FIGURE 3.4
(a) Show corrupted mammogram image with 70% of impulse noise. (b) Show corrupted ultrasound with 70% of impulse noise.

Figures 3.5 and 3.6 represent the visual observation of the denoising filter and denoising filter with ABC and BFO algorithm for mammogram image. Figure 3.6 represents the visual observation of the denoising filter and denoising filter with ABC and BFO algorithm for ultrasound image, respectively. The proposed parameters for the BFO algorithm with ASWMF filter show the better visual outcome than the other noise reduction filter. The interior region and edges are restored well with our proposed framework and the image edges are more prominent when our proposed method compared with the other filter with ABC algorithm.

3.10 Conclusion

The proposed work introduced the denoising filter cascaded with the optimization algorithms such as ABC and BFO. The optimized denoising filter is applied to medical images which are affected by impulse noise candidate. The efficiency and performance of the filter is estimated both qualitatively and quantitatively by the metrics SSIM and PSNR. From the visual and analytical results, the ASWMF filter that is made to cascade with BFO algorithm gives the good result when compared to other optimized filters. Therefore, it gives take away computational complexity at a very lower level and superior over the performance. However, when the noise level increases in an ultrasound image, it faces the serious effect with the image quality which may limit the efficiency of the proposed work and that can be further enhanced in future work.

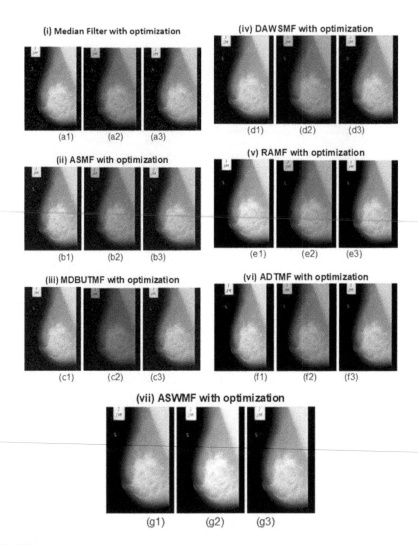

FIGURE 3.5

(i)–(vii) represent the visual result of various denoising filters and denoising filter with ABC and BFO optimization algorithm for mammogram images. In (i), (a1) show Median filter image, (a2) show resultant image of Median filter with ABC optimization, (a3) show resultant image of Median filter with BFO algorithm. In (ii), (b1) depicts the ASMF denoising filter image, (b2) shows resultant image of ASMF with ABC optimization, (b3) shows resultant image of ASMF with BFO algorithm. In (iii), (c1) shows MDBUTMF denoising filter image, (c2) shows resultant image of MDBUTMF with ABC optimization, (c3) shows resultant image of MDBUTMF with BFO algorithm. In (iv), (d1) shows DAWSMF denoising filter output image, (d2) represents resultant image of DAWSMF with ABC optimization, (d3) shows resultant image of DAWSMF with BFO algorithm. In (v), (e1) shows RAMF denoising filter output image, (e2) shows resultant image of RAMF with ABC optimization, (e3) shows resultant image of RAMF with BFO algorithm. In (vi), (f1) represents ADTMF denoising filter output image, (f2) shows resultant image of ADTMF with ABC optimization, (f3) shows resultant image of ADTMF with BFO algorithm. In (vii), (g1) shows ASWMF denoising filter output image, (g2) represents resultant image of ASWMF with ABC optimization, (g3) shows resultant image of ASWMF with BFO algorithm.

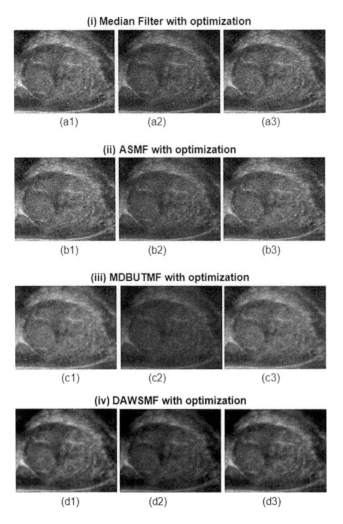

FIGURE 3.6
(i)–(vii) represents the visual result of various denoising filters and denoising filter with ABC and BFO optimization algorithm for ultrasound images. In (i), (a1) shows Median filter image, (a2) shows resultant image of Median filter with ABC optimization, (a3) shows resultant image of Median filter with BFO algorithm. In (ii), (b1) depicts the ASMF denoising filter image, (b2) shows resultant image of ASMF with ABC optimization, (b3) shows resultant image of ASMF with BFO algorithm. In (iii), (c1) shows MDBUTMF denoising filter image, (c2) shows resultant image of MDBUTMF with ABC optimization, (c3) shows resultant image of MDBUTMF with BFO algorithm. In (iv), (d1) shows DAWSMF denoising filter output image, (d2) represents resultant image of DAWSMF with ABC optimization, (d3) shows resultant image of DAWSMF with BFO algorithm. In (v), (e1) shows RAMF denoising filter output image, (e2) shows resultant image of RAMF with ABC optimization, (e3) shows resultant image of RAMF with BFO algorithm. In (vi), (f1) represents ADTMF denoising filter output image, (f2) shows resultant image of ADTMF with ABC optimization, (f3) shows resultant image of ADTMF with BFO algorithm. In (vii), (g1) shows ASWMF denoising filter output image, (g2) represents resultant image of ASWMF with ABC optimization, (g3) shows resultant image of ASWMF with BFO algorithm. *(Continued)*

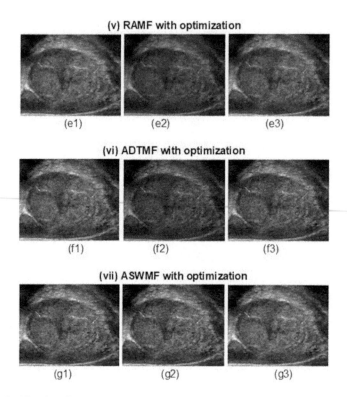

FIGURE 3.6 *(Continued)*

References

[1] Agrawal, V., Sharma, H. and Bansal, J., 2012. Bacterial foraging optimization: A survey. In *Proceedings of the International Conference on Soft Computing for Problem Solving (SocProS 2011) December 20-22, 2011* (pp. 227–242). Springer Berlin/ Heidelberg.

[2] Brownlee, J., 2019. "A gentle introduction to object recognition with deep learning", Deep Learning for Computer Vision, May 22, 2019.

[3] Nair, M.S. and Mol, P.A., 2013. Direction based adaptive weighted switching median filter for removing high density impulse noise. *Computers & Electrical Engineering*, 39(2), pp. 663–689.

[4] Ramya, A., Murugan, V. and Murugan, D., 2017. Non-linear directive contrast filter for mammogram images to enhance pleomorphic calcification. *International Journal of Computer Applications*, 163(7).

[5] Yaduwanshi, S. and Sidhu, J.S., 2013. Application of bacterial foraging optimisation as a de-noising filter. *International Journal of Engineering Trends and Technology (IJETT)*, 13(4), 600–612.

[6] Wilson, G. and Cook, D.J., 2020. "A survey of unsupervised deep domain adaptation", Machine Learning (cs.LG); Machine Learning (stat.ML), Submitted on 6 Dec 2018 (v1), last revised 6 Feb 2020 (this version, v3).

[7] Frost, V.S., et al., 1982. A model for radar images and its application to adaptive digital filtering of multiplicative noise. *IEEE Transactions on Pattern Analysis and Machine Intelligence*, 2, pp. 157–166.

[8] Gulo, C.A., de Arruda, H.F., de Araujo, A.F., Sementille, A.C., and Tavares, J.M.R. (2019). Efficient parallelization on GPU of an image smoothing method based on a variational model. *Journal of Real-Time Image Processing*, 16(4), pp. 1249–1261.

[9] Kushwaha, S. and Singh, R.K., 2017. An efficient approach for denoising ultrasound images using anisotropic diffusion and teaching learning based optimization. *Biomedical and Pharmacology Journal*, 10(2), pp. 805–816.

[10] Wang, Z., Bovik, A., Sheikh, H. and Simoncelli, E., 2004. Image quality assessment: From error visibility to structural similarity, *IEEE Trans. Image Process*, 13(4), pp. 600–612.

[11] Csurka, G. (Ed.). (2017). *Domain Adaptation in Computer Vision Applications* (Vol. 8). Cham: Springer.

[12] Redko, I., Morvant, E., Habrard, A., Sebban, M. and Bennani, Y., 2020. "A survey on domain adaptation theory: Learning bounds and theoretical guarantees", Machine Learning (cs.LG); Machine Learning (stat.ML), Submitted on 24 Apr 2020 (v1), last revised 6 Aug 2020 (this version, v5).

[13] Hsieh, M.-H., et al., 2013. Fast and efficient median filter for removing 1–99% levels of salt-and-pepper noise in images. *Engineering Applications of Artificial Intelligence* 26(4), pp. 1333–1338.

[14] Buades, A., Coll, B. and Morel, J.-M., 2005. A non-local algorithm for image denoising. *Computer Vision and Pattern Recognition, 2005. CVPR 2005. IEEE Computer Society Conference on*. Vol. 2. IEEE.

[15] de Araujo, A.F., Constantinou, C.E., and Tavares, J.M.R., 2016. Smoothing of ultrasound images using a new selective average filter. *Expert Systems with Applications*, 60, pp. 96–106.

[16] Das, S., Biswas, A., Dasgupta, S. and Abraham, A., 2009. Bacterial foraging optimization algorithm: theoretical foundations, analysis, and applications. *Foundations of Computational Intelligence*, 3, pp. 23–55.

[17] de Araujo, A.F., Constantinou, C.E., & Tavares, J.M.R., 2014. New artificial life model for image enhancement. *Expert Systems with Applications*, 41(13), pp. 5892–5906.

[18] Mathieu, M., Zhao, J., Sprechmann, P., Ramesh, A., LeCun, Y., 2016. "Disentangling factors of variation in deep representations using adversarial training", Conference paper in NIPS 2016, Machine Learning (cs.LG); Machine Learning (stat.ML) 10 Nov 2016.

[19] Lan, X. and Zuo, Z., 2014. Random-valued impulse noise removal by the adaptive switching median detectors and detail-preserving regularization. *Optik-International Journal for Light and Electron Optics*, 125(3), pp. 1101–1105.

[20] Dey, N., Ashour, A.S., Beagum, S., Pistola, D.S., Gospodinov, M., Gospodinova, E.P., and Tavares, J.M.R., 2015. Parameter optimization for local polynomial approximation based intersection confidence interval filter using genetic algorithm: an application for brain MRI image de-noising. *Journal of Imaging*, 1(1), pp. 60–84.

[21] Devila, S., Pattnaika, S.S., Duttab, M., Sastrya, G.V.R.S., Patraa, P.K. and Sagara, C.V., *Image Denoising using Bacterial Foraging Optimization Technique*, 2008.

[22] Akkoul, S., Ledee, R., Leconge, R. and Harba, R., 2010. A new adaptive switching median filter. *IEEE Signal Processing Letters*, 17(6), pp. 587–590.

[23] Kaur, A. and Goyal, S., 2011. A survey on the applications of bee colony optimization techniques. *International Journal on Computer Science and Engineering*, 3(8), p. 3037.

[24] Bakwad, K.M., Pattnaik, S.S., Sohi, B.S., Devi, S., Panigrahi, B.K. and Gollapudi, S.V., 2009. Bacterial foraging optimization technique cascaded with adaptive filter to enhance peak signal to noise ratio from single image. *IETE Journal of Research*, 55(4), pp. 173–179.

[25] Bhandari, A.K., Kumar, A., Singh, G.K. and Soni, V., 2016. Performance study of evolutionary algorithm for different wavelet filters for satellite image denoising using sub-band adaptive threshold. *Journal of Experimental & Theoretical Artificial Intelligence*, 28(1–2), pp. 71–95.

[26] Liu, Y. and Passino, K.M., 2002. Biomimicry of social foraging bacteria for distributed optimization: models, principles, and emergent behaviors. *Journal of Optimization Theory and Applications*, 115(3), pp. 603–628.

[27] Thanh, D.N., Hai, N.H., Prasath, V.S., Hieu, L.M. and Tavares, J.M.R. (2020). A two-stage filter for high density salt and pepper denoising. *Multimedia Tools and Applications*.

[28] Bhadouria, V.S., Tanase, A., Schmid, M., Hannig, F., Teich, J. and Ghoshal, D., 2017. A novel image impulse noise removal algorithm optimized for hardware accelerators. *Journal of Signal Processing Systems*, 89(2), pp. 225–242.

[29] Faragallah, O.S. and Ibrahem, H.M., 2016. Adaptive switching weighted median filter framework for suppressing salt-and-pepper noise. *AEU – International Journal of Electronics and Communications*, 70(8), pp. 1034–1040.

[30] Gupta, V., Chaurasia, V. and Shandilya, M., 2015. Random-valued impulse noise removal using adaptive dual threshold median filter. *Journal of Visual Communication and Image Representation*, 26, pp. 296–304.

[31] Meher, S.K. and Singhawat, B., 2014. An improved recursive and adaptive median filter for high density impulse noise. *AEU – International Journal of Electronics and Communications*, 68(12), pp. 1173–1179.

[32] Florencio, D.A.F. and Schafer, R.W., 1994. Decision-based median filter using local signal statistics. In *Visual Communications and Image Processing'94, 2308*, pp. 268–275.

[33] Karaboga, D., Gorkemli, B., Ozturk, C. and Karaboga, N., 2014. A comprehensive survey: Artificial bee colony (ABC) algorithm and applications. *Artificial Intelligence Review*, 42(1), pp. 21–57.

[34] Latifoğlu, F., 2013. A novel approach to speckle noise filtering based on artificial bee colony algorithm: An ultrasound image application. *Computer Methods and Programs in Biomedicine*, 111(3), pp. 561–569.

[35] Kaliraj, G. and S. Baskar, 2010. An efficient approach for the removal of impulse noise from the corrupted image using neural network based impulse detector. *Image and Vision Computing*, 28(3), pp. 458–466.

[36] Lu, C.-T. and Chou, T.-C., 2012. Denoising of salt-and-pepper noise corrupted image using modified directional-weighted-median filter. *Pattern Recognition Letters*, 33(10), pp. 1287–1295.

[37] Chen, H., Zhu, Y. and Hu, K., 2011, March. Adaptive bacterial foraging optimization. *Abstract and Applied Analysis, 2011.*

[38] Chan, R.H., Ho, C.-W. and Nikolova, M., 2005. Salt-and-pepper noise removal by median-type noise detectors and detail-preserving regularization. *IEEE Transactions on Image Processing 14*(10), pp. 1479–1485.

[39] Wang, J. and Zhang, D., 2015. Image denoising based on artificial bee colony and BP neural network. *TELKOMNIKA (Telecommunication Computing Electronics and Control), 13*(2), pp. 614–623.

[40] Esakkirajan, S., Veerakumar, T., Subramanyam, A.N. and PremChand, C.H., 2011. Removal of high density salt and pepper noise through modified decision based unsymmetric trimmed median filter. *IEEE Signal Processing Letters, 18*(5), pp. 287–290.

4

Construction of Deep Representations

Anitha Julian and R. Ramyadevi

4.1 Introduction

Section 4.2 explains the concept of representation learning, also termed feature learning, as a collection of procedures that allows automatic discovery of representations required for detecting features or performs classification from available raw data. This section also gives an overview of the traditional feature learning.

Section 4.3 elaborately discusses the first type of feature learning technique, supervised feature learning. As the name suggests, this set of algorithms indicates the presence of a supervisor or teacher through which the machine is trained with date already labeled or tagged with the correct answer. On the event of the machine being given a new set of data, the learning algorithm analyzes the trained data and produces correct answer from the tagged data that comprises two categories: classification and regression. Supervised dictionary learning (SDL) (develops a dictionary of representative elements for a given input data) and neural networks (belong to the family of learning algorithms that use a network consisting of multiple layers of interconnected nodes, it is developed under the inspiration of the animal nervous system) are also covered in detail with practical real-time scenarios for better understanding of the concepts.

Section 4.4 covers the second type of feature learning, i.e., unsupervised feature learning where features are learnt from unlabeled data. The goal is to discover low-dimensional features that capture some structure underlying the high-dimensional input data that comprises two categories: clustering and association. The section also gives a detailed overview on k-means clustering, principal component analysis (PCA), local linear embedding, independent component analysis (ICA), and unsupervised dictionary learning.

Section 4.5 gives information on learning in neural networks which covers single-layer learning that is a stepwise procedure for building and training a neural network. This approach makes the learning process easier for classifications tasks. The section also gives a brief note of the various learning algorithms.

DOI: 10.1201/9781003126898-4

Section 4.6 illustrates PCA as a dimensionality reduction technique in domains like facial recognition, computer vision, image compression, and pattern finding in high-dimensional data in various fields of study.

Each section concludes with real-time application illustrations related to the learned algorithms so that the learner gains in-depth knowledge on the topics covered in this chapter.

4.2 Feature Learning

In machine learning, feature learning or representation learning is a set of techniques that extract useful data from the raw input and convert it into a representation using mathematics, statistics, and domain knowledge in machine learning tasks. Figure 4.1 gives an overview of data representation learning over past decades [1]. A machine is said to be learning, with respect to a set of tasks, from past data that is fed in, and the performance for a given task improves with experience. A feature is an individual measurable property or attribute of a mechanism being observed in pattern recognition. Features are also referred to as independent variables, predictors, and attributes.

The crucial step for effective algorithms in pattern recognition is to facilitate the subsequent classification, retrieval, and recommendation tasks, choosing information, discriminating, and independent features. For large-scale applications, the important challenge is how to learn the intrinsic structure of data and discover valuable information from data. Features are usually numerical, but in syntactic pattern recognition, structural characteristics such as strings and graphs are used. The definition of "feature" is similar to

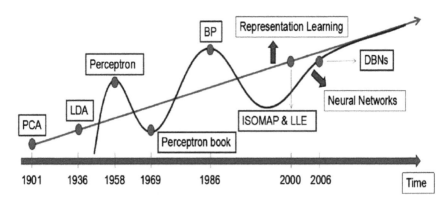

FIGURE 4.1
An overview on data representation learning

that used in statistical techniques, such as linear regression, as an explanatory variable.

4.2.1 Feature Engineering (Manual)/Traditional Feature Learning

Feature engineering in the field of machine learning and data analysis is an important area. It is a process of allowing a machine to automatically detect the meaningful features by learning both a specific task (using the features) and the features themselves. Data scientists and analysts need to spend much of their time on data cleaning, which is reduced by the use of feature engineering. Some examples of feature engineering techniques are:

1. Outlier detection and removal
2. One-hot encoding
3. Log transform
4. Dimensionality reduction
5. Handling missing values
6. Scaling

The fact that machine learning tasks, such as classification often require data, are mathematically and computationally easy to process, motivates feature learning. Real-world data such as measurement of images, video, and sensors, however, is typically complex, redundant, and highly variable. Thus, there is a need to discover useful features or representations from raw data. Traditional manually defined features often require costly human labor and often rely on technical expertise and they do not generalize well. Feature engineering/learning/selection are just self-explanatory words related to transforming, understanding, and selecting features.

Performing feature engineering in machine learning depends on the algorithm used and on the assumptions that the algorithm makes and how it uses the variables. It is the process of developing features that make machine learning algorithms work by using domain knowledge of the data. If feature engineering is done properly, it improves the predictive ability of algorithms for machine learning by creating features from raw data that help accelerate the process of machine learning. Feature engineering is an art. It denotes the construction of new features. The reduction is called variable selection or dimension reduction. There are two questions here, about feature selection and about feature extraction.

Feature selection, using less than all features available, can in many cases prevent overfitting and improve model results. Some algorithms are more resilient to irrelevant features than others. In some cases, proper regularization can limit the damage from redundant/irrelevant features but not all. Tree-based models are usually fairly resilient and yet they too can be harmed.

In many cases, we want to allow leaves for with a fairly small amount of samples (single digit) and in that scenario if we have many irrelevant features, it becomes likely that one of them be selected at the lowest split just by chance even if there is another feature with slightly less gain on the branch but much more overall.

Feature extraction is another matter altogether. This is the creative part and often requires understanding the problem and domain expertise. That said there are some generic tricks applicable to a wide range of problems, for example, bag-of-words encoding for text, stemming words, one-hot encoding of categorical variables, multiplying with indicator variable for linear models, summing a few variables for tree-based models, log normalization, and z score.

4.2.2 Feature Detection or Classification

Steps that are involved while solving any problem in machine learning are as follows:

- Gathering data
- Cleaning data
- Feature engineering
- Defining model
- Training, testing model, and predicting the output

Feature engineering is the most important art in machine learning that creates the huge difference between a good model and a bad model.

The interquartile range (IQR) is one of the values which helps in detecting and removing outliers in datasets. An outlier is an observation in a random sample of a population that is an abnormal distance from other values. For statistical studies, outliers are troublesome because they can cause experiments to either miss important findings or misrepresent real results. In a statistical dispersion, the total data-points are divided into four more or less equal parts called quarters or quartiles named Q_1, Q_2, Q_3, and Q_4 which signifies, 25th, 50th, 75th, and 100th percentile, respectively. IQR is calculated at the difference between Q_3 and Q_1. Using IQR, the upper and lower limits are calculated as:

$$\text{low}_{\text{limit}} = Q_1 - 1.5 \times \text{IQR} \tag{4.1}$$

$$\text{high}_{\text{limit}} = Q_3 + 1.5 \times \text{IQR} \tag{4.2}$$

Any value in the data-point that falls below the $\text{low}_{\text{limit}}$ or is higher than the $\text{high}_{\text{limit}}$ can be considered as an outlier. The implementation of this is

TABLE 4.1

Display for df.describe () in Python

	height
count	20.000000
mean	8.390000
std	8.782812
min	1.200000
25%	5.350000
50%	5.700000
75%	6.275000
max	40.200000

illustrated here in Python. A dataset having *heights* of students is considered from heights.csv file as shown in Table 4.1.

```
import pd.read_csv ("heights.csv")
df.describe()
```

To detect and remove the outlier,

```
Q1 = df.heights.quantile (0.25)
Q3 = df.heights.quantile (0.75)
IQR = Q3 – Q1
low_limit = Q1 – 1.5 * IQR
high_limit = Q3 + 1.5 * IQR
df[df.height < low_limit) | (df.height > high_limit)]
df
df_no_outlier = df[df.height < low_limit) & (df.height > high_limit)]
df_no_outlier
```

When the presence of some features degrades the performance of the model, their removal from a dataset is also included as feature engineering shown in Table 4.2. To summarize, the steps involved in feature engineering are:

1. Brainstorming on the list of features
2. If needed creating new features

TABLE 4.2

Display for df_no_outlier in Python

	Name	height
2	sakib	4.9
3	tao	5.1
4	virat	5.2
5	khubu	5.4
6	dmitry	5.5
7	selena	5.5
8	john	5.6
9	imran	5.6
10	jose	5.8
11	deepika	5.9
12	yoseph	6.0
13	binod	6.1
14	gulshan	6.2
15	johnson	6.5
16	donald	7-1

3. Checking the working of the model with the included features

4. Steps 1 to 3 can be repeated for better performance of the model

4.3 Supervised Feature Learning

There are many learning techniques through which computer can learn from the past data or experiences, identifying from the patterns and making new prediction for the new data. Types of learning algorithms can be classified as:

- Supervised
- Unsupervised
- Semi-supervised
- Reinforcement

Feature learning is classified as supervised and unsupervised similar to these types in machine learning. When features are learned with labeled input data, it is termed as supervised learning. Similarly, when features are learned with unlabeled input data, it is termed as unsupervised feature learning. Examples include dictionary learning, ICA, autoencoders, and various forms of clustering.

Learning with supervised features is learning features from labeled data. Data label plays an important role in computing an error term. The degree to which the system fails to produce the label is used as feedback to reduce or minimize errors in the learning process. The approaches included are:

- Classification (labels are defined)
- Regression (labels are not defined)

When the model is trained on a labeled dataset, it is termed as supervised learning. A labeled dataset is one which has input and output parameters. Here, the training as well as the validation datasets are labeled.

4.3.1 Supervised Dictionary Learning

Sparse data which alters the efficiency of algorithms and their ability to calculate precise predictions is a common problem in machine learning. When some predicted values are absent in a dataset, data is called sparse, which is a common occurrence in large-scale data analysis in general. For example, a region might sell only particular products and thus might not have data for other products. To represent such data, sparse representation is recommended.

Sparse representations aim to represent values with as few significant coefficients as possible. A matrix with fewer nonzero elements is called a sparse matrix. For example, if a matrix of size 1000×1000 contains only 100 nonzero elements, it is obvious that only 10 spaces of the matrix are filled with nonzero values and remaining spaces are filled with zero. In a sparse matrix representation, instead of storing zeroes with nonzero elements, only the nonzero elements are stored with triples, namely (Row, Column, Value), as shown in Table 4.3. A significant amount of memory can be saved and processing of data can be sped up by using sparse matrices to store data containing a large number of zero-value elements.

Dictionary learning is a branch of signal processing and machine learning that aims to find a frame in which a sparse representation is accepted by

TABLE 4.3

Sparse matrix representation

$$\begin{bmatrix} 2 & 0 & 0 & 0 & 3 \\ 0 & 1 & 0 & 0 & 0 \\ 5 & 0 & 0 & 0 & 0 \\ 0 & 7 & 0 & 0 & 8 \\ 0 & 0 & 4 & 0 & 0 \\ 0 & 6 & 0 & 0 & 0 \end{bmatrix} \Rightarrow$$

Row	Column	Value
6	5	8
0	0	2
0	4	3
1	1	1
2	0	5
3	1	7
4	2	4
5	1	6

some training data. The frame may also be referred to as a dictionary. The dictionary is characterized to be superior if the representation is sparser. It is a technique that helps to recreate a sample from a sparse atomic dictionary. The technique is similar to principal components but does not include constraints about the independence. The dictionary design for the sparse representations is done by iterating following two stages:

- Computing the sparse representations for the fixed dictionary and
- Updating the dictionary by using the fixed representations

Given the input dataset $X = [x_1, ..., x_K]$, $x_i \in R^d$, to find a dictionary $D \in R^{d \times n} : D = [d_1, ..., d_n]$ and a representation $R = [r_1, ..., r_K]$, $r_i \in R^n$ such that $\|X - D\ R\|_F^2$ is minimized and the representation r_i are sparse enough. This is formulated as an optimization problem as follows:

$$\underset{D \in C,\ \eta_i \in R^n}{\text{argmin}} \sum_{i=1}^{K} \|x_i - Dr_i\|_2^2 + \lambda \|r_i\|_0, \text{ where } C \equiv \left\{ D \in R^{d \times n} : \|d_i\|_2 \leq 1 \forall_i = 1, ..., n \right\}, \lambda > 0$$

(4.3)

C is required to constrain D so that its atoms will not reach arbitrarily high values allowing for arbitrarily low (but nonzero) values of r_i. The value λ controls the trade-off between the sparsity and the minimization error [1].

The dictionary can be *undercomplete if n < d* or *overcomplete if n > d* with the latter condition being the typical assumption for a sparse dictionary learning problem. From a representational point of view, the case of a complete dictionary does not offer any improvement and so it is not considered. Some of the algorithms that can describe this optimization problem are:

- Method of optimal directions (MOD)
- K-SVD
- Stochastic gradient descent
- Lagrange dual method
- LASSO

The description and explanations to these algorithms are beyond the scope of this chapter and the reader is suggested to refer content for these topics in Ref. [2] for detailed understanding.

In current recognition systems, supervised sparse coding has become a commonly used module, which unifies classifier training and dictionary learning to implement discrimination in sparse codes. The representation of items by the strong activation of a relatively small collection of neurons is termed as sparse coding. Authors in Ref. [3] have integrated multiple classifier training along with dictionary learning to deal with issue of supervised classification methods being unable to discriminate classes when dealt with high-complexity data. An ensemble of classifiers (linear classifiers) for predicting and a dictionary for representing are jointly learned by a minimized model that is developed. Each linear classifier is associated with a group of atoms and applied to the sparse codes, which enables the dictionary and all the classifiers to be simultaneously updated when trained. Such a method of supervised dictionary approach produces a compact dictionary with better discrimination also equipping the classifiers with improved robustness.

The SDL can be performed in three different approaches that are:

1. Reconstructive approach
2. Generative approach
3. Discriminative approach

Dictionary learning finds its use in image processing, video processing, signal processing, machine learning, medical imaging, and more varied fields. The technique can be applied to classification problems in such a way that the input signal can be categorized by finding the dictionary corresponding to the sparsest representation if unique dictionaries have been developed for each class. It also has characteristics that are useful for signal denoising since the meaningful part of the input signal can typically be represented in a sparse way by a dictionary, but the noise in the input would have a much less sparse representation [4]. Texture synthesis [5] and unsupervised clustering [6] have been successfully implemented using sparse dictionary learning. Sparse coding has been found empirically to outperform other coding methods on object category recognition tasks in assessments using the bag-of-words model [7]. Dictionary learning is used to interpret medical signals in depth. These medical signals include those from electroencephalography (EEG), electrocardiography (ECG), magnetic resonance imaging (MRI), functional MRI (fMRI), and computer tomography ultrasound (USCT), which are used to interpret each signal using different assumptions.

4.4 Unsupervised Learning

4.4.1 *k*-Means Clustering

Clustering is process that is used to identify classes of observations (known as clusters) that are identical for a given dataset. *k*-Means clustering is an immensely powerful unsupervised machine learning algorithm that is used to solve many complex unsupervised machine learning problems. The algorithm groups similar items in the dataset to form clusters, where the number of clusters formed is represented by k. The algorithm works as follows:

1. In accordance with the value of k, centroids are modeled randomly.
2. Each data-point in the dataset is assigned to the nearest centroid and tries to reduce the Euclidean distance (shortest distance between two points) between the data-points. If the data-point is nearer to the center of that cluster than to any other cluster center, data-points are said to be present in that cluster.
3. k-Means iteratively determines the centroid by finding mean of all data-points in a cluster. This helps to reduce the variance of the intra-cluster distances.
4. Steps 2 and 3 are repeated until sum of distances between the data-points and their respective centroids are diminished such that there is no variation in the cluster center value.

Euclidean distance is calculated by using the formula:

$$d = \left(\left(x_1 - y_1 \right)^2 + \left(x_2 - y_2 \right)^2 \right)^{1/2} \tag{4.4}$$

The formula is generalized for an n-dimensional space as:

$$D_e = \left(\sum_{i=1}^{n} \left(x_i - y_i \right)^2 \right)^{1/2} \tag{4.5}$$

where n is the number of dimensions and (x_i, y_i) are the coordinates of the data-points under consideration.

k-Means algorithm is easier to implement and is scalable faster to huge datasets. In terms of perception and resolution, the algorithm operates exceptionally smooth. It performs faster than other clustering algorithms for datasets that have many variables. The algorithm can work on unlabeled numerical data.

k-Means is sensitive when the dataset has outliers. An outlier is an observation in a random sample of a population that is an abnormal distance from other values. For statistical studies, outliers are troublesome because they can cause experiments to either miss important findings or misrepresent real results. The choice of an optimal value for k is a challenge. As the dimensions of the dataset increase, the scalability of the algorithm decreases.

k-Means algorithm finds its application in identifying varying conditions in health screenings, identifying traffic models under specified conditions, distinguishing automated activity from human activity, and segregating users into differing target markets. In general, k-means can be used for classification problems.

4.4.2 Principal Component Analysis

PCA is a tool that is used widely in exploratory data analysis (EDA) which comprises dimension reduction, feature extraction, and data visualization. In applications of artificial intelligence that use machine learning algorithms, PCA is useful for creating predictive models. PCA is also an unsupervised statistical technique and it is useful in examining the interrelations among a set of variables [8].

The performance of machine learning algorithms is seen as wonder working when the dataset provided for training is large and concise. The larger the size of data, it allows to build better predictive models as more data is available to train the machine. However, large datasets certainly have a pitfall in terms of dimensionality, or in other words, large dimensional datasets have lots of inconsistencies in the features or lots of redundant features in the dataset. This gradually increases the computation time and makes data processing and EDA more complex.

To address the issues in dimensionality, a process called dimensionality reduction is suggested, which consists of techniques that can filter out a limited number of significant features alone that are needed for training.

PCA is a dimensionality reduction technique that identifies correlations and patterns in a dataset and transforms it into a dataset of significantly lower dimension without loss of any important information.

Dimensionality reduction can be performed using PCA through the following steps:

1. Standardization of the data
2. Computation of the covariance matrix
3. Calculation of the eigenvectors and eigenvalues
4. Computation of the principal components
5. Dimensions of the dataset are reduced

A detailed description of this topic is dealt with in Section 4.6. However, as an eye-opener, some of the applications of PCA are listed here.

1. *Image compression* – An image is a matrix of pixels that are represented by red, green, blue (RGB) color values. PCA is used to reduce the dimensions of the image (matrix) and project the reformed image with new dimensions and of smaller k-weight, however, retaining its original qualities.
2. *Customer profiling/market segmentation* – Using the demographics data as well as the intellect of customers in purchasing, the positive and negative features in the dataset that lead to profiling/segmentation can be identified. Also, customer perception toward brands can also be analyzed.

3. *Cluster pattern and discrimination analysis in organic materials* – PCA is also used by researchers and scientists in food science, e.g., for finding the percentage oil in the pastry, density, crispiness, fracturability, and hardness of food products.

4. *Finance/banking* – PCA is useful in analyzing stocks quantitatively, forecasting portfolio returns, interest rate implantation, exploring applicants applied for loans, credit cards, etc., in banks.

5. *Health-care applications* – PCA has been used on medical data to show correlation of vital parameters. It can also be used to explore and analyze patient insurance data that consists of multiple sources and a huge number of variables that are correlated to each other.

The applications of PCA are also found in fields such as detection and visualization of computer network attacks, anomaly detection, facial recognition, computer vision, data mining, bioinformatics, psychology, etc.

4.4.3 Locally Linear Embedding

Locally linear embedding (LLE) algorithm is an unsupervised method proposed by Sam T. Roweis and Lawrence K. Saul in 2000 to minimize nonlinear dimensionality in their article [9]. The algorithm, by maintaining the geometric characteristics of the original nonlinear feature structure, attempts to reduce the n-dimensions in the data.

In any given application, to predict the output, machine learning algorithms use the features on which they were trained. The major issue faced with these algorithms is that of overfitting (the model fits the training data perfectly, but it is unable to predict the real-life test data accurately). Overfitting happens when a large number of features are used to train the data as the model gets more complex and enables the model to fit the data very well. Dimensionality reduction helps minimize the complexity of the machine learning model thereby helping to reduce overfitting to a greater degree. Dimensionality reduction allows to preserve the most relevant features in the data by reducing the number of features needed to predict the performance.

For every data-point, LLE algorithm initially finds the *k-nearest neighbors*. Next, it approximates each data vector as a weighted linear combination of its *k*-nearest neighbors. The weights that best reconstruct the vectors from its neighbors are then constructed thereby to deliver the low-dimensional vectors best reconstructed by these weights. The steps in the algorithm can be traced as follows:

1. The algorithm has only one parameter for tuning, the value of k, which is the number of nearest neighbors to be considered for forming the cluster. The choice of k should not be too small or too big as

it will not accommodate the entire geometry of the original data. For each data-point, k-nearest neighbors are computed.

2. To construct a new point, a weighted aggregation of the neighbors of each point is done, trying to minimize the cost function for jth nearest neighbor for the point X_i.

$$E(W) = \sum_i \left| X_i - \sum_j W_{ij} \, X_j \right|^2 \quad \text{such that} \quad \sum_j W_{ij} = 1 \qquad (4.6)$$

3. The new vector space Y is defined such that the cost for Y is minimized.

$$C(Y) = \sum_i \left| Y_i - \sum_j W_{ij} \, Y_j \right|^2 \qquad (4.7)$$

The advantages of LLE over other similar dimensionality reduction algorithms are in terms of the consideration of the nonlinearity of the structure and better computational time as shown in Figure 4.2.

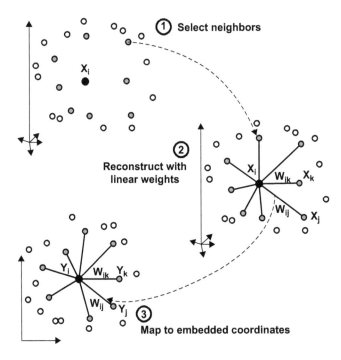

FIGURE 4.2
LLE algorithm procedure (Source: Ref. [10])

The brain–computer interface (BCI)-based robotic-assisted rehabilitation system is an applicable option for stroke survivors with a poorly functioning hemiparetic arm. Motor imagery EEG (MI-EEG) feature extraction, which is a nonlinear time-varying and nonstationary signal with a remarkable time-frequency characteristic, is the primary recovery device technique normally used. Authors in Ref. [11] have suggested a novel feature extraction method that is based on the LLE algorithm and discrete wavelet transform. To extract the nonlinear characteristics, LLE is applied to the approximation components, and the statistics of the detailed components are determined to obtain the time-frequency characteristics. The two features are then combined serially and the genetic algorithm optimizes a backpropagation neural network and employs it as a classifier to determine the efficacy of the proposed process. The results of the tenfold cross-validation experiment on a public BCI competition dataset show that the nonlinear features visually present obvious distribution of clustering and the fused features enhance the accuracy and stability of the classification.

Authors in Ref. [12] have proposed a modified LLE, namely, locally linear discriminate embedding (LLDE). LLDE retains a high-dimensional local linear structure and obtains a compact data representation in the embedding space (low dimensional) as accurately as possible before identification. The radial basis function (RBF) classifier is integrated with the LLDE for machine simplicity and fast processing. In relation to the variance of the data, the RBF classifier is carried out on low-dimensional embedding. The CMU-PIE database was used to test the proposed procedure, and experiments performed in this study demonstrated the efficacy of the proposed techniques in face recognition compared to linear and nonlinear approaches.

4.4.4 Independent Component Analysis

A recent and effective addition to the tools available to scientists and engineers to explore large datasets in high-dimensional spaces is ICA. It takes a broad dataset of several variables and reduces it to smaller dimensions that can be interpreted as self-organized functional networks [13].

Several application fields use ICA for its analysis and interpretation of data. It is a statistical technique for splitting a multivariate signal into additive subcomponents in signal processing. ICA is a tool of machine learning to distinguish a mixed signal from independent sources.

The separation of signals is a recurrent problem and is fundamental to the processing of statistical signals, which has a wide variety of applications in several technical fields ranging from audio and image processing to biomedical signal processing, telecommunications, and econometrics. As an illustration, assuming here is a conference hall with an audience and two speakers delivering presentations simultaneously. Audiences as normal are making comments and noises in the background. At different locations, there are two microphones that record the voices of the speakers and the noise coming from the audience. The goal is to isolate each speaker's voice while avoiding the background noise.

The shared illustration is a typical example of ICA, a well-established stochastic approach with applications in many technical fields such as audio and image processing, biomedical signal processing, telecommunications, and econometrics. ICA can be used as a blind source separation tool, meaning that independent signals can be isolated from linear mixtures with essentially no previous knowledge of the signals.

The data $x_i(t)$ assumed to consist of a number of variables m that are observed by T observations together, where the indices take the values $i = 1, ..., m$ and $t = 1, ..., T$ and m and T can be very large values. Such m-dimensional data is usually represented as linear functions as it is simpler for interpretation of the representation and also for computation. Thus, every component, say y_i, can be expressed as a linear combination of the observed variables as:

$$y_i(t) = \sum_j w_{ij} x_j(t), \text{ for } i = 1, ..., n, \ j = 1, ..., m \quad (4.8)$$

where w_{ij} are coefficients that define the representation. The equation can be expressed as a matrix multiplication by using linear algebra, by collecting the coefficients w_{ij} in a matrix W. The new equation is:

$$\begin{pmatrix} y_1(t) \\ y_2(t) \\ ... \\ y_n(t) \end{pmatrix} = W \begin{pmatrix} x_1(t) \\ x_2(t) \\ ... \\ x_n(t) \end{pmatrix} \quad (4.9)$$

Taking this same understanding for ICA too, given a set of observations of random variables $\big((x_1(t), x_2(t), ..., x_n(t)\big)$, t is the time or sample index. Assuming that the samples are generated as a linear mixture of independent components, we get the following equation:

$$\begin{pmatrix} x_1(t) \\ x_2(t) \\ ... \\ x_n(t) \end{pmatrix} = A \begin{pmatrix} s_1(t) \\ s_2(t) \\ ... \\ s_n(t) \end{pmatrix} \quad (4.10)$$

where A is an unknown matrix and ICA consists of estimating both the matrix A and the sample $s_i(t)$, when only $x_i(t)$ is observed.

Alternatively, ICA can be defined as *finding a linear transformation given by a matrix W as in () such that the random variables y_i, $i = 1, ..., n$ are as independent as possible*. This formulation is almost the same as the previous one, as after estimating A, its inverse gives W. The important point to be noted is that the mentioned model can be estimated if and only if the components s_i are *non-Gaussian*. The *Gaussian function* is given here for better understanding, which is a function of the form:

$$f(x) = a \cdot exp\left(-\frac{(x-b)^2}{2c^2}\right) \tag{4.11}$$

where a, b, and *nonzero c* are arbitrary constants, and the graph is a characteristic symmetric "bell curve" shape. The parameter a is the height of the curve's peak, b is the position of the center of the peak, and c is the standard deviation that controls the width of the "bell" in the curve.

The separation of mixed signals using ICA gives very good results only if the two assumptions are met:

1. The source signals are independent of each other.
2. The values in each source signal have non-Gaussian distributions.

In the research work in Ref. [14], the author has shown that ICA breaks down a two-dimensional (2D) data matrix (e.g., time-voxels) into distinct components with distinct characteristics in its basic form. It is used in fMRI to recognize hidden fMRI signals, such as activations. This approach has been an important tool for data exploration in cognitive and clinical neuroscience since the first application of ICA to fMRI in 1998.

Research has shown that ICA filters for natural images can be designed and based on the ICA decomposition, noise can be removed from images corrupted with additive Gaussian noise [15].

A comparison between PCA and ICA has been made and is summarized in Table 4.4.

TABLE 4.4

Differences between PCA and ICA

Principal Component Analysis	Independent Component Analysis
To prevent overfitting, it reduces the dimensions	It decomposes the mixed signal into the signals of its independent sources
Deals with the principal components	Deals with the independent components
Focuses on maximizing the variance	Do not focus on the issue of variance among the data-points
Focuses on the mutual orthogonality property of the principal components	Do not focus on the mutual orthogonality of the components
Do not focus on the mutual independence of the components	Focuses on the mutual independence of the components

4.4.5 Unsupervised Dictionary Learning

SDL has been discussed in Section 4.3.1 and the discussion for unsupervised dictionary learning refers to the same dictionary definitions given in that section.

Semi-supervised dictionary algorithms are initiated by using a classification algorithm to train a dictionary with labeled data. Later, the dictionary is used in unsupervised mode to classify and learn from real-time input data. Upon creation, the dictionaries used by the unsupervised dictionary algorithm do not guarantee correctly ordered dictionaries. Hence, each dictionary is associated with the label that produces the highest number of correct labeled training input occurrences.

Authors of Ref. [16] have considered supervised and unsupervised clustering algorithms. When experimenting unsupervised clustering, the authors have combined spectral clustering and dictionary learning. The experimental results as illustrated through MATLAB code available at Ref. [17] have shown that the unsupervised dictionary learning with k-means algorithm gives slightly better results than plain unsupervised clustering algorithms in terms of classification of labels.

Authors of Ref. [18] have employed dictionary learning to anomaly detection applications such as the absence of supervision, online formulations, and reducing false-positive rates.

4.5 Learning in Neural Networks

4.5.1 Single-Layer Learning

Single-layer learning refers to the setup consisting of a single-layer neural network, representing the simplest form of neural network, having only one layer of input nodes. The input nodes send weighted inputs to a subsequent layer of receiving node(s). Figure 4.3 illustrates the single-layer architecture, where x_i ($i = 1, 2, ..., n$) are the inputs to the network, o_j ($j = 1, 2, ..., m$) are the outputs from the network, $f(\Sigma)$ is the activation function, and w_{ij} is the weight that connects the input x_i to the neuron j that is associated with the output o_j.

The training algorithm for the single-layer architecture can be summarized as follows:

1. Weights w_{ij} to be initialized to arbitrary values
2. Repeat
   a. Training sample (x,o) is chosen where x is the input and o is the expected output
   b. For each neuron, sum is computed as $S_j = \sum_{i=1}^{n} w_{ij} x_i$

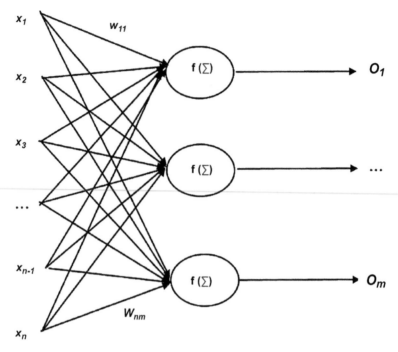

FIGURE 4.3
Single-layer architecture

---

    c. The outputs of the network are computed as $o_j = f(S)$ along with error δ_j for each output

    d. Each synaptic weight of the network is updated as $w_{ij} = w_{ij} + \delta_j \cdot x_i \cdot df(S)/dS$

  3. Until the training set is empty

An example of the usage of the single-layer architecture for a classification problem can be illustrated. Assuming a dataset with points $X = (x, y)$ being associated with either a Class A or a Class B depending on the value being either +1 or –1, respectively.

Since the output of the hyperbolic function is between –1 and +1, it has been chosen. Thus, the output is interpreted in terms of binary Classes A and B. The output of the network is +1 when tanh is positive indicating that the data-point belongs to Class A. The output of the network is –1 when tanh is negative indicating that the data-point belongs to Class B.

The transfer function of the given single-layer network is:

$$O = xw_1 + yw_2 + w_3 \tag{4.12}$$

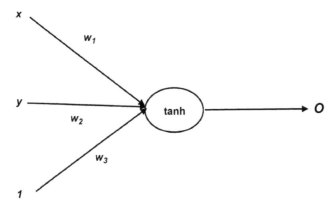

FIGURE 4.4
Single-layer architecture with hyperbolic tangent as the activation function

which is a linear model, as shown by the separator line between the zeros and ones. Taking the example of the XOR function, which is a nonlinear problem, it cannot be classified with this linear model. Hence, multilayer perceptron (MLP) is used to overcome such issues arising with nonlinear problems as shown in Figure 4.4.

4.5.2 Learning Algorithms

Learning rule or a learning process that define algorithms for the purpose are methods applied over the artificial neural network to improve its

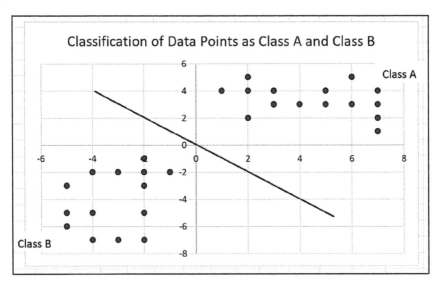

FIGURE 4.5
Classification of data-points as Class A and Class B

performance as shown in Figure 4.5. By simulating a network in a particular data environment, learning rules update the weights and bias levels of a network. The application of these rules is an iterative process, and it helps the neural network to improve its performance by learning from the existing conditions. Some of the learning rules in neural networks are discussed in the following sections:

4.5.2.1 Hebbian Learning Rule

The Hebbian rule is the first learning rule framed for unsupervised neural networks. It can be used to identify ways to improve the weights of nodes in a network. The rule states that if two neighboring neurons are activated and deactivated simultaneously, the weights connecting the neurons are likely to increase. Similarly, the weights between them are likely to decrease if the neurons are operating in the opposite phase. In case of no signal correlation, the weight is likely to remain the same.

Initially, all the weights are set to zero. When the inputs of two nodes are the same that is both are positive or both are negative, the weight between the nodes is strongly positive. If the input of one of the nodes is positive and the other is negative, the weight between the nodes is strongly negative. The mathematical formula for Hebbian learning rule is given by:

$$w_{ij} = x_i \times x_j \tag{4.13}$$

The rule fits under the category of unsupervised learning as the desired responses of the neurons are not considered for the learning process. Authors in Ref. [19] have put forth an evaluation technique that considers all the factors and perspectives that affect the design process in the best way and allows one to take suitable decisions. The decision process searches for a balance among the options in relation to the aims and interests of a specific design project based on Hebbian learning rule. A real-time application that implements the proposed technique is also presented to demonstrate its applicability in evaluating industrial designs.

4.5.2.2 Perceptron Learning Rule

The perceptron learning rule [20] states that the algorithm can learn the optimal weight coefficients automatically. To decide whether a neuron fires or not, the input features are then multiplied with these weights. As shown in Figure 4.6, inputs are approved by a perceptron, moderated by some weight values, and then the transformation function is applied to the final product.

The weights of the different inputs are adjusted, each time checking to see if the error function has increased or decreased. It is an example of supervised learning as the assigning of weights to the nodes is according to the user's desire.

The perceptron is a supervised learning algorithm of binary classifiers. The aim of the algorithm is to find the w vector that classifies positive inputs and negative inputs in the data perfectly.

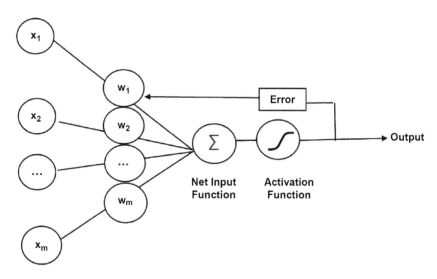

FIGURE 4.6
Single-layer perceptron model

The perceptron algorithm is ideally suited for problems with complex datasets, such as image recognition in comparison with other algorithms such as *k*NN. For problems with complex datasets, MLPs are ideal. In the perceptron learning algorithm, the activation function is a crucial factor and different activation functions can be used if the learning rate is slow at each of the multilayers as shown in Figure 4.6.

4.5.2.3 Delta Learning Rule

The delta rule developed by *Widrow* and *Hoff is* one of the most common learning rules that depend on supervised learning.

When the activation functions are linear, their units are called linear units. Any network that has a single linear unit is termed ADALINE (Adaptive Linear Neuron). Here the relationship between the inputs and output is linear and it uses a bipolar activation for the input signals and target output. The weights are adjustable between input and output, and it has only one output unit. The delta learning rule can be used to train the ADALINE network. This rule is also called least mean square (LMS) rule of Widrow–Hoff rule. The rule is very similar to the Perception learning rule; however, it is found to be differing in the fact that it minimizes the mean-squared error between the activation and the target value. The formula is given by:

$$w = w_{old} + \eta \delta x \tag{4.14}$$

where δ is the error expressed as $O_{target} - O$ and η is a constant that controls the learning rate, which is the amount of increment/update Δw at each training step. Unlike in perceptron learning rule, the error δ in the delta rule is not restricted to having values of 0, 1, or –1. It can have any value. Authors of Ref. [21] have discussed the use of the delta learning rule in the feedforward neural networks.

4.5.2.4 Correlation Learning Rule

The rule of correlation learning is based on a theory close to the rule of Hebbian learning. When the inputs of two nodes are the same that is both are positive or both are negative, the weight between the nodes is strongly positive. If the input of one of the nodes is positive and the other is negative, the weight between the nodes is strongly negative. Contrary to the Hebbian rule, the correlation rule is that of supervised learning and is expressed as:

$$\Delta w_{ij} = \eta x_i d_j \tag{4.15}$$

where d_j is the desired response of the output signal, and this is used in the weight-change calculation instead of the actual response o_j. At the start of the algorithm, the weights are initialized to zero.

4.5.2.5 Outstar Learning Rule

When it is assumed that nodes or neurons in a network are arranged in a layer, the Outstar learning (also called Grossberg learning rule) rule can be used. The rule states that the weights connected to a particular node should be equal to the desired outputs for the neurons connected through these weights and the rule produces the desired response for the layer of n nodes. This learning is then applied to all the nodes in a particular layer and the weights are updated. The Outstar rule is expressed as for two nodes j and k,

$$w_{jk} = \begin{cases} \eta(y_k - w_{jk}) \text{ if node j wins the competition} \\ 0 \text{ if the node j loses the competition} \end{cases} \tag{4.16}$$

As the desired outputs must be known, this rule comes under supervised learning algorithms. The artificial neural network's most promising function is its ability to learn. There are several artificial neural network training algorithms with their own pros and cons.

4.6 Principal Component Analysis

As already introduced in Section 4.4.2, PCA is a dimensionality reduction technique. It identifies correlations and patterns in a dataset and transforms the dataset of much lesser dimension without loss to any of the crucial information. This process is very crucial in solving complex data-driven problems that involve the use of high-dimensional datasets.

The reducing of the number of variables in any dataset generally comes at the cost of accuracy. Dimensionality reduction must be cleverly implemented to trade little of accuracy for simplicity. When the datasets consist of lesser number of variables, it is easier to explore and visualize data at a faster rate by the machine learning algorithms, as it need not process extraneous variables.

4.6.1 Objectives

The objectives of using PCA can be summarized as follows:

- It finds a sequence of linear combinations of the non-correlated variables.
- It can deal with multicollinearity well before the model is developed.
- It reduces the number of dimensions/features (dimensionality reduction) in the data and it converts any set of correlated variables to non-correlated variables called principal components.
- PCA is useful for explaining maximum amount of variance with least number of principal components.
- High-dimensional data can be visualized in a better way by using PCA as a tool (e.g., heatmaps can be created to show the correlation between each component identified using PCA)

PCA can thus be used in situations wherein:

1. In a large dataset with many variables when it is needed to reduce the number of variables, and if not able to identify which variables to remove.
2. It is needed to ensure that data variables in the given data are independent of each other.
3. When it is needed to interpret data and variable selection from the given data.

Dimensionality reduction can be implemented using either of the two broad categories, feature elimination and feature extraction. PCA uses feature extraction. It combines all the input variables in a specific way, such that the least essential variables can be dropped yet still retaining the most significant parts of all the variables.

A simple understanding of PCA can be visualized by studying its usefulness through an example. The example taken is that of measuring the transcription of genes in different mice. If only one gene is measured, the values can be plotted on a number line summarized in Table 4.5.

TABLE 4.5

Gene-1 for Seven Mice

	Mouse 1	Mouse 2	Mouse 3	Mouse 4	Mouse 5	Mouse 6	Mouse 7
Gene-1	9	12	7	4	1	1	3

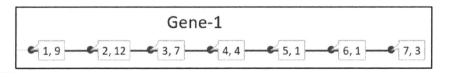

FIGURE 4.7
Number line depicting values for Gene-1

The number line clearly shows that mice 1, 2, and 3 have relatively high values and mice 4, 5, 6, and 7 have relatively low values, thus the inference that mice 1, 2, and 3 are more similar to each other than they are to 4, 5, 6, and 7. If two genes are measured, the data can be plotted on a 2D graph as shown in Figure 4.7.

When a third gene is measured, it can be represented as a three-dimensional graph, with a similar mapping.

But beyond this if the genes are measured that is beyond 3, it is not possible to represent them as a graph. However, PCA can take four or more gene measurements that is to say it can take four or more dimensions of data and can generate a 2D PCA plot.

As depicted in Table 4.7 and Figure 4.9, using PCA, it can be inferred that the values of Gene-3 are responsible for separating the samples across the *x*-axis.

4.6.2 Interpretation of PCA

To minimize dimensionality using PCA, the steps next need to be followed.

1. *Standardization of the data* – is the procedure of scaling the data such that all the variables and their values lie within a similar range as mentioned in Table 4.6. When the ranges of initial variables vary widely, those variables with wider ranges will dominate those with small ranges For example, a variable between 100 and 50,000 is dominant

TABLE 4.6

Gene-1 and Gene-2 for Seven Mice

	Mouse 1	Mouse 2	Mouse 3	Mouse 4	Mouse 5	Mouse 6	Mouse 7
Gene-1	9	12	7	4	1	1	3
Gene-2	7	5	4	3	2	2	1

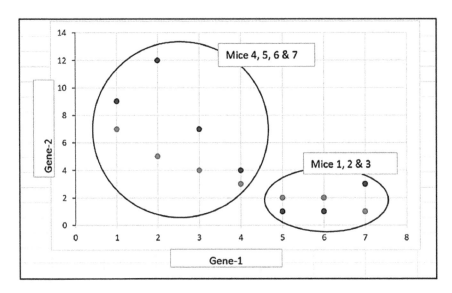

FIGURE 4.8
X–Y plot depicting values for Gene-1 and Gene-2

over a variable between 0 and 100. The wider range would have a more noticeable effect on the result. To avoid this, all data-points are standardized. By subtracting each value in the data from the mean and dividing it by the total variance in the data collection, standardization is carried out as shown in Figure 4.8.

$$z = \frac{\text{data} - \text{point value} - \text{mean}}{\text{standard deviation}} \tag{4.17}$$

On standardization, all the variables are transformed to a same scale.

2. *Computing the covariance matrix* – As already discussed through the example of measuring genes, the correlation and dependencies among the features in a dataset can be assessed using PCA by means of the covariance matrix. Heavy dependencies among the variables indicate the presence of biased and redundant information that tends to decrease the overall performance of the model. The covariance matrix is a symmetric matrix of $p \times p$ (where p is the number of

TABLE 4.7

Gene-1, Gene-2, and Gene-3 for Seven Mice

	Mouse 1	Mouse 2	Mouse 3	Mouse 4	Mouse 5	Mouse 6	Mouse 7
Gene-1	9	12	7	4	1	1	3
Gene-2	7	5	4	3	2	2	1
Gene-3	12	9	10	2	1	2	3

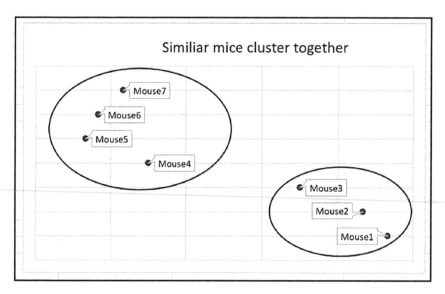

FIGURE 4.9
Similar mice are seen to be clustered together

dimensions) with the covariances associated with all possible pairs of the original variables as entries. Considering a n-dimensional dataset with variables $a_1, a_2, \ldots, a_n$, the covariance matrix for the dataset is a $n \times n$ matrix, namely,

$$
\begin{bmatrix}
a_{11} & a_{12} & \ldots & a_{1n} \\
a_{21} & a_{22} & \ldots & a_{2n} \\
\ldots & \ldots & \ldots & \ldots \\
a_{n1} & a_{n2} & \ldots & a_{nn}
\end{bmatrix}
\tag{4.18}
$$

where a_{11} represents the covariance of the variable a_{11} with itself, as indicated by the diagonal of the matrix. The element a_{12} represents the covariance of the variable a_1 with respect to the variable a_2. The covariance is of commutative property and hence *covariance of a_{12} is equal to the covariance of a_{21}*. If the sign of the covariance is positive then, the two variables are correlated and increase or decrease together. If the sign of the covariance is negative then, the two variables are inversely correlated and thus, when one increases, the other decreases.

3. *Calculating the eigenvectors and eigenvalues* – Eigenvectors and eigenvalues are the linear algebraic formulations that are always computed as a pair (for every eigenvector, there is an eigenvalue). The number of eigenvectors that need to be computed is equal to the

dimension of the dataset. From the covariance matrix, which defines the main components of the results, eigenvectors and eigenvalues are computed.

4. *Computing the principal components* – The eigenvectors and eigenvalues are arranged in descending order and the eigenvector with the largest eigenvalue is considered as the most significant and is termed the *first principal component*, normally indicated as PC1. To reduce the dimensions of the data, the principal components of lower importance may thus be removed. A *feature matrix* that contains all the significant data variables that possess maximum information about the data is formed.

5. *Reducing the dimensions of the dataset* – The final step in PCA is to rearrange the original data with the main components that represent the dataset's maximum and most relevant details. The feature vector that is formed using the eigenvectors and eigenvalues of the covariance matrix is used to reorient the data from its original axes to those represented by the principal components. This transformation is implemented by multiplying the transpose of the original dataset by the transpose of the feature vector.

4.6.3 Real-Time Applications that can Benefit from PCA

The research work in Ref. [22], with the use of PCA, has assessed the presence of contamination in soil and vegetables due to long-lasting mining activities. The varied parameters, namely, contents in heavy metals and some of the agrochemical parameters that characterize the contamination in soil have been considered. PCA has helped in optimizing the number and type of data that are best in extracting the heavy metal contamination of the soil and vegetables. It has also helped to identify the vegetable species that present the highest/minimum risk of a negative impact on the food chain and human health.

Stock price prediction is based upon the assumption that market patterns recur over time and that prices are always tied to several macroeconomic variables and fundamental variables such as book to market ratio and earnings yield, which could be examined for predictive purposes and all these rely on covariance information. Some other applications of PCA in this field include:

- Analyzing the shape of the revenue curve
- Hedging fixed income portfolios
- Implementation of interest rate models
- Forecasting portfolio returns
- Developing asset allocation algorithms
- Developing long-short equity trading algorithms

In neuroscience, PCA is often used to classify the basic properties of a stimulus that increase the likelihood of an action being produced by a neuron.

4.7 Conclusion

This chapter has given an overview of the techniques used in the construction of deep representations, mainly supervised learning and unsupervised learning. Feature learning has been explained in detail and its role in supervised learning has been included. Under supervised learning, dictionary learning concepts and the implementation of neural networks have been studied. Unsupervised learning techniques such as k-means clustering, local linear embedding, ICA, and unsupervised dictionary learning have been discussed with relevant examples. It has also given a detailed coverage on PCA, which is an important dimension reduction technique used in deep representations.

References

[1] Zhong, G., Wang, L.-N., Ling, X., Dong, J. An overview on data representation learning: From traditional feature learning to recent deep learning. The Journal of Finance and Data Science, 2(4), pages 265–278, 2016.

[2] https://en.wikipedia.org/wiki/Sparse_dictionary_learning

[3] Dumitrescu, B., Irofti, P. Dictionary Learning Algorithms and Applications. Romania: Springer, 2018.

[4] Mairal, J., Bach, F., Ponce, J., Sapiro, G., Zisserman, A. Supervised dictionary learning. In NIPS'08, pages 1033–1040, NIPS Foundation, 2009.

[5] Aharon, M., Elad, M., Bruckstein, A. K-SVD: An algorithm for designing overcomplete dictionaries for sparse representation. IEEE Transactions on Signal Processing, 54(11), pages 4311–4322, 2006.

[6] Peyré, G. Sparse modeling of textures. Journal of Mathematical Imaging and Vision, 34(1), pages 17–31, 2008.

[7] Ramirez, I., Sprechmann, P., Sapiro, G. Classification and clustering via dictionary learning with structured incoherence and shared features. In IEEE Conference on Computer Vision and Pattern Recognition, pages 3501–3508, Los Alamitos, CA: IEEE Computer Society, 2014.

[8] Koniusz, P., Yan, F., Gosselin, P.H., Mikolajczyk, K. Higher-order occurrence pooling for bags-of-words: Visual concept detection. IEEE Transactions on Pattern Analysis and Machine Intelligence, 39(2), pages 313–326, 2017.

[9] Roweis, S.T., Saul, L.K. Nonlinear dimensionality reduction by locally linear embedding. Science, 290(5500), pages 2323–2326, 2000.

[10] Roweis, S.T., Saul, L.K. Nonlinear dimensionality reduction by locally linear embedding. Science, 290(5500), pages 2323–2326, 2000.

[11] Li, M., Luo, X., Yang, J., Sun, Y. Applying a locally linear embedding algorithm for feature extraction and visualization of MI-EEG. Journal of Sensors, 2016, 9 pages, 2016, Article ID 7481946.

[12] Abusham, E.E., Wong, E.K. Locally linear discriminate embedding for face recognition. Discrete Dynamics in Nature and Society, 2009, 8 pages, 2009, Article ID 916382.

[13] Beckmann, C., Smith, S. Probabilistic independent component analysis for functional magnetic resonance imaging. IEEE Transactions on Medical Imaging, 23(2), pages 137–152, 2004.

[14] Beckmann, C.F. Modelling with independent components. Neuroimage, 62, pages 891–901, 2012.

[15] Hyvärinen, A. Sparse code shrinkage: Denoising of non-Gaussian data by maximum likelihood estimation. Neural Computation, 11(7), pages 1739–1768, 1999.

[16] Bufford, T., Chen, Y., Horning, M., Shee, L. When Dictionary Learning Meets Classification, 2013.

[17] https://tools.ipol.im/wiki/www/dev.ipol.im/

[18] Irofti, P., Băltoiu, A. "Unsupervised dictionary learning for anomaly detection." arXiv preprint arXiv:2003.00293, (2020).

[19] Comesaña-Campos, A., Bouza-Rodríguez, J.B. An application of Hebbian learning in the design process decision-making. Journal of Intelligent Manufacturing, 27, pages 487–506, 2016.

[20] Chakraverty, S., Sahoo, D.M., Mahato, N.R. Perceptron learning rule. In Concepts of Soft Computing. Singapore: Springer, 2019.

[21] Chakraverty, S., Sahoo, D.M., Mahato, N.R. Delta learning rule and back-propagation rule for multilayer perceptron. In Concepts of Soft Computing. Singapore: Springer, 2019.

[22] Gergen, I., Harmanescu, M. Application of principal component analysis in the pollution assessment with heavy metals of vegetable food chain in the old mining areas. Chemistry Central Journal, 6, page 156, 2012.

5

Knowledge Representation Using Probabilistic Model and Reconstruction-Based Algorithms

Shruti Dambhare, Sanjay Kumar, and Sandya Katiyar

5.1 Introduction to Learning Models

A US visionary of computer games and artificial intelligence, Arthur Samuel (1901–1990), coined in 1959 the word "machine learning" [1–3]. He identified it as "a study field that allows computers to learn without having to be programmed explicitly."

Machine learning since then went through a lot of systematic changes and new research and application in various areas with the evergrowing demands of humans lead to a bloom of this field that found its separate path from its mother branch artificial intelligence [4, 5].

A basic question set off the so-called machine learning revolution: could a computer learn without being specifically instructed how? The field of artificial intelligence developed machine learning models by integrating mathematical information with the computer's ability to transfer vast quantities of data faster than anyone else could. These models may take raw data, identify a pattern influencing it, and adapt to new circumstances what they learned. Computers, in other words, may discover the hidden truths in the data by themselves.

A machine learning model depicts the patterns hidden in data. Machine learning model can also be stated as mathematical representation, which exhibits the pattern found within a set of data. When the machine learning model is trained (or constructed or adapted) to the training data, some ruling function is observed within those. The ruling function is then transformed or stated into rules that can be used for predictions in novel environments as shown in Figure 5.1 [6].

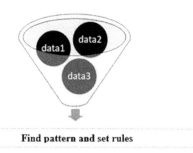

Find pattern and set rules

FIGURE 5.1
Machine learning model

5.2 The Training Process Steps for Machine Learning Model

There are standard steps that are followed by a typical machine learning model which are to be followed for any application that is to be used right from smart remote monitoring, weather prediction model, to a model for diagnosing health aliments based on health parameters; in any case, the steps will be the same as given next [7]:

1. Getting input dataset
2. Bifurcate data into training and test datasets
3. Fit algorithm to training data
4. Evaluate the model
5. Use the model in real life

Connection of graphical model in the machine learning domain:
The quantity of base area knowledge required to solve a problem is one of the major differences between machine training (ML) and deep learning (DL). Machine learning algorithms use domain knowledge on a daily basis. However, if the information is incomplete, the solution can be biased. We can solve problems more easily; however, if done correctly. **A ML branch using a graph describing a domain problem is the graphic model (GM).** Graphical models amalgamate concepts of graph and probability theories in a bid to give a modifiable framework for modeling huge batch of random variables with complicated interactions [8–10].

In the recent decades, the fields of statistics and computer science have usually accompanied different directions, each field offering helpful features to the other, albeit with no intersection of core objectives. However, the long-term priorities of the two areas have become increasingly apparent in recent years. Statistics are now more concerned with computational aspects.

Models and inference procedures, both theoretical and practical. Researchers increasingly deal with systems communicating with the outside world and interpreting unknown information as far as simple probabilistic models are concerned. These trends are most prominent in the area of probabilistic graphical model (PGM) [11].

5.3 Knowledge Representation

A PGM also termed as structured probabilistic model is a probabilistic model or, in simple word, it is called graphical model. In this model, a graph facilitates the expression of conditional dependence structure between random variables. Conventionally, graphical models have been widely used in statistics particularly in Bayesian network (BN). They have also been implied in machine learning and various applications of graph theory. With an objective to encode a distribution in a multidimensional PGMs applies graphical representations.

The two most common forms of graphical models are as follows:

1. Directed graphical models (DGMs)
2. Undirected graphical models

5.3.1 Directed Graphical Models

As the name already suggests, DGMs [12] can be represented by a graph with its vertices serving as random variables and directed edges serving as dependency relationships between them (see Figure 5.2).

In Figure 5.2, two examples of DGMs are stated. **While the model in (a) is cyclic, (b) is a directed acyclic graph (DAG) and could represent a BN.** The direction of the edges determines the influence of one random variable on

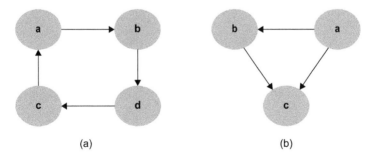

(a)   (b)

FIGURE 5.2
DGMs-cyclic and Bayesian network

another. If the graph does not contain cycles (a number of vertices connected in a closed chain), it is usually referred to as a DAG [13–15]. Inference on these graphs may be performed exactly using algorithms such as belief propagation (BP) [16] or variable elimination.

5.3.2 Bayesian Networks (BNs)

An example of a DGM is the BN. The BN [17–19] is a DAG with vertices (random variables) representing observable or latent variables of the model. The directed edges ("arrows") of a BN represent conditional distributions. If the values of the vertices are binary, for example, the conditional distributions may be Bernoulli distributions. In the case of continuous values, the conditional distributions may be Gaussian. The joint probability distribution is formulated as a product of conditional or marginal probabilities. For instance, when modeling the probability of wet grass, given if it is raining or the sprinkler is on, we might represent it using a DAG such as the one shown in Figure 5.3:

In Figure 5.3, an example of a BN is depicted. It encodes the following logic: the probability that the grass is wet is dependent on turning on the sprinkler and the rain. The probability that the sprinkler is on is itself dependent on the rain (you wouldn't turn on the sprinkler during rain).

This DAG represents the (factorized) probability distribution

$$p(S,R,G) = p(R)p(S|R)p(G|S,R)$$

where R is the random variable for rain, S for the sprinkler and G for the wet grass. By examining the graph, you quickly see that the only independent variable in the model is R. The other two variables are conditioned on the probability of rain and/or the sprinkler. In general, the joint distribution for a BN is the product of the conditional probabilities for every node, given its parents:

$$p(X) = \prod_{i=1}^{N} p(X_i \,|\, \mathrm{Parents}(X_i))$$

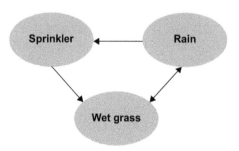

FIGURE 5.3
Bayesian network example

Since most nodes have far fewer parents than the total number of nodes, the graph is usually sparse.

Although this is not required, BNs are often used to model causal relationships. If the direction of edges in a BN represents causality, the causal do-calculus introduced by Judea Pearl allows one to modify the graph by performing a simulated intervention and predict the impact of an external intervention (please see this great post if you like to know more).

5.3.3 Inference in BNs

Let us return to the wet grass example and figure out the probability that the grass is wet, i.e. the marginal probability $p(G)$. This task is known as inference. In order to determine the marginal probability of a variable, you must, in general, sum over all its parents in the graph. In this case, the marginal probability would be

$$p(G) = \sum_R \sum_S p(S,R,G) = \sum_R \sum_S p(R)p(S|R)p(G|S,R)$$

In this case, we need to sum over all the factors. However, for more complicated graphs, it might be possible to pull some factors out of the sum and simplify the calculation greatly, making use of the sparse graph structure. Another task we may be interested in is to calculate the conditional probability that the grass will be wet, given that it is not raining. In this case, we would proceed as follows:

$$p(G|R) = \sum_S p(S,G|R) = \sum_S p(S|R)p(G|S,R)$$

In this case, we only have to marginalize over S since R is already assumed as given. This procedure is called variable elimination. Variable elimination [20] is an exact inference algorithm. It can also be used to figure out the state of the network that has maximum probability by simply exchanging the sums by max functions. Its downside is that, for large BNs, it might be computationally intractable. Approximate inference algorithms such as Gibbs or rejection sampling might be used in these cases.

5.3.4 Figuring Out Independence in BNs

To determine if two nodes in a BN are independent, given another node, next is the introduction to the concept of d-separation:

There are three rules of d-separation:

Consider two nodes, "X" and "Y" and they are considered to be d-separated if there is no unidirectional path (any sequence of edges regardless of their directionality) between them.

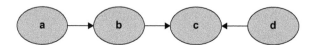

FIGURE 5.4
Rule 1: d-separation

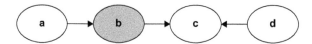

FIGURE 5.5
Rule 2: d-separation

In this example, node a and c are d-connected, whereas node a and d or node b and d are d-separated, since b and d are both parents of c as shown in Figures 5.4 and 5.5.

X and Y are d-separated; in the case of the other set of a node is Z, if Z "blocks" any unidirectional path between them.

In this case, b blocks the path between a and c, causing them to be d-separated.

If a collider or its descendants is in the set Z, it breaks the d-separation of its parents.

This one requires some explanation: a collider is a node, which has two or more parents. If the collider is observed, its parents, although previously independent, become dependent. For instance, if we are dealing with binary variables, the knowledge of the collider makes the probability of its parents more or less likely. In the image as shown in Figure 5.6, b breaks the d-separation between a and c.

5.4 Undirected Graphical Models (UGMs) or Markov Random Fields (MRFs)

Similar to BNs, Markov random fields (MRFs) are used to describe dependencies between random variables using a graph [21]. However, MRFs use

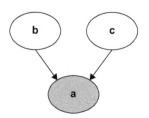

FIGURE 5.6
Rule 3

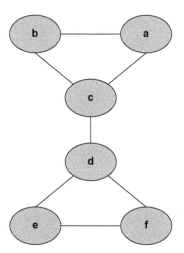

FIGURE 5.7
MRFs with three cliques

undirected instead of directed edges [22]. They may also contain cycles, unlike BNs. Thus, MRFs can describe a different set of dependency relationships than their BN counterparts [23]. Note that MRFs are not a superset of DGMs since there are relationships (like causal relationships) that can only be described by DGMs [24–25].

While the edges of BNs represent conditional dependencies, the undirected edges of MRFs represent joint probabilities of cliques in the graph. Take a look at the following MRF as shown in Figures 5.6 and 5.7.

This graph describes a joint probability function of six variables in three distinct cliques. Thus, it factorizes into the following product of distributions:

$$p(X) = p(X_a, X_b, X_c)p(X_c, X_d)p(X_d, X_e, X_f)$$

A fundamental property of MRFs is that they satisfy the pairwise, local and global Markov properties. These properties share a deep connection with the d-separation rules for BNs. In particular, d-separation defines the Markov properties on directed graphs.

As per the pairwise Markov property, it is deduced that if non-neighboring variables are conditionally independent, given all other variables:

$$X_a \perp X_b \mid X_{G \setminus \{a,b\}}$$

with X_a and X_b defining any two non-neighboring variables and X_G being the set of all variables.

The local Markov property introduces the concept of the neighborhood of a variable:

$$X_a \perp X_{G \setminus N(a)} \mid X_{N(a)}$$

where $N(a)$ is the neighborhood of X_a. In other words, any variable is conditionally independent of any other variables, given its neighborhood.

Finally, the global Markov property states that any set of variables X_A is independent of any other set X_B, given a separating subset X_S:

$$X_A \perp X_B \mid X_S$$

In general, the pairwise Markov property follows from the local Markov property, which in turn follows from the global Markov property. However, for strictly positive probability distributions, the statements are equivalent.

Another important result for MRFs is the Hammersley-Clifford theorem [26]. Informally, this theorem states that a strictly positive probability distribution that satisfies one (or equivalently all) of the Markov properties may be represented as a Gibbs measure. Hereby, the Gibbs measure is a strictly positive function factorized over the cliques of the graph:

$$p(X) = \frac{1}{Z} \prod_{c \in C_G} \phi_c(X_c)$$

where Z is an appropriate normalization constant (also called partition function), c are the (maximal) cliques of the graph, ϕ is the factorized function on the clique (not necessarily normalized), and X is the set of random variables. MRFs are also often used in fields such as image processing, where they describe the relationships between individual pixels. For instance, they may enforce a certain smoothness of a desired solution by requiring that neighboring pixels have similar intensities.

5.5 Boltzmann Machines

A Boltzmann machine is made up of a network of several units that resemble neurons that are connected in a symmetric way. It [27, 28] takes (nondeterministic) stochastic decisions about whether to be on or off. It helps to find out interesting features in datasets, which are made of binary vectors [29, 30].

Working principle:
A Boltzmann machine looks like the one shown in Figure 5.8:

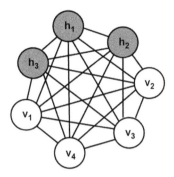

FIGURE 5.8
Boltzmann machine

They have two nodes "hidden" and "visible" only with no output nodes that make them demonstrate the nondeterministic nature. What makes them unique is that they show patterns without the need for typical 1 or 0 output. Another thing that is remarkable to note is that they have connections among the input nodes. Various conventional networks do not possess such connection between input nodes. It is this interconnectivity between all nodes, whether hidden or visible.

Such interconnectivity gives them the distinct ability to transfer data and also generate data at a later stage. Data that is there on both visible and hidden nodes is measured.

5.6 Restricted Boltzmann Machines (RBMs)

Restricted Boltzmann machines (RBMs) are compositional artificial neural networks that have two layers. One of the layers is a transparent layer and the other is a hidden layer, with a completely bipartite graph linking the two layers. This can clarify the fact that each neuron in the visible layer is not connected to each neuron in the same layer. Rather, each neuron of hidden layer is inversely connected to each neuron of transparent layer but not within the same layer. This limitation paves the way to effective training algorithms than those implementable for Boltzmann machines in a conventional way, such as the gradient-based contrastive divergence algorithm [31]. They are capable of learning a probability distribution from a collection of inputs. Geoffrey Hinton developed RBMs, which can be used for dimensionality reduction, sorting, regression, collective filtering, function learning, and subject modeling, among other things. RBMs are a kind of Boltzmann machine that has links between the visible and hidden

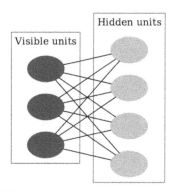

FIGURE 5.9
Restricted Boltzmann machine

units that are restricted [32]. When compared to Boltzmann machines, this makes them easier to execute. A typical RBM looks like the one shown in Figure 5.9:

5.7 Generalizations of the RBM to Real-Valued Data

A lot of work has been done recently in stating generalizations of RBM, which encompass real-valued data. Most importantly, data is real-valued image data, where the input values are appropriately modeled via conditional covariance. Motivated by the spectrum of inference and learning in the RBMs has paved the way for various data researchers and analysts to model them to varied data distribution [30]. Gaussian RBM (GRBM) is one of the easiest ways to train real value–based data within the RBM framework. In GRBM "the only change in the RBM energy function is to the visible units biases, by adding a bias term that is quadratic in the visible units x" [31–32].

5.8 Autoencoders

Autoencoders are a form of unsupervised learning technique that uses neural networks to learn representations. We'll build a neural network architecture in such a manner that we force a compact information representation of the initial input led by adding a bottleneck in the network. This compression and resulting restoration would be incredibly difficult if the input features

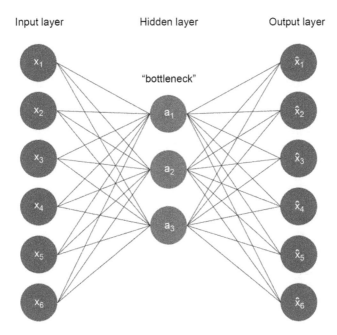

FIGURE 5.10
Auto encoder- Neural Network

were all independent of one another. If there is some corelation in the data structure, this structure can be trained and used to push the input via the network's bottleneck. We may frame an unlabeled dataset as a supervised learning problem with the goal of outputting x, a reconstruction of the original input x, as seen earlier. The reconstruction error, $L(x,x)$, which calculates the variations between our original input and the subsequent reconstruction, can be used to train this network. The existence of a knowledge bottleneck is a core feature of our network design; without it, our network might quickly learn to simply memorize the input values by moving them along the network (Figure 5.10).

A bottleneck limits the volume of data that can cross the entire network, allowing the incoming data to be compressed, sensitive enough to produce a reliable reconstruction from the inputs. The model is insensitive enough to the inputs that it does not memorize or overfit the training results. This exchange requires the model to keep only the data variations needed to rebuild the input, rather than keeping redundancies in the input. In several cases, this requires implementing a loss function in which one term allows our model to be adaptive to the inputs (e.g. reconstruction loss $L(x,x)$) and a second term discourages memorization/overfitting (e.g. reconstruction loss $L(x,x)$) (i.e. an added regularizer).

5.9 Conclusion

This chapter has given a detailed description of knowledge representation using the probabilistic models, an insight into the directed and undirected graphical learning model. This chapter gives a review of the probabilistic models, the reconstruction-based algorithms like autoencoders. Finding active relations amidst these modeling techniques is presently an important place of research and shall aid in generating a new model.

References

[1] McCarthy, J., & Feigenbaum, E. A. (1990). In memoriam: Arthur Samuel: Pioneer in machine learning. *AI Magazine, 11*(3), 10.

[2] Samuel, A. L. (1959). Some studies in machine learning using the game of checkers. *IBM Journal of Research and Development, 3*(3), 210–229.

[3] Lee, A., Taylor, P., Kalpathy-Cramer, J., & Tufail, A. (2017). Machine learning has arrived! *Ophthalmology, 124*(12), 1726–1728.

[4] El Naqa, I., & Murphy, M. J. (2015). What is machine learning? In *Machine learning in radiation oncology* (pp. 3–11). Springer, Cham.

[5] Russell, S., & Norvig, P. (2002). Artificial intelligence: a modern approach. https://storage.googleapis.com/pub-tools-public-publication-data/pdf/27702.pdf

[6] Nickel, M., Murphy, K., Tresp, V., & Gabrilovich, E. (2015). A review of relational machine learning for knowledge graphs. *Proceedings of the IEEE, 104*(1), 11–33.

[7] Bunke, H. (2003). Graph-based tools for data mining and machine learning. In International *workshop on machine learning and data mining in pattern recognition* (pp. 7–19). Springer, Berlin, Heidelberg.

[8] Chami, I., Abu-El-Haija, S., Perozzi, B., Ré, C., & Murphy, K. (2020). Machine learning on graphs: A model and comprehensive taxonomy. *arXiv preprint, arXiv:2005.03675.*

[9] Pernkopf, F., Peharz, R., & Tschiatschek, S. Introduction to probabilistic graphical models. In *Academic Press Library in Signal Processing*, vol. 1, pp. 989–1064. Elsevier, 2014.

[10] Amari, Shun'ichi. *The handbook of brain theory and neural networks.* MIT press, 2003.

[11] Shrier, I., & Platt, R. W. (2008). Reducing bias through directed acyclic graphs. *BMC Medical Research Methodology, 8*(1), 1–15.

[12] Healy, P., & Nikolov, N. S. (2001). How to layer a directed acyclic graph. In International *symposium on graph drawing* (pp. 16–30). Springer, Berlin, Heidelberg.

[13] Shrier, I., & Platt, R. W. (2008). Reducing bias through directed acyclic graphs. *BMC Medical Research Methodology, 8*(1), 1–15.

[14] Yedidia, J. S., Freeman, W. T., & Weiss, Y. (2003). Understanding belief propagation and its generalizations. *Exploring Artificial Intelligence in the New Millennium*, 8, 236–239.

[15] Margaritis, D. (2003). *Learning Bayesian network model structure from data.* Carnegie-Mellon University, Pittsburgh, PA.

[16] Friedman, N., Geiger, D., & Goldszmidt, M. (1997). Bayesian network classifiers. *Machine Learning*, 29(2), 131–163.

[17] Jensen, F. V. (1996). *An introduction to Bayesian networks* (Vol. 210, pp. 1–178). UCL Press, London.

[18] Stracuzzi, D. J., & Utgoff, P. E. (2004). Randomized variable elimination. *The Journal of Machine Learning Research*, 5, 1331–1362.

[19] Clifford, P. (1990). Markov random fields in statistics. In *Disorder in physical systems: A volume in honour of John M. Hammersley* (pp. 19–32).

[20] Blake, A., Kohli, P., & Rother, C. eds. *Markov random fields for vision and image processing*. MIT press, 2011.

[21] Zhang, H., Kamath, G., Kulkarni, J., & Wu, S. (2020). Privately learning Markov random fields. In International *conference on machine learning* (pp. 11129–11140). PMLR.

[22] Shah, A., Shah, D., & Wornell, G. (2021). On learning continuous pairwise Markov random fields. In International *conference on artificial intelligence and statistics* (pp. 1153–1161). PMLR.

[23] Sidén, P., & Lindsten, F. (2020). Deep Gaussian Markov random fields. In International *conference on machine learning* (pp. 8916–8926). PMLR.

[24] Walenciuk, O. M. (2020). *Undirected graphical models* (Doctoral dissertation, Zakład Rachunku Prawdopodobieństwa i Statystyki Matematycznej).

[25] Vrábel, J., Pořízka, P., & Kaiser, J. (2020). Restricted Boltzmann machine method for dimensionality reduction of large spectroscopic data. *Spectrochimica Acta Part B: Atomic Spectroscopy*, 167, 105849.

[26] Tao, Y., Sornette, D., & Lin, L. (2021). Emerging social brain: A collective self-motivated Boltzmann machine. *Chaos, Solitons & Fractals*, 143, 110543.

[27] Harrington, P. B. (2020). Enhanced zippy restricted Boltzmann machine for feature expansion and improved classification of analytical data. *Journal of Chemometrics*, 34(3), e3228.

[28] Yair, Omer, and Tomer Michaeli. "Contrastive Divergence Learning is a Time Reversal Adversarial Game." *arXiv preprint arXiv:2012.03295* (2020).

[29] Melko, R. G., Carleo, G., Carrasquilla, J., & Cirac, J. I. (2019). Restricted Boltzmann machines in quantum physics. *Nature Physics*, 15(9), 887–892.

[30] Lee, S., & Jo, J. (2021). Compression phase is not necessary for generalization in representation learning. *arXiv preprint arXiv:2102.07402*.

[31] Hinton, Geoffrey E. "A practical guide to training restricted Boltzmann machines." In *Neural networks: Tricks of the trade*, pp. 599–619. Springer, Berlin, Heidelberg, 2012.

[32] Deshwal, D., & Sangwan, P. (2021). A comprehensive study of deep neural networks for unsupervised deep learning. In *Artificial intelligence for sustainable development: Theory, practice and future applications* (pp. 101–126). Springer, Cham.

6

Multi-Ontology Mapping for Internet of Things (MOMI)

Varun M. Tayur and R. Suchithra

6.1 Introduction

Internet of Things (IoT) includes a massive number of devices and an equally diverse set of technologies. The communication between such devices produces a lot of data, and by nature, they are heterogenous. The devices can interoperate by means of various protocols that take care of communication needs. The data that is produced itself can be gleamed upon to improve intelligence of the operational domain. Annotation of such device data enables automated extraction of intelligence; this is where ontologies play an important role in solidifying the semantic and operational rules for the devices and the domain in general. An ontology formally models the knowledge of the domain by defining the concepts, the properties describing a concept and the relationships between two concepts. Over time and due to different interpretations, a concept in different ontologies could be defined with different terminologies and contexts. This has led to a fragmented semantic space and made machine-to-machine communication more difficult while also increasing the challenges in expressing intelligence in higher levels of applications.

Over the last few years, the IoT research community has produced up to 200 ontologies encoding knowledge [1], justified by the steady increase in research and the growth of data that is being collected in all related areas of IoT. Not only is the number of ontologies increasing and their size growing, but their relevance in IoT research is also rising [2] as they contribute to the interpretation of the IoT data and enable inference from their encoding. However, many of the ontologies exhibit overlapping information (e.g., oneM2M ontology and SSN both define sensing concepts), which imposes the task of ontology alignment, i.e. finding mappings or correspondences between concepts and relations in different ontologies that are remarked as important.

Ontology alignment, in general, has been performed using various methods, including rule-based and statistical methods. More recently, neural methods for incorporating contextual and background information have been applied to ontology alignment as well. In Ref. [3], a two-way Gated Recurrent Unit (GRU) neural model is used to align concepts from different ontologies and generate inference rules from external definitions and context information, while in Ref. [4], the OntoPhil approach uses lexical and structural matchers to find suitable alignments between the ontologies. However, all the above approaches determine probable concept matches using word embeddings of the concepts in each ontology; neither of them forms the embeddings for entities and relationships contained in the ontologies. IoT ontologies encode knowledge by capturing domain-level expertise in the form of the knowledge graph of structured relations. Knowledge graph embeddings [5] allow the representation of the structured knowledge from a knowledge graph into concept and relation embeddings.

As in Ref. [6], producing knowledge graph embeddings for the biomedical ontologies has shown that ontology can be successfully expressed as real-valued vectors associated with concepts and relations. Furthermore, these vectors are used that to produce alignments between two ontologies. An adversarial learning framework is used to produce alignments between two ontologies. The "generator-discriminator" operator in a feedback loop works together to produce the ontology alignment. For this purpose, multi-ontology mapping for IoT (MOMI) algorithm has been proposed. The generator part is called "OntoGenerator", while the discriminator is called "OntoCNN". The OntoGenerator of MOMI uses the concept embeddings of the IoT ontologies to produce the most probable triples that are asserted for validity within the discriminator. The novel OntoCNN discriminator network is useful here to classify the produced triples. It uses a relation attention mechanism and entity relation descriptions to improve the classification score. The classified relations are used to iteratively predict new alignments based on the confidence score of the discriminator. MOMI differs from Ref. [6] in many ways: (1) it uses a system of generators weighted on name, label, comments, properties, instance descriptions, concept attributes and the neighborhood of nearby concepts in the knowledge graph and (2) a novel convolution neural network (CNN) discriminator to classify the generated tuples.

6.2 Data

In this work, the focus is on producing alignments of three ontologies, Smart Applications REFerence (SAREF) [7], oneM2M [8] and SSN [9]. The SAREF ontology is a shared model of consensus that facilitates the matching of existing assets in the smart applications domain. SAREF provides building blocks that allow separation and recombination of different parts of the ontology depending on specific needs. oneM2M specifications provide a framework to support applications and services such as the smart grid, connected car, home automation, public safety and health. It is built for extension by individual organizations as they deem fit to promote reuse and interoperations. SSN ontology provides an encoding of sensor descriptions and observation data along with enabling more expressive representation, advanced access and formal analysis of sensor resources. For the lack of having a universal ontology in IoT space, IoT-O is considered a reference alignment for evaluating the quality of the learned knowledge alignments.

6.3 MOMI

In MOMI, knowledge alignments are learned using the structure of the ontologies, i.e. relying on (1) the conceptual names, (2) relation-spanning concepts and (3) the attributes of concepts. To describe the functionality of MOMI, first, the way in which alignments between ontologies are learned and produced is provided and then details on how MOMI generates a view of the aligned ontologies are presented. Figure 6.1 illustrates the steps of MOMI algorithm. Several ontologies are input to the algorithm; they are preprocessed (normalized) first and later the matching and aligning of the concepts and relations are performed followed by the manual selection/approval by humans to ensure there is no invalid relation being accepted into the aligned ontology. The output aligned ontology with the new relations can be utilized dynamically when queries are to be issued across related operating domains.

6.3.1 MOMI Algorithm

Figure 6.2 illustrates the MOMI architecture. The generator-discriminator system in a feedback loop allows continuous learning within the system. The likely concepts of the input ontologies are used to produce relation triples with an aim to fool the discriminator. The discriminator is trained independently of the input ontologies using a special CNN that utilizes the entity descriptions and relation data between the concepts. Data is obtained from Wikidata/Freebase for ascertaining the entity descriptions. Figure 6.3 illustrates the high-level steps followed in the algorithm.

FIGURE 6.1
Architecture of the MOMI

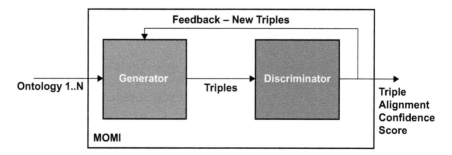

FIGURE 6.2
MOMI algorithm high-level architecture

6.3.2 Preprocessing

The preprocessing step is concerned with the normalization of the input ontologies. The system extracts and integrates all the ontologies in the matching process by mapping only the entities such as concepts, instances and properties. The basic precondition for the preprocessing step is that the input must be in Web Ontology Language (OWL) format because it makes the ontologies more flexible, shareable and easily manageable.

The preprocessing stage consists of various different steps:

- Standardization of the punctuation signs, such as the spaces, numbers and special characters of ontologies, is removed.

Input: Ontology 1… Ontology N

Output: Ontology1… Ontology N alignments

Steps:

1. Preprocess (Ontology1… Ontology N)

2. Do (Train MOMI (generator, discriminator))

    Discriminator := Train Model Onto CNN (Ontology<i…N>, Wikidata)

    Generator := Train Model Onto Generator (Ontology, … Ontology<N>)

   Until (no new alignments found)

3. Extract top-N triples from the discriminator model to produce alignments

4. Selected top-N triples are validated (manually)

FIGURE 6.3
MOMI algorithm

- Normalization is applied where the text is run through the following normalization methods, namely, lemmatization, lowercase conversion, Stop_Words and Delete_Links.
- Transforming ontological data into numerical vectors to allow submission into a neural network.
- Data preselection to reduce scope for data explosion.

6.4 Ontological Data Transformation

In order for a machine learning model to work, the input ontology must be transformed into a set of numerical vectors, which a model can use as input.

First, the structure of each ontology is extracted using Apache Jena. All the classes in the ontology will be extracted for the label, and labels of its immediate super-classes are also extracted. Comments, properties, instance descriptions and concept attributes are also extracted. Each of the extracted aspects is utilized by the generator; however, before this can be utilized by the generator, vector embeddings of these extracted aspects of ontology are generated. The discriminator utilizes, in general, all the information related to classes' description to build the entity descriptions and the properties to influence the relation attention module.

A neural network model cannot take strings of characters as direct input. Hence, characters must be converted to numbers. A simple character encoding could have been used but character embeddings are used. These embeddings provide a representation vector for each possible character. The embedding dimension is set to 300 characters. Each provided value is normalized between 0 and 1. De-noising of the data is achieved by using lower case on every class label and replacing underscores with spaces.

6.5 Data Preselection

In order to prevent combinatorial explosion when comparing classes from both ontologies and extracting relations from it, obvious examples need to be removed before passing input data to the neural network model. Two cases are as follows:

- Trivial positive examples: across two different ontologies, some classes have identical names and properties. When this happens, these classes are automatically considered equivalent.

- Trivial negative examples: to avoid many completely different classes from being selected for comparison, distance-based preselection is used. If the Levenshtein distance between the labels of two classes is large, these classes are considered different. This can be overcome by choosing to weigh the Levenshtein distance with a factor that is inversely proportional to the length of the labels: the shorter the labels, the greater is the final distance.

Let a and b be the labels of the two classes that need to be compared. Let L_a and L_b be their respective lengths. The following index i is computed:

$$i = \frac{\text{levenshtien}(a,b)}{L_a \times L_b} \tag{6.1}$$

A threshold t_h is defined, and if $i > t_h$, the two classes are classified as different.

6.6 Data Creation

For every class, comments, label, instance descriptions properties and a term vector are created. In particular, properties of a class, namely, ID, label, comments, properties' descriptions and instances' descriptions, are used to produce the term vector using Word2Vec [10] approach. Using the similar approach, vectors are also produced for the properties' ID, label, domain and its range (or its textual value when the property is a data-type property), and the instances' ID, label and their properties' values.

Word	Vector
Sensor	[Sensing, Temperature, ...]
Actuator	[Actuating, Sensing, Actor, ...]
...	

Since characters cannot be input to a machine learning algorithm, a binary term vector is created for each entity with elements 1 and 0, which refer to the existence and inexistence of a specific word, respectively.

Word	Vector
ID:611	[1, 0, 1, 1, ...]
ID:729	[0, 1, 0, 0, ...]
...	

6.7 Matching and Alignment

6.7.1 Generator

Formally, let C_x and C_y denote the set of concepts encoded in ontologies X and Y, respectively. An alignment $A = \{(c_x, c_y) \in C_X \times C_Y \mid C_x \equiv C_y\}$, which is a set of pairs of concepts from X and Y that represent equivalent concepts from both ontologies. For example, the concept "system" from SSN represents the same concept as "device" in SAREF, which is the same as "device" in the reference ontology IoT-O, so there would be a pair (system, device) in A. It should be noted that $c_1 \equiv c_2$ cannot hold if c_1 and c_2 are from the same ontology; so a concept c_x from X can be aligned with at most one concept c_y from Y and vice versa. Subset of A, A', is considered training data. This allows to model alignment as a classification problem where the probability $q(c_y \mid c_x)$ of a concept c_y being aligned with a concept c_x is a function of the similarity to their concept embeddings:

$$q(c_y \mid c_x) = \text{softmax}\left(\text{sim}\left(c_x, c_y\right)\right) = \frac{e^{\text{sim}(c_x, c_y)}}{\displaystyle\sum_{j \in Y} e^{\text{sim}(c_x, c_y)}} \tag{6.2}$$

$$\text{where } \text{sim}\left(c_x, c_y\right) = \frac{\vec{v}\left(c_x\right) \cdot \vec{v}\left(c_y\right)}{\left\|\vec{v}\left(c_x\right)\right\|_2 \left\|\vec{v}\left(c_y\right)\right\|_2} \tag{6.3}$$

where $\vec{v}(c_x)$ represents the concept embedding for (c_x), whereas sim is computed by the cosine similarity.

Inspired by Ref. [6], a contextualized concept embedding method is adopted that is particularly well suited to knowledge graph alignment. Concept embeddings for (1) name, (2) label, (3) comments, (4) properties, (5) instance descriptions, (6) concept attributes and (7) the neighborhood of nearby concepts in the knowledge graph are generated. In ontology, concept attributes encode auxiliary information via attribute triples of the form <c,t,v> where c represents a concept, t represents an attribute type and v represents the attribute value, usually a string. To further contextualize each concept embedding, nearby concept embeddings are aggregated using random walks in the knowledge graph. Formally, the embedding v(c) for the concept c in MOMI is calculated as:

$$\begin{aligned}
\vec{v}(c) = \sigma \, \big(& \vec{v_0}(c) + W_n E_n(c) \\
& + W_l E_l(c) + W_c E_c(c) \\
& + W_{pd} E_{pd}(c) + W_{inst} E_{inst}(c) \\
& + W_a E_a(c) + W_{nc} E_{nc}(c) \big)
\end{aligned} \tag{6.4}$$

where σ is the sigmoid function, $\vec{v}_0(c) \in R^d$ is an initial d-dimension embedding of c, $E_n(c)$ is the aggregate name embedding of c, $E_l(c)$ is the aggregate label embedding of c, $E_c(c)$ is the aggregate encoding of comments of c, $E_{pd}(c)$ is the aggregate embeddings of property descriptions of c, $E_{inst}(c)$ is the aggregate embeddings of instance descriptions of c, $E_a(c)$ is the aggregate embeddings of attributes of c, $E_{nc}(c)$ is the aggregate neighborhood context embedding of c, while W_n, W_l, W_c, W_{pd}, W_{inst}, W_a and $W_{nc} \in R^{d \times d}$ are weight matrices. More specifically:

- The aggregate name, label and comments are computed by max-pooling over the embeddings.
- An attribute embedding a is calculated by passing an attribute-type embedding a_t and an attribute value embedding a_v through a fully connected sigmoid layer, $a = \sigma(W_t a_t + W_v a_v)$, where W_t and $W_v \in R^{d \times d}$ are weight matrices.
- The aggregate neighborhood context embedding W_n is computed by averaging the initial embedding vectors $\vec{v}_0(c)$ for each concept c_i in the neighborhood of c. The neighborhood of a concept c is approximated as the set of concepts other than c encountered on k random walks of length l executed when starting at c.

The quality of the predicted alignment according to q using cross-entropy is found using the concept embeddings $q(c_y|c_x) \ \forall \ (c_x, c_y) \in C_X \times C_Y$:

$$-\sum_{x \in X} \sum_{y \in Y} 1_{[c_x \equiv c_y]} \log q(c_y | c_x) \tag{6.5}$$

Equation 6.5 only measures how well the model captures the similarity between concepts aligned in the training data, which represents a small subset of $C_X \times C_Y$. Equation 6.6 is extended to incorporate uncertainty for unlabeled alignments using the function $\phi(c_x, c_y)$ in place of the indicator function of Equation 6.5.

$$\phi(c_x, c_y) = \begin{cases} 1_{[c_x \equiv c_y]} & \text{if } c_x \text{ is aligned in the training data} \\ \dfrac{1}{N_{unl}} & \text{if } c_x \text{ is unlabeled} \end{cases} \tag{6.6}$$

where N_{unl} is the number of currently unaligned concepts from Y. $\dfrac{1}{N_{unl}}$, which represents a uniform distribution over the possible alignment candidate for c_x and serves to bias the system against erroneous alignments. Using ϕ in the cross-entropy calculation of Equation 6.5 in place of the indicator function, the alignment classification loss is obtained:

$$\mathcal{L}_G = -\sum_{x \in X}\sum_{y \in Y}\phi\left(c_x, c_y\right)\log q\left(c_y \mid c_x\right) \tag{6.7}$$

By minimizing $\mathcal{L}_G$, MOMI shows the probability alignment function, q, which enables the maximum likelihood alignment between X and Y to be found. For each concept pair $< c_x, c_y >$, for which $q(c_y \mid c_x)$ is above a certain threshold, the alignment can be considered. It should be noted that this represents a max-weighted, one-to-one matching between subsets of X and Y with maximum total likelihood according to q. MOMI shows alignment-oriented knowledge embeddings for each concept in $C_X \cup C_Y$ using the feedback from the discriminator described in the next section, after which the alignments are learned, and new concept matches are added to A'_{i+1}. If a more likely matching emerges for a particular concept according to q, the less likely matching is simply replaced. MOMI terminates when no new concept matchings are added to the alignment. Figure 6.4 provides the high-level steps followed within the generator.

6.7.2 Discriminator

In this section, the discriminator uses a CNN called ontology CNN (OCNN) that improves traditional CNN network classification by injecting an attention module that deals with relation properties and entity descriptions to find the most probable relation tuple between the ontologies. Attention to

Method: Generator
Input: Ontology 1, Ontology 2
Output: New Triples combining Ontology 1 and Ontology 2
Steps:

1. Extract ontology triples <ci,cj,k> from both ontologies 1, 2. Let S_1 represent all triples from Ontology 1 and S_2 represent all triples from Ontology 2 $S_1 = \{< C_{x1}, C_{x2}, k >, < C_{x1}, C_{x3}, k >, ... < C_{xm}, C_{x(m-1)}, k > \mid C_{xm} \neq C_{x(m+1)}\}$ and $S_2 = \{< C_{y1}, C_{y2}, k >, < C_{y1}, C_{y3}, k >, ... < C_{yn}, C_{y(n-1)}, k > \mid C_{yi} \neq C_{y(i+1)}\}$
2. Two concepts are aligned when they are semantically similar. Semantic similarity can be obtained by the function of similarity of the concepts, i.e. $q(c_y \mid c_x) = f(\text{similarity (concept)})$. Where concept similarity is obtained as a function of the similarity of the concept embeddings $softmax\left(sim(c_x, c_y)\right)$
   a. Produce embeddings for each of the classes in S_1 and S_2 using the following attributes of the classes (a) name of the classes (b) labels of the classes (c) immediate super-class and subclass (d) attributes of the classes
3. Step 2 gives pairs of concepts that are similar, Output ontology triples using the similar conceptual pairs across ontologies minimizing the Loss $\mathcal{L}_G$

FIGURE 6.4
Generator algorithm

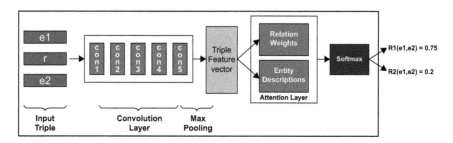

FIGURE 6.5
Discriminator architecture

relation properties enables our model to select multiple valid instances for training, so that full use of the supervision information is made possible. Entity descriptions provide more background knowledge about the entities, which could improve the performance of our model and bring better entity representations for attention module.

Figure 6.5 shows the neural network architecture of our model OCNNs. It consists of two parts: OCNN module and resource properties attention module. OCNN module includes vector representation, convolution and piecewise max-pooling. Resource properties attention module is composed of attention layer and softmax classifier. The parts of the discriminator are explained in detail in Figure 6.5.

6.8 OCNN Module

This module is used to extract feature vector of a relation property from a bag. In order to provide inputs to this module, a vector representation/ embedding of the ontology parameters has been chosen. The convolution layer uses five feature maps to capture the name, label, comments, property and instance descriptions of a particular concept.

6.8.1 Vector Representation

Since a neural network model is used to do the task, transformation of the word tokens into low-dimensional vectors is essential. In the current method, words are transformed into vectors by looking up to the pre-trained word embeddings. The method as described in Section 6.6 is used for obtaining the vector representation.

Word embeddings are distributed representations of words that map each word in text to a low-dimensional vector. It has been proved to be very effective in many Natural Language Processing (NLP) tasks. $\mathbf{E}$ denotes the trained word embeddings using the suggested approach.

6.8.2 Convolution

Assume that $\mathbf{A} = \left(a_{ij}\right)_{m \times n}$ and $\mathbf{B} = \left(b_{ij}\right)_{m \times n}$, then the convolution of $\mathbf{A}$ and $\mathbf{B}$ is defined as $\mathbf{A} \otimes \mathbf{B} = \sum_{i=1}^{m}\sum_{j=1}^{n} a_{ij}b_{ij}$.

An input triple is denoted by $S = \left\{s_1, s_2, \ldots, s_{|S|}\right\}$ where s_i is the ith word and uses $s_1 \in R^k$ to represent its vector. $S_{i:j}$ is used to represent the matrix concatenated by sequence $[s_1, s_2, \ldots, s_j]$ ($[x_1 : x_2]$), which denotes the horizontal concatenation of x_1, x_2. The length of filter is represented by w, the weight matrix of the filter is $W \in R^{w \times k}$, and the convolution operation between the filter and triple S results in another vector $c \in R^{|S|- w+1}$

$$c_j = W \otimes S_{(j-w+1):j} \qquad (6.8)$$

where $1 \leq j \leq |S| - w + 1$.

In experiments, n ($n>1$) filters (or feature maps) are used to capture different features of an instance. Therefore, n weight matrices $\widehat{W} = \{W_1, W_2, \ldots, W_n\}$ are also required, so that all the convolution operations can be expressed by

$$c_{ij} = \mathbf{W}_i \otimes \mathbf{S}_{(j-w+1):j} \qquad (6.9)$$

where $1 \leq i \leq n$ and $1 \leq j \leq |S| - w + 1$. Through the convolution layer, the results are captured in vector $C = \{c_1, c_2, \ldots, c_n\}$.

6.8.3 Max-Pooling

Max-pooling operation is applied to each of the outputs of the convolution vectors C to extract the most significant features in feature maps. In order to capture the structural information and fine-grained features, OCNN divides an instance into segments according to the given entity pair for the names, labels, comments etc. and then a max-pooling operation on each segment is performed. For the result vector c_i of convolution operations, it can be divided into n parts, for example, $c_i = \left\{c_{i,1}, c_{i,2}, c_{i,3}\right\}$. Then piecewise max-pooling procedure is $p_{ij} = \max\left\{c_{i,j}\right\}$, where $1 \leq i \leq n$ and $j=1, 2, 3$ etc. After that, all the vectors $p_i = \left[p_{i,1}, p_{i,2}, p_{i,3}\right]$ ($i=1, 2, 3, \ldots, n$) are concatenated to obtain vector $p \in R^{3n}$. Furthermore, computation of the feature vector $b_s = \tanh(p)$ for the concept C is performed.

6.8.4 Attention Module

Attention mechanism is one of the most important parts of the OntoCNN. The attention model can represent higher weights for valid instances and lower weights for the invalid ones. Once the convolution layer outputs have been computed, it is fed into a softmax classifier. Relation classification for knowledge graph embedding approach is treated as a translation from entity ($e1$) to tail entity ($e2$). The relation can be expressed as a triplet in the form of $r(e1, e2)$. In Ref. [6], the embeddings are expressed as $e_1 + r \times e_2$. Motivated by Ref. [11], feature embeddings considered are related by the absolute difference between the feature embeddings of entities defined by $v_{relation} = e_1 - e_2$. Every instance in the bag may express the relation r or another relation. If an instance expresses the relation r, its feature vector should have higher similarity with $v_{relation}$, otherwise lower similarity. $\{b_1, b_2, \ldots, b_q\}$ are feature vectors computed by OCNN; $v_{relation} = e_1 - e_2$ is used to denote the relation between e_1 and e_2. Based on Ref. [12], formulas are used to compute the attention weight (similarity or relatedness) between each instance's feature vector and $v_{relation}$.

$$\alpha_i = \frac{\exp(\omega_i)}{\sum\limits_{j=1}^{q} \exp(\omega_b)} \tag{6.10}$$

$$\omega_i = W_a^\top \left(\tanh \left[b_i ; v_{relation} \right] \right) + b_a \tag{6.11}$$

where $[x_1 : x_2]$ denotes the vertical concatenation of x_1, x_2, $1 \le i \le q$, $W_a \in R^{1 \times (3n + k)}$ is an intermediate matrix and b_a is an offset value. $\alpha = \{\alpha_1, \alpha_2, \ldots, \alpha_q\}$ that are the weight vectors of all instances in the bag. Then the bag features can be computed as follows.

$$\bar{b} = \sum\limits_{i=1}^{q} \alpha_i b_i \tag{6.12}$$

where $\bar{b} \in R^{3n}$.

6.8.5 Entity Descriptions

Entity descriptions provide supplementary information about the concept under study. Here, another traditional CNN that uses a convolution layer and a single max-pooling layer is used to extract features from entity descriptions. The pair of (entity, description) is denoted by $D = \{(e_i, d_i) \mid i = 1, 2, \ldots, |D|\}$. The vectors of e_i and words in descriptions can be obtained by looking up to the word embeddings E. The vectors of d_i are computed by a CNNs, the weight matrices of which are denoted by $\widehat{W}_d$. In this method, the vectors of entities are chosen to be close to the descriptions. The errors are defined as follows:

$$\mathcal{L}_e = \sum\limits_{i=1}^{|D|} \|e_i - d_i\|_2^2 \tag{6.13}$$

The background knowledge extracted from descriptions not only provides more information for prediction relations but also brings better representations of entities for the attention module.

6.8.6 Softmax

To compute the confidence of each relation, the feature vector $\bar{b}$ is fed into a softmax classifier. $o = W_s\bar{b} + b_s$, where $o \in R^{n_o}$ is the output, $W_s \in R^{n_o \times 3n}$ is the weight matrix and $b_s \in R^{n_o}$ is the bias. Let $\theta=(E, \widehat{W}, PF_1, PF_2, W_a, W_b)$ to denote all parameters and B represents a bag. Then the conditional probability of ith relation is

$$p\left(r_i \mid B;\theta\right) = \frac{\exp(O_i)}{\sum_{j=1}^{n_o} \exp(o_j)}. \qquad (6.14)$$

6.8.7 Training Objective

N bags in training set $\{B_1, B_2,\dots, B_N\}$ and their labels are relations $\{r_1, r_2,\dots, r_N\}$, which are used to analyze the effects of relation attention mechanism and entity descriptions, respectively. The model is trained in two modes. First, the OntoCNNs are trained using only relation-level attention module (no entity descriptions); the loss function is found using cross-entropy as follows:

$$\min \mathcal{L}_R = \sum_{i=1}^{N} \log p\left(r_i \mid B_i, \theta\right) \qquad (6.15)$$

where $\Theta = \&\left(\mathbf{E}, \widehat{\mathbf{W}}, \mathbf{PF}_1, \mathbf{PF}_2, \mathbf{W}_a, \mathbf{W}_s\right)$

Second, both relation-level attention module and entity descriptions are enabled for training. The loss function hence will be $\min \mathcal{L}_D = \mathcal{L}_R + \lambda \mathcal{L}_e$, where $\lambda>0$ is the weight of $\mathcal{L}_e$. In the experiments, dropout strategy and ADADELTA to train are proposed to train the model. Figure 6.6 provides the steps in the discriminator algorithm.

6.8.8 Selection

The output from the MOMI algorithm is the plausible relation triple. The algorithm continues to train until no more triples are generated and validated. The model obtained after the iteration is the real output that can be used further. The top 100 triples obtained in the model are presented to the experts for assertion; once approved they can be used to answer queries when several domains and concepts are in operation.

Method: Discriminator
Input: Ontology 1, Ontology 2
Output: Probabilities of the validity of Triple combining Ontology 1 and Ontology 2
Steps:

1. Train a simple CNN to derive entity descriptions required for the attention layer
2. Obtain relation-weights by using $v_{relation} = e_1 - e_2$
3. Train a Ontology CNN (OCNN) network individually on Ontology 1 and Ontology 2 relations triples independently together with the knowledge of relation pairs from Wikidata, Freebase.

FIGURE 6.6
Discriminator algorithm

6.9 Aligned Ontology

Figure 6.7 illustrates the aligned ontology in action; for a request from a user or a machine, the knowledge base (KB) is used to resolve the query as the concepts and relations across various ontologies and related domains are established using MOMI. The KB enables a user to learn and resolve the queries from across ontologies, provided the axioms are established and rule inference engines are updated to look across the ontologies. The MOMI algorithm augments the inference mechanism to look beyond just one ontology and transparently provides replacements for the concepts and the relations.

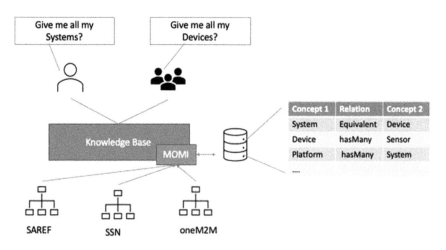

FIGURE 6.7
MOMI aligned ontology

6.10 Discussion

A unique combination of generator based on probabilistic classifier and discriminator based on a novel CNN with relation attention assisted by entity descriptions will be able to produce the best possible alignment between ontologies. In the IoT space, lack of a generic universal ontology will be a big gap to fill compared to other domains such as biomedicine where Unified Modelling Language (UMLs) provides a reference ontology for matching and alignments. IoT-O has been selected as the reference ontology in this work because it is the most comprehensive ontology covering several important concepts in IoT space. SSN covers only sensors and actuators, while SAREF and oneM2M cover only certain concepts of IoT domains. An aligned ontology in such a scenario where there is lot of fragmentation and incompleteness is very important to build an intelligent M2M communication system.

The discriminator being the central part of the whole solution is different from all the existing works in many ways; it is an algorithm that is built for the alignment of ontologies as it is fine tuned to relate concepts and relations not just within a given ontology but against several ontologies. This is possible only when the algorithm can consider several important parts of the ontology for alignment like the name, label, comments, properties, instance descriptions and context around the class. The learning of the concepts and relations is improved to a large extent by adding the relation weights and entity descriptions that augment the learning process and they are crucial as they bring in knowledge from across several domains (distant supervision).

Training the generator-discriminator network is the hard part as convergence is hard to identify. In the first round, the generator is programmed to output the fake triples using the concepts from both ontologies, while the discriminator is trained using both the fake and real concept triples. In the second round, the generator is programmed to output more fake triples, which is the only input provided to the discriminator for training. This ensures the discriminator is able to fully realize the fake from the real triples. Such a training optimization ensures MOMI is able to represent the triples correctly when new related ontologies are fed into the algorithm. Also, MOMI is able to produce new triples in the process of alignment of the ontologies that can be used to extract information across varied related domains.

6.11 Conclusion and Future Work

MOMI algorithm took a step toward alignment of related ontologies, thus enabling extension of the KB, which otherwise would have not been possible as it is impossible for a human expert to be able to glean knowledge across related similar domains. The ability to automatically infer aligned concepts and relations enables reasoning to be extended across domain boundaries, allowing machines to progress the intelligence beyond a single domain of operation.

Several features of the ontology such as name and label are selected manually; the selection of these features must be recognized by algorithm/process itself instead of manual identification as several ontologies might not have all of those features defined. An automatic feature selection algorithm can precede the MOMI algorithm execution to enable more accurate detection of the required feature to compare while aligning the ontologies. Another area of work is the extension of the alignments produced to arrive at a shared embedding space so that ontology alignments can be easily made available for broader use such as in automated ontology construction.

References

[1] A. Gyrard, C. Bonnet, K. Boudaoud, and M. Serrano, "LOV4IoT: A second life for ontology-based domain knowledge to build semantic web of things applications," Proc. – 2016 IEEE 4th Int. Conf. Futur. Internet Things Cloud, FiCloud 2016, pp. 254–261, 2016.

[2] G. Bajaj, R. Agarwal, P. Singh, N. Georgantas, and V. Issarny, "A study of existing Ontologies in the IoT-domain," 2017.

[3] J. Liu, X. Zhang, Y. Li, J. Wang, and H. J. Kim, "Deep learning-based reasoning with multi-ontology for IoT applications," *IEEE Access*, vol. 7, pp. 124688–124701, 2019.

[4] L. Otero-Cerdeira, F. J. Rodríguez-Martínez, and A. Gómez-Rodríguez, "Definition of an ontology matching algorithm for context integration in smart cities," *Sensors (Switzerland)*, vol. 14, no. 12, pp. 23581–23619, 2014.

[5] M. Palmonari and M. Palmonari. "Knowledge graph embeddings and explainable AI." *Knowledge Graphs for Explainable Artificial Intelligence: Foundations, Applications and Challenges*, IOS Press, Amsterdam (2020): 49–72.

[6] R. M. Maldonado and S. M. Harabagiu, "Bootstrapping adversarial learning of biomedical ontology alignments," *AMIA … Annual Symposium proceedings/ AMIA Symposium. AMIA Symposium*, vol. 2019, pp. 627–636, 2019.

[7] ETSI, "SAREF," 2020. [Online]. Available: https://saref.etsi.org/core/v3.1.1/saref.rdf.

[8] "oneM2M Ontology," 2018. [Online]. Available: https://git.onem2m.org/MAS/BaseOntology/blob/master/base_ontology.owl.

[9] "SSN Ontology." Available: https://www.w3.org/TR/vocab-ssn/#:~:text=The%20Semantic%20Sensor%20Network%20%28SSN%29%20ontology%20is%20an,and%20the%20observed%20properties%2C%20as%20well%20as%20actuators.

[10] T. Mikolov, K. Chen, G. Corrado, and J. Dean, "Efficient estimation of word representations in vector space," *1st Int. Conf. Learn. Represent. ICLR 2013 – Work. Track Proc.*, pp. 1–12, 2013.

[11] G. Ji, K. Liu, S. He, and J. Zhao, "Distant supervision for relation extraction with sentence-level attention and entity descriptions," *31st AAAI Conf. Artif. Intell. AAAI 2017*, pp. 3060–3066, 2017.

[12] M.-T. Luong, H. Pham, and C. D. Manning, "Effective approaches to attention-based neural machine translation," *arXiv*, 2015.

7

Higher Level Abstraction of Deep Architecture

C. Ramesh Kumar

7.1 Introduction

Machine learning focuses primarily on the representation of input data and the general use for future invisible data. The quality of data depiction greatly influences the machine-student's performance on the data: a poor data representation will likely reduce the performance of even a sophisticated, complex learner, while good data depiction could lead to high performance for a relatively simple machine to student (De Haan et al., 2020). Functional engineering, which concentrates on building features and representing raw data, is an important component of machine learning. Feature engineering uses a large part of the effort in the machine learning work and typically involves considerable human input and is quite domain specific (Lee et al., 2019). The oriented gradient histogram (HOG) and the scale invariant transform feature (SIFT) are popular feature engineering algorithms specifically developed for the computer viewing domain. Performing more automated and generally based feature engineering that could be an important breakthrough in machine learning, because it would automatically enable practitioners to extract these features without direct human input (Saha & Manickavasagan, 2021).

Deep learning algorithms are one promising path to automated data extraction (features) at high levels of abstraction. Such algorithms develop a layered, hierarchical learning architecture and data representing higher level characteristics (more abstract) with lower level (less abstract) characteristics defined (Diro & Chilamkurti, 2018). Deep Learning is a part of the machine learning algorithms inspired by the structure and function of the system called artificial intelligence, emulating the deep, layered learning process in the primary sensory areas of the neocortex in the human brain, where features and abstractions automatically are extracted from the underlying data. When dealing with learning a large amount of uncontrolling data, deep learning algorithms are very beneficial and usually gloomy-faced

DOI: 10.1201/9781003126898-7

representations of data. Empirical studies have shown that data representation obtained by stacking nonlinear feature extractors (as with deep learning) often leads to better machine learning outcomes, e.g. improving the classification modeling of improved sample quality with generational probabilistic models and the invariant properties of data representations (Mecheter et al., 2020). In various machine learning applications, including computer vision, speech recognition and natural language processing, deep learning solutions have produced exceptional results, a detailed overview is presented (Deng, 2014).

Big data represents the general range of problems and technologies used to collect and maintain massive amounts of raw data for domain-specific data analysis for application domains. The development of big data science has been greatly contributed by modern data-intensive technologies and increased computational and data-storage resources (AlQuraishi, 2019). Tech companies such as Google, Yahoo, Microsoft and Amazon have collected and maintained exabyte measured data. In addition, social media organizations like Facebook, YouTube and Twitter have trillions of users constantly generating a huge amount of information. Different companies have invested in the development of big data analytics products (Khan & Yairi, 2018), addressing their monitoring, experimentation, data analyses, simulations and other knowledge and business needs.

At the heart, big data analytics is the exploitation and extraction of meaningful patterns from massive data input for decision-making and prediction. Big data analytics also presents other unique challenges for machine learning and data analysis in addition to analysis of massive data volumes, including format variation for raw data, quick streaming data, confident data analysis, high-distributed sources of inputs (Fiorucci et al., 2020), bruising data and poor-quality data, high dimensionality, algorithm scalability, imbalanced input data, unmonitored and poorly analyzed data. Additional key issues in big data analytics include adequate data storage, indexing/tagging and quick data recovery. To work with big data, innovative analytical data and data administration solutions are therefore guaranteed. In a recent study, for example, we examined the high dimensions of bioinformatics domain data and examined feature selection techniques to deal with the problem (Fiorucci et al., 2020).

In the context of big data analytics, the information gained from (and made available by) deep learning algorithms is largely untapped. Certain big data domains have been used to greatly improve classification modeling results, such as computer vision and speech recognition. It is attractive for Big data analytics as the ability of deep learning to extract high-level, complex abstractions and data representation from large amounts of data (Tsirikoglou et al., 2020), especially from uncontrolled data. More specifically, large data issues such as semantic indexing, data tagging, fast retrieval of information and discriminatory modeling with the help of deep learning can be improved. More traditional engineering algorithms and machine learning aren't efficient enough to extract the complex and nonlinear patterns generally seen in big data. Deep learning allows for the use of relatively simple linear models for big data analyses, such as grading and prediction, which are important for the development of big data-scale models. The new feature of this study is the application of deep learning algorithms in big data analysis to address key problems that motivate more targeted research by experts in both fields (Wang et al., 2021).

The chapter focuses upon two main topics: (1) how deep learning can help specific big data analytics challenges and (2) how specific deep learning areas can be improved to reflect certain big data analytics challenges. With regard to the first topic, we explore the use of deep learning for particular large data analytics. This includes learning from massive data volumes, memantine indexing, discriminatory tasks and information tagging (Mohammadi et al., 2018). Our second topic research focuses on specific challenges facing deep learning, due to the problems in big data analytics, including learning from data streaming, the high dimension of data, the model scalability and distributed and parallel computing. We conclude by identifying important future areas of innovation in big data analytics deep learning, including data sampling for useful high-level abstraction, domain adaptation (data distribution), criteria defining the extracting of good data representations for descriptive and indexing tasks, semi-controlled learning and active learning (Yang et al., 2020).

The rest of the chapter has the following structures: Section 7.3 provides an overview of deep learning for data analysis in the field of data mining and machine learning: big data analytics, with the key characteristics of big data and identification of specific data analysis problems facing big data analytics. Section 7.5 discusses some challenges that deep learning experts face due to their specific data analysis needs. The future work on big data analytics provides our insight into further work that is needed to extend the application of deep learning in big data, and questions key field experts.

7.2 Deep Learning Architectures

In deep learning, there is wide and varied number of architectures and algorithms used. This section discusses 6 of the last 20 years of profound learning architecture (Yadav & Vishwakarma, 2020). Long-term memory (LSTM) and coevolutionary neural networks (CNNs) are two of the oldest and two most widely applied approaches in this list as shown in Figure 7.1.

This chapter classifies the architecture of profound learning into supervised and uncontrollable learning and offers several popular architectures for depth learning (Levine et al., 2019), such as neural network convolutions, recurring neural networks and long-term recurrent memory/equipment

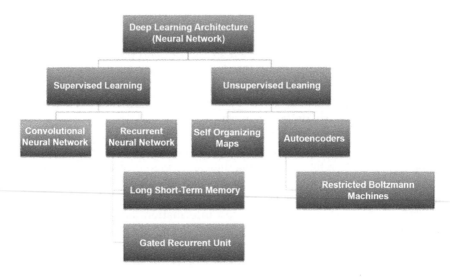

FIGURE 7.1
Architecture of deep learning

units (GRU) (RBM). It also provides an overview of DBN and deep networks (DSNs).

7.2.1 Supervised Deep Learning

Supervised learning refers to the problem area in the data used for training, in which the target to be forecast is clearly marked (Li et al., 2019).

In this area, we present two of the most popular supervised architectures for deep learning at high level – CNNs and recurrent neural networks (RNNs) and some of their variants (Ouali et al., 2020).

7.2.1.1 Convolutional Neural Networks

A CNN is an animal visual cortex-inspired multi-layered neuronal network. In image processing applications, the architecture is particularly useful. Yann LeCun was the first to show CNN; the design at that time focused on the recognition of handwritten characters (Gu et al., 2018), such as the interpretation of postal code. Early strata identify features (like edge) as a DSN and later strata are recombined into higher input attributes as illustrated in Figure 7.2.

The LeNet CNN architecture consists of several layers that extract features and then classify them (see Figure 7.2) (Qian et al., 2020). The picture is divided into receptive fields that flow into a coevolutionary layer, where the functions are extracted from the image input. The next step is to pool the extracted features (by down-sampling) with the retention of the most

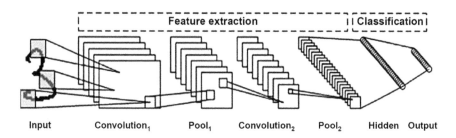

FIGURE 7.2
CNN architecture for learning

important information (typically, through max pooling). A further step of convolution, which feeds into a totally connected multilayer perceptron, will then be carried out. A set of nodes that identify image features is the last output layer of the network (in this case, a node per identified number). Use back-propagation to train the network (Zhou, 2020).

By using deep processing layers, convolutions, bundling and a fully connected classification layer, various new applications of deep learning neural networks are opening the door (Tian, 2020). In addition to image processing, video identification and various tasks within the processing of natural languages have been successfully carried out by CNN.

7.2.1.2 Recurrent Neural Networks

The RNN is one of the basic architectures in the network of other architectures. The main difference between a typical multilayer network and a recurrent network is that a recurrent network could be connected to previous layers, rather than fully feed-forward connections (or into the same layer) (Schuster & Paliwal, 1997). This feedback allows RNNs to keep memory of previous inputs and models problems in due course.

RNNs are rich in architecture (we will look at one of the popular LSTM topologies). Feedback from a hidden layer, the output layer or a certain combination of the network can be the main differentiator (Ceni et al., 2020).

RNNs can be developed in time, trained with standard back-breeding or with a variant of back-breeding called back-breeding in time (BPTT) (Manchev & Spratling, 2020), as shown in Figure 7.3. Furthermore, it can be used.

7.2.2 Unsupervised Deep Learning

Unattended learning refers to the area in which the data that are used for training are not subject to a target label (Cui et al., 2019).

This section addresses three uncontrolled architectures for deep learning: self-organized maps (SOMs), autoencoders and Boltzmann-restricted

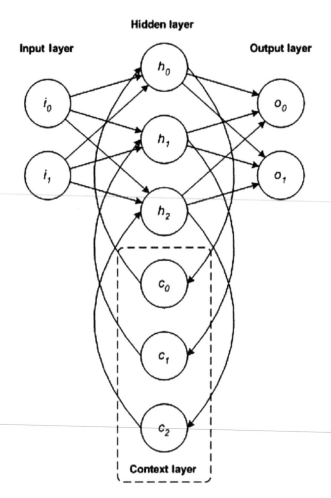

FIGURE 7.3
Recurrent neural networks for learning

machines. We also discuss the building of deep belief and stacking networks based on the underlying unattended architecture (Ou et al., 2019).

7.2.2.1 Self-Organized Maps

In 1982, Dr. Teuvo Kohonen invented the SOM and was commonly referred to as the Kohonen Map (Xue et al., 2019). SOM is a neural network unchecked that creates input data clusters by reducing the input size. SOMs are quite different shown in Figure 7.4 from the traditional artificial neural network.

The first important variation is that weights are a feature of the node. After normalizing the inputs, a random input is selected first. Each feature of the input record is initialized with random weights close to zero (Raza & Singh,

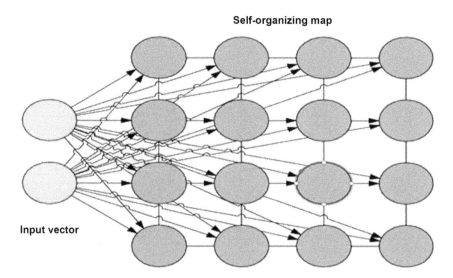

Self-organizing map

Input vector

FIGURE 7.4
Self-organized map for unsupervised learning

2018). The weights are now the node of input. Variations in the input node occur in several combinations of these random weights. The Euclidean distance is calculated between each of these input nodes. The lowest distance node is declared to be the most accurate input display and marked as the most appropriate unit or BMU. These BMUs as centers also calculate other units and are assigned them to the cluster from which they are located. Radius of points around BMU weights are updated based on proximity (Liu et al., 2019).

There is no activating function in the SOM next and there is no concept of error calculation and propagation in the back because there are no target labels to compare it with (dos Santos Ferreira et al., 2019).

Examples of applications are as follows: reduced dimensionality, clustering of high-dimensional inputs to two-dimensional output, result radiant and visualization of the cluster.

7.2.2.2 Deep Belief Networks

The DBN is a typical network architecture but has a new algorithm for training. The DBN is a multilayered network with RBM in each pair of connected layers (typically deep, including many hidden layers). A DBN is thus represented as an RBM stack (Zhao & Jia, 2020).

The input layer in the DBN shows the raw sensory input, and the abstracted representations of this input are found on each hidden layer. The network classification is implemented by the output layer, which is somewhat different than the other layers (Huang et al., 2019). There are two training

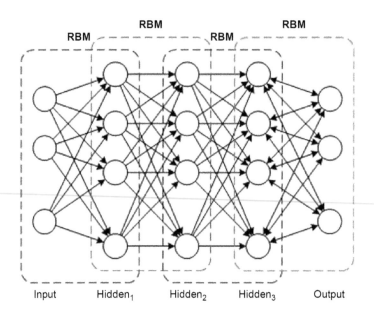

FIGURE 7.5
Deep belief networks for learning

steps: pretraining unattended and fine adjustment supervised as illustrated in Figure 7.5.

Each RBM is trained to reconstruct its input during unchecked pretraining (for example, the first RBM reconstructs the input layer to the first hidden layer). The next RBM is similarly trained; the first layer of the RBM is called the visible, or input, layer, and the second is the hidden layer (Wang & Cha, 2021). This process continues to be pretrained for each layer. Once the pre-workout is over, finishing starts. The output nodes are used to provide them with significance in this phase (what they represent in the context of the network). Full network training is then used to complete the training process by means of either graduation or back-propagation (Oh et al., 2020).

Examples are as follows: image recognition, information collection, understanding of natural languages and prediction for failure.

7.3 Deep Learning in Data Mining and Machine Learning

Automating data extraction from representatives (abstractions) is the principal concept in deeply lean algorithms. Deep learning algorithms are used to automatically extract complex representation by a huge number of unattended data. The main motivation for these algorithms is AI that emulates the human brain's ability to observe, analyses, learn and decide, especially for extremely complex problems (Wang, 2017). Testing to emulate the hierarchical learning approach of the human brain has been a major motivation behind deep learning algorithms. Models based on poor study architectures like decision trees, vector support machines and case-oriented reasoning may fail to extract useful information from complex input structures and relationships (Nguyen et al., 2019a). Deep learning, on the other hand, can generalize learning patterns and relationships beyond the immediate neighbors in data in a nonlocal and global manner. In fact, profound learning is an important step toward AI. It offers complex data representations that are suitable for AI tasks as well as independence from human knowledge, which is AI's ultimate objective. It extracts representations without human interference directly from unchecked data (Wu et al., 2021).

A key concept behind the deep learning methods is distributed representations of data, which allow for the compact representation of each sample and lead to greater generalization, in a large number of possible configurations of abstract features of data input. Extensively linked to the number of extracted abstract features is the number of possible configurations (Belhadi et al., 2020). It is possible to describe additional (unsensed) data patterns via new configurations of the factors learned and patterns if the observed data are generated by interactions of several known/unknown factors. The data pattern is potentiated by certain configurations of learning factors (Ramasamy Ramamurthy & Roy, 2018). The number of patterns is obtainable by means of a distributed representation scales quickly with the number of learning factors compared to learning based on local generalizations.

Deep learning algorithms lead to abstract representations, since more abstract representations are often built on less abstract representations. An important benefit of more abstract representations is that the local changes of the input data can be invariant. To learn these invariant features is an important objective in recognition of patterns (for example, learning features that are invariant to the face orientation in a face recognition task) (Hassanien et al., 2020). In addition to being invariant, the factors of variation in data can also be separated. The real data used for AI-related tasks come mainly from complex interactions between a number of sources. An image consists, for instance, of different variation sources such as light, object shapes and object materials. Deep learning algorithms can separate the abstract representations from the different sources of data variations (Kivrak et al., 2021).

In actual fact, deeper learning algorithms are deep, consecutive layer architectures. Each layer transforms its input in a nonlinear way and gives its output a representation. Its aim is to learn how to represent the data in a complicated and abstract way through multiple transformation layers in a hierarchical way. The sensing data are fed into the first layer, for example, pixels in an image. As an input for its next layer, therefore, the output of every layer is provided (Lan et al., 2018).

The basic concept in deep learning algorithms is to store the nonlinear transformation layers. The deeper the layers the data pass through, the more complex the nonlinear transformations are. These transformations represent the data such that deep learning can be seen as a special case of algorithms of representation learning (Gómez-Pulid et al., 2020), in which data are represented in a deep architecture with multiple levels of representation. A highly nonlinear feature of the input data is the achieved final representation.

Learning the parameters in a deep architecture is a complex process of optimization, for example, learning the parameters of several hidden layer neural networks. In 2006, in an uncontrolled, selfish way of learning, Hinton suggested learning deep architectural structures. Initially, sensory data are fed to the first layer as learning data (Zuo et al., 2019). The first layer is then trained on the basis of these figures and the output from the first layer is provided as learning data for the second layer. This is achieved before you have the optimal number of layers. The DSN is being trained at this stage. For different tasks, you can use representations on the last layer. When the task is a classification task, a different supervised layer is normally placed on the top of the last layer (either randomly or by using supervised data and keeping the rest of the network fixed). At the end of the day, the entire network is optimized with supervised data (Witten et al., 2016).

Another uncontrolled single-layer learning algorithm is the Boltzmann-restricted computer, which is a building block in deep belief networks (RBM). RBMs are probably Boltzmann's most common version. They have one layer visible and one layer concealed. The limit is that the units of the same layer cannot communicate, and the interactions are exclusively between units of different layers. The Boltzmann computer trained mainly using the contrastive divergence algorithm.

7.4 Applications of Deep Learning in Big Data Analytics

As previously stated, deep learning algorithms extract meaningful abstract representations of raw data through the use of a hierarchical multilevel learning approach, which is based on the less abstract concepts and representations in the lower level of learning hierarchy and at the higher level more abstract and complex representations are learnt (Wang et al., 2018). If deep learning is available in sufficiently large quantities to learn from labeled data, it is mainly attractive to learn from large volumes of non-labeled/unmonitored data and to extract meaningful representations and patterns from big data (Najafabadi et al., 2015).

Upon learning of hierarchical data abstracts using deep learning, the use of comparatively fewer supervised/labeled data-points, where labeled data are generally collected by human/expert input, is trained more conventionally discriminative models. Deep learning algorithms are better suited than relatively low learning architectures (Elsayed & Zulkernine, 2020) to extract nonlocal and global relations and patterns in the data. Other useful features of deep learning's learned abstraction include (1) relatively simple linear models can work effectively with the knowledge gained from more complex and abstract data representations, (2) enhanced automation of unattended data representation extraction, allowing its broad application to different types of data, such as images, textures. Although there are other useful aspects (Mohammadi et al., 2018) of data representation based on deep learning, the abovementioned special features are of particular importance for big data analytics.

In view of each of the four Vs of big data, i.e. volume, diversity, speed and veracity, the deep learning algorithms and architectures are more suitable in addressing volume and variety issues related to the big data analytics. The deep learning (Prabhu, 2019) exploits inherently the availability of massive data, i.e. big data volume, which does not explore and understand the high complexity of data patterns through algorithms with superficial learning hierarchies. In addition, given that deep learning addresses data abstraction and representations, it will probably be suitable for the analysis of raw data in (Sun & Scanlon, 2019) different formats and/or from different sources, i.e. variety in large data, and may minimize the need to extract data features from every new type of data observed in large data by human experts. Big data analytics presents a significant opportunity to develop new algorithms and models to address specific questions concerning big data while posing various challenges in terms of more conventional data analytics approaches.

In the rest of this section, we summarize important work in the field of algorithms and architectures of deep learning, including semantic indexing, discrimination and data tagging. We focus on the novel applicability of deep learning in big data analytics by introducing these works in deep learning, especially as certain application (Phinyomark & Scheme, 2018) areas in the works being presented involve large-scale data. Deep learning algorithms apply to various types of input information; in this section, however, we focus on image, textual and audio-data applications.

7.4.1 Semantic Indexing

The information recovery is a key task in connection with big data analytics. Big data is increasingly problematic for efficient data retrieval and storage, in particular as very large amounts of data like text, images, video (Phinyomark & Scheme, 2018) and audio are collected and made available over a variety of fields, including social networks, safety systems, shopping and marketing systems, defense systems, fraud detection and cyber traffic monitoring. The massive volumes of data and various data representations, both associated with big data, challenge previous strategies and solutions for storage and recovery of information. Massive amounts of data are available on these systems requiring semantic indexing instead of being saved as data bit strings. Semantic indexation presents data in a more efficient manner (Pandey & Janghel, 2019) and helps to find and understand knowledge by making search engines work faster and more efficiently, for instance.

Deep learning can be used on other types of data, similar to textual data, to extract semantic representations from the input corpus (Bhandari et al., 2020), to enable the semantic indexing of that data. Given the recent emergence of profound learning, there has to be additional efforts to use its hierarchical learning strategy as a way to index big data semantically. One remaining open question is which criteria are used when attempted to extract data representations for indexing purposes to define "similar" (recall, data-points that are semantically similar will have similar data representations in a specific distance space).

7.4.2 Discriminative Tasks and Semantic Tagging

Deep learning algorithms can be used to extract complicated nonlinear features from the crude data when performing discriminative tasks in big data analysis and then use simple linear models to perform discriminative tasks with extracted features as input. This approach has two advantages: (1) extracting features with deep learning add a more computationally effective approach, which closely associates discriminative tasks with AI and (2) applying relatively simple linear analytical models on extractions. A comprehensive literature study has examined the problem of developing efficient linear models for big data analytics. Thus, the development of nonlinear characteristics based on massive (Nguyen et al., 2019b) input data allows data analysts to take advantage of the available knowledge in large quantities of data by applying the knowledge learned to simple linear models for further analysis. This is an important advantage for practitioners in large data analysis using deep learning to perform complex tasks relating to AI, such as image understanding, image object recognition, etc., with simpler models. In large data analytics, therefore, the use of deep learning algorithms makes discriminatory tasks relatively easy.

7.5 Deep Learning Challenges in Big Data Analytics

Although in-depth learning techniques are best proven, and different complex applications with multiple layers and high abstraction have been resolved. It is certainly agreed that deep learning systems are almost the same for accuracy, accuracy, receptive capacity and accuracy or sometimes exceeding human experts. The technology must take on many challenges to feel the joy of victory in today's scenario. There is therefore a list of challenges to be overcome by deep learning:

- Input data must be continuously administered by deep learning algorithms.
- Algorithms must ensure that the conclusion is transparent.
- Resources are high-performance technology such as GPUs and storage requirements.
- Enhanced big data analytics methods. DSNs are known as networks in black boxes.
- The presence of over-the-top parameters and complicated design.
- Local minima suffer.
- Intractable for computers.
- A lot of data are required.
- Costly for the difficult issues and calculations.
- There is no solid theoretical basis.
- It's hard to find topology and profound learning training parameters.
- Deep learning provides new data calculation tools and infrastructures and makes it possible for computers to learn objects and images.

Large-scale deep learning models are perfectly suited for the handling of large volumes of data input and they also learn complex data patterns from large volumes of data, as shown in above work. Determination and improvement of the computational practicability of such large-size models pose challenges in deep learning for big data analytics. In addition to the problem of massive data handling, large-scale big data analytics deep learning models must also address other big data issues like domain adaptation (see next section) and streaming data. This makes further innovations in large-scale deep learning models necessary for algorithms and architectures.

7.6 Future Work on Deep Learning in Big Data Analytics

In the preceding sections, we addressed some recent deep learning algorithms for big data analytics applications, as well as some areas where deep learning technology needs to be further explored to solve specific big data analysis problems. Given deep learning's immaturity, we believe there is still a lot of work to be done. In this section, we share our thoughts on some unanswered questions in deep learning research, particularly work needed to improve machine learning and formulate high-level abstractions and data representations for big data.

When using deep learning algorithms to analyze data, one important question is whether to use the entire big data input corpus available. The overall goal is to use deep learning algorithms to train high-level data representation patterns using a portion of the available input corpus, and then use the remaining input corpus combined with the learned patterns to extract data abstractions and representations. In the context of this issue, one question to investigate is how much data is required to train useful (good) data representations using deep learning algorithms, which can then be generalized to new data in the big data application domain.

Future aspects of deep learning includes:

- Working of DSNs with sophisticated and non-static noisy scenarios and with numerous noise types are among the future aspects of deep learning.
- Improving the diversity of features in DSNs to improve their performance?
- Deep neural networks' compatibility in an online unsupervised learning environment.
- Deep reinforcement learning will be the way of the future.
- Factors like inferences, performance and accuracies would be desirable in the future with DSNs.
- Keeping a large data archive up to date.
- For the parametric speech recognition system, create deep generative models with superior and advanced temporal modeling abilities.
- Deep learning is used to automatically assess the ECG signal.
- Deep neural networks are used to detect and monitor objects in images.
- Completely automated driving using a deep neural network.

7.7 Conclusion

Deep learning, in comparison to more traditional machine learning and feature engineering algorithms, has the advantage of potentially offering a solution to data processing and learning problems contained in large amounts of data. It assists in the automated extraction of complex data representations from vast quantities of unsupervised data. This makes it a useful method for big data analytics, which entails analyzing data from very large sets of unsupervised and un-categorized raw data. Deep learning's hierarchical learning and extraction of different levels of complex data abstractions simplifies big data analytics tasks, especially for analyzing large amounts of data, semantic indexing, data labeling, information retrieval and discriminative tasks like classification and prediction.

Deep learning is a rapidly expanding machine learning technology. Deep learning algorithms' rapid adoption in a variety of fields demonstrates their performance and flexibility. Deep learning's accomplishments and increased accuracy rates demonstrate the technology's importance, highlighting the technology's development and the potential for future advancement and study. Furthermore, it is essential to emphasize that the hierarchy of layers and learning supervision are the most important factors in developing an effective deep learning application. The explanation for this is that the hierarchy is needed for proper data classification, and the supervisor recognizes the value of database maintenance.

Deep learning is based on the optimization of existing machine learning applications and on their innovativeness in manipulating hierarchical layers. Profound learning can produce efficient results for different applications, such as digital imaging and language recognition. Throughout this current and future period, the combined facial recognition and speech recognition of deep learning can be used as a useful safety tool. Digital image processing is also a sort of field of study that can be used in many fields. Deep learning is an exciting contemporary topic of AI to demonstrate that it is a genuine optimization. Finally, we conclude here that if we pursue the wave of progress, with more data and computer resources available, the application of deep learning will truly be able to be accepted in many applications. The technology is truly ephebic, young and unique, and in the coming years, rapid progress in deep learning is expected to achieve objectives and high levels of triumph and satisfaction in ever more applications with great success, e.g. natural language processing, remote sensing and medical care.

It is argued that in any domain where traditional machine learning techniques were applicable, the deep learning methods are quite interesting. Finally, profound learning is the most effective, monitored and enhanced approach to master learning. Researchers can quickly evaluate the unknown and unbelievable problems associated with the application to achieve better and reliable performance.

References

AlQuraishi, M. (2019). ProteinNet: A standardized data set for machine learning of protein structure. BMC Bioinformatics. https://doi.org/10.1186/s12859-019-2932-0

Belhadi, A., Djenouri, Y., Djenouri, D., Michalak, T., & Lin, J. C. W. (2020). Deep learning versus traditional solutions for group trajectory outliers. IEEE Transactions on Cybernetics. https://doi.org/10.1109/TCYB.2020.3029338

Bhandari, M., Zeffiro, T., & Reddiboina, M. (2020). Artificial intelligence and robotic surgery: Current perspective and future directions. Current Opinion in Urology. https://doi.org/10.1097/MOU.0000000000000692

Ceni, A., Ashwin, P., & Livi, L. (2020). Interpreting recurrent neural networks behaviour via excitable network attractors. Cognitive Computation. https://doi.org/10.1007/s12559-019-09634-2

Cui, J., Gong, K., Guo, N., Wu, C., Meng, X., Kim, K., Zheng, K., Wu, Z., Fu, L., Xu, B., Zhu, Z., Tian, J., Liu, H., & Li, Q. (2019). PET image denoising using unsupervised deep learning. European Journal of Nuclear Medicine and Molecular Imaging. https://doi.org/10.1007/s00259-019-04468-4

De Haan, K., Rivenson, Y., Wu, Y., & Ozcan, A. (2020). Deep-learning-based image reconstruction and enhancement in optical microscopy. Proceedings of the IEEE. https://doi.org/10.1109/JPROC.2019.2949575

Deng, L. (2014). A tutorial survey of architectures, algorithms, and applications for deep learning. APSIPA Transactions on Signal and Information Processing. https://doi.org/10.1017/atsip.2013.9

Diro, A. A., & Chilamkurti, N. (2018). Distributed attack detection scheme using deep learning approach for Internet of Things. Future Generation Computer Systems. https://doi.org/10.1016/j.future.2017.08.043

dos Santos Ferreira, A., Freitas, D. M., da Silva, G. G., Pistori, H., & Folhes, M. T. (2019). Unsupervised deep learning and semi-automatic data labeling in weed discrimination. Computers and Electronics in Agriculture. https://doi.org/10.1016/j.compag.2019.104963

Elsayed, M. A., & Zulkernine, M. (2020). PredictDeep: Security analytics as a service for anomaly detection and prediction. IEEE Access. https://doi.org/10.1109/ACCESS.2020.2977325

Fiorucci, M., Khoroshiltseva, M., Pontil, M., Traviglia, A., Del Bue, A., & James, S. (2020). Machine learning for cultural heritage: A survey. Pattern Recognition Letters. https://doi.org/10.1016/j.patrec.2020.02.017

Gómez-Pulid, J. A., Park, Y., & Soto, R. (2020). Advanced techniques in the analysis and prediction of students' behaviour in technology-enhanced learning contexts. Applied Sciences (Switzerland). https://doi.org/10.3390/APP10186178

Gu, J., Wang, Z., Kuen, J., Ma, L., Shahroudy, A., Shuai, B., Liu, T., Wang, X., Wang, G., Cai, J., & Chen, T. (2018). Recent advances in convolutional neural networks. Pattern Recognition. https://doi.org/10.1016/j.patcog.2017.10.013

Hassanien, A. E., Darwish, A., & Abdelghafar, S. (2020). Machine learning in telemetry data mining of space mission: Basics, challenging and future directions. Artificial Intelligence Review. https://doi.org/10.1007/s10462-019-09760-1

Huang, J., Dong, Q., Gong, S., & Zhu, X. (2019). Unsupervised deep learning by neighbourhood discovery. 36th International Conference on Machine Learning, ICML 2019.

Khan, S., & Yairi, T. (2018). A review on the application of deep learning in system health management. Mechanical Systems and Signal Processing. https://doi.org/10.1016/j.ymssp.2017.11.024

Kivrak, M., Guldogan, E., & Colak, C. (2021). Prediction of death status on the course of treatment in SARS-COV-2 patients with deep learning and machine learning methods. Computer Methods and Programs in Biomedicine. https://doi.org/10.1016/j.cmpb.2021.105951

Lan, K., Wang, D. T., Fong, S., Liu, L. S., Wong, K. K. L., & Dey, N. (2018). A survey of data mining and deep learning in bioinformatics. Journal of Medical Systems. https://doi.org/10.1007/s10916-018-1003-9

Lee, S. M., Seo, J. B., Yun, J., Cho, Y. H., Vogel-Claussen, J., Schiebler, M. L., Gefter, W. B., Van Beek, E. J. R., Goo, J. M., Lee, K. S., Hatabu, H., Gee, J., & Kim, N. (2019). Deep learning applications in chest radiography and computed tomography. Journal of Thoracic Imaging. https://doi.org/10.1097/RTI.0000000000000387

Levine, Y., Sharir, O., Cohen, N., & Shashua, A. (2019). Quantum entanglement in deep learning architectures. Physical Review Letters. https://doi.org/10.1103/PhysRevLett.122.065301

Li, Z., Ko, B. S., & Choi, H. J. (2019). Naive semi-supervised deep learning using pseudo-label. Peer-to-Peer Networking and Applications. https://doi.org/10.1007/s12083-018-0702-9

Liu, Q., Li, R., Hu, H., & Gu, D. (2019). Using unsupervised deep learning technique for monocular visual odometry. IEEE Access. https://doi.org/10.1109/ACCESS.2019.2896988

Manchev, N., & Spratling, M. (2020). Target propagation in recurrent neural networks. Journal of Machine Learning Research. 21 (2020): 7–1.

Mecheter, I., Alic, L., Abbod, M., Amira, A., & Ji, J. (2020). MR image-based attenuation correction of brain PET imaging: Review of literature on machine learning approaches for segmentation. Journal of Digital Imaging. https://doi.org/10.1007/s10278-020-00361-x

Mohammadi, M., Al-Fuqaha, A., Sorour, S., & Guizani, M. (2018). Deep learning for IoT big data and streaming analytics: A survey. IEEE Communications Surveys and Tutorials. https://doi.org/10.1109/COMST.2018.2844341

Najafabadi, M. M., Villanustre, F., Khoshgoftaar, T. M., Seliya, N., Wald, R., & Muharemagic, E. (2015). Deep learning applications and challenges in big data analytics. Journal of Big Data. https://doi.org/10.1186/s40537-014-0007-7

Nguyen, G., Dlugolinsky, S., Bobák, M., Tran, V., López García, Á., Heredia, I., Malík, P., & Hluchý, L. (2019a). Machine learning and deep learning frameworks and libraries for large-scale data mining: A survey. Artificial Intelligence Review. https://doi.org/10.1007/s10462-018-09679-z

Nguyen, T. T., Nguyen, C. M., Nguyen, D. T., Nguyen, D. T., & Nahavandi, S. (2019b). Deep learning for deepfakes creation and detection. arXiv.

Oh, G., Bae, H., Ahn, H. S., Park, S. H., & Ye, J. C. (2020). CycleQSM: Unsupervised QSM deep learning using physics-informed CycleGAN. arXiv.

Ou, C., Yang, J., Du, Z., Zhang, X., & Zhu, D. (2019). Integrating cellular automata with unsupervised deep-learning algorithms: A case study of urban-sprawl simulation in the Jingjintang urban agglomeration, China. Sustainability (Switzerland). https://doi.org/10.3390/su11092464

Ouali, Y., Hudelot, C., & Tami, M. (2020). An overview of deep semi-supervised learning. arXiv.

Pandey, S. K., & Janghel, R. R. (2019). Recent deep learning techniques, challenges and its applications for medical healthcare system: A review. Neural Processing Letters. https://doi.org/10.1007/s11063-018-09976-2

Phinyomark, A., & Scheme, E. (2018). EMG pattern recognition in the era of big data and deep learning. Big Data and Cognitive Computing. https://doi.org/10.3390/bdcc2030021

Prabhu, C. S. R. (2019). Fog computing, deep learning and big data analytics-research directions. Fog Computing, Deep Learning and Big Data Analytics-Research Directions. https://doi.org/10.1007/978-981-13-3209-8

Qian, B., Xiao, Y., Zheng, Z., Zhou, M., Zhuang, W., Li, S., & Ma, Q. (2020). Dynamic multi-scale convolutional neural network for time series classification. IEEE Access. https://doi.org/10.1109/ACCESS.2020.3002095

Ramasamy Ramamurthy, S., & Roy, N. (2018). Recent trends in machine learning for human activity recognition—A survey. Wiley Interdisciplinary Reviews: Data Mining and Knowledge Discovery. https://doi.org/10.1002/widm.1254

Raza, K., & Singh, N. K. (2018). A tour of unsupervised deep learning for medical image analysis. arXiv. https://doi.org/10.2174/1573405617666210127154257

Saha, D., & Manickavasagan, A. (2021). Machine learning techniques for analysis of hyperspectral images to determine quality of food products: A review. Current Research in Food Science. https://doi.org/10.1016/j.crfs.2021.01.002

Schuster, M., & Paliwal, K. K. (1997). Bidirectional recurrent neural networks. IEEE Transactions on Signal Processing. https://doi.org/10.1109/78.650093

Sun, A. Y., & Scanlon, B. R. (2019). How can big data and machine learning benefit environment and water management: A survey of methods, applications, and future directions. Environmental Research Letters. https://doi.org/10.1088/1748-9326/ab1b7d

Tian, Y. (2020). Artificial intelligence image recognition method based on convolutional neural network algorithm. IEEE Access. https://doi.org/10.1109/ACCESS.2020.3006097

Tsirikoglou, A., Eilertsen, G., & Unger, J. (2020). A survey of image synthesis methods for visual machine learning. Computer Graphics Forum. https://doi.org/10.1111/cgf.14047

Wang, J., Ma, Y., Zhang, L., Gao, R. X., & Wu, D. (2018). Deep learning for smart manufacturing: Methods and applications. Journal of Manufacturing Systems. https://doi.org/10.1016/j.jmsy.2018.01.003

Wang, L. (2017). Data mining, machine learning and big data analytics. International Transaction of Electrical and Computer Engineers System. https://doi.org/10.12691/iteces-4-2-2

Wang, Q., Jiao, W., Wang, P., & Zhang, Y. M. (2021). A tutorial on deep learning-based data analytics in manufacturing through a welding case study. Journal of Manufacturing Processes. https://doi.org/10.1016/j.jmapro.2020.04.044

Wang, Z., & Cha, Y. J. (2021). Unsupervised deep learning approach using a deep autoencoder with a one-class support vector machine to detect damage. Structural Health Monitoring. https://doi.org/10.1177/1475921720934051

Witten, I. H., Frank, E., Hall, M. A., & Pal, C. J. (2016). Data mining: Practical machine learning tools and techniques. Data Mining: Practical Machine Learning Tools and Techniques. https://doi.org/10.1016/c2009-0-19715-5

Wu, Z., Pan, S., Chen, F., Long, G., Zhang, C., & Yu, P. S. (2021). A comprehensive survey on graph neural networks. IEEE Transactions on Neural Networks and Learning Systems. https://doi.org/10.1109/TNNLS.2020.2978386

Xue, S., Ma, Y., Yi, N., & Tafazolli, R. (2019). Unsupervised deep learning for musimo joint transmitter and noncoherent receiver design. IEEE Wireless Communications Letters. https://doi.org/10.1109/LWC.2018.2865563

Yadav, A., & Vishwakarma, D. K. (2020). Sentiment analysis using deep learning architectures: A review. Artificial Intelligence Review. https://doi.org/10.1007/s10462-019-09794-5

Yang, M., Nazir, S., Xu, Q., Ali, S., & Uddin, M. I. (2020). Deep learning algorithms and multicriteria decision-making used in big data: A systematic literature review. Complexity. https://doi.org/10.1155/2020/2836064

Zhao, X., & Jia, M. (2020). A novel unsupervised deep learning network for intelligent fault diagnosis of rotating machinery. Structural Health Monitoring. https://doi.org/10.1177/1475921719897317

Zhou, D. X. (2020). Universality of deep convolutional neural networks. Applied and Computational Harmonic Analysis. https://doi.org/10.1016/j.acha.2019.06.004

Zuo, R., Xiong, Y., Wang, J., & Carranza, E. J. M. (2019). Deep learning and its application in geochemical mapping. Earth-Science Reviews. https://doi.org/10.1016/j.earscirev.2019.02.023

8

Knowledge Representation and Learning Mechanism Based on Networks of Spiking Neurons

Rathi Karuppasamy, K. Geetha, and Priti Rishi

8.1 Introduction

In contemporary times, we perceive how a Neuralink plans to enhance the brain's computation through embedding a minuscule interconnection onto the human brain. The electrodes with the BCI (brain-computer interface) convert the neuronal data to instructions that are capable of controlling the external systems. The biggest query that emerges is how the signals in our brain will be handled.

To apprehend this, we want to recognize how neurons are structured in the human brain and how they transfer the data. Everybody who has been succeeding in the modern machine learning tendency is aware of the second-generation artificial neural network (ANN). ANN deals with continuous values, but spiking neural network (SNN) deals with discrete values. ANNs have made extremely good developments in lots of fields.

Yet, they do not emulate the process of the human brain's neurons. The subsequent era of neural network and SNN objectives to ease the utility of machine learning in neuroscience.

8.2 Realize How Neurons Transfer the Information Within the Brain?

Neurons ought to transmit data for conveying information among themselves. Transmissions of the data are completed in the neuron or from one neuron to a different one. Within the human brain, the dendrites generally obtain information from the sensory receptors. The data acquired is transmitted to

DOI: 10.1201/9781003126898-8

Neuron

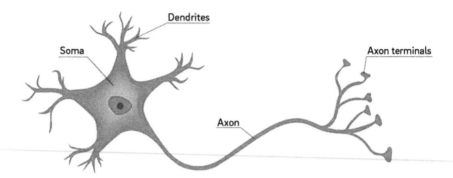

FIGURE 8.1
Neuron cell (Source: Ref. [1])

the axon along the cell body. Instantly, as the data reaches the axon, it moves throughout the axon's full length as an electrical signal called nerve impulse. On extending the top of the axon, data must be transmitted to subsequent neuron's dendrites, if needed. There is a synaptic gap in existing amid the axon and therefore the dendrites of subsequent neuron. This gap is often filled on its own or with the assistance of neurotransmitters as shown in Figure 8.1.

8.3 Spiking Neural Network (SNN)

An SNN [2] is distinct from popular neural networks familiar within the machine learning society. SNN utilizes spikes. Spikes are the discrete events happening at explicit points of your time. Thus, it's distinct from ANN that uses the continuous values. Differential equations denote several biological processes within the event of a spike. One of the foremost critical processes is the membrane capacity of the neuron. A neuron spikes when it reaches a selected potential. After a neuron spike, the potential is again re-established for that neuron. It takes a while for a neuron to return to its stable state after firing a nerve impulse. The interval after reaching membrane potential is understood and is thus called biological time (refractory period). In the biological time, triggering another nerve impulse is a sort of difficulty albeit the excitatory inputs are strong. The most used model is leaky integrate-and-fire (LIF). SNNs are not densely connected.

8.3.1 Differential Equation for LIF Model

In the SNN, neurons aren't discharged at each propagation cycle. The ejecting of neurons is mere as the membrane potential extends to a particular value.

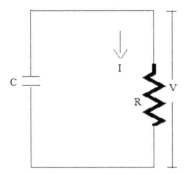

FIGURE 8.2
Leaky integrate-and-fire neuron (Source: Ref. [5])

Instantly, as a neuron is ejected, it gives a signal. This signal outreaches the other neurons and exchanges their potential with membranes. Spike train brings us to enlarge potential to operate spatiotemporal information. Spatial characteristic of neuron is that they are connected to each other and process as CNN (convolutional neural network). A temporal characteristic of a spike takes place at a specific time. The data is adrift in binary encoding and is retrieved from the spikes (Figure 8.2).

8.3.2 SNN and STDP Learning

A LIF [3, 4] neuron that is made up of a resistor (R) in parallel accompanied by a capacitor (C) operated by an external current $I_i(t)$. The external current can be considered the current for presynaptic neurons. The latent $u_i(t)$ over the C and R is explained even as membrane potential. For coherence, the scale of voltage is selected so that $u_i(t)=0$ is the idle potential.

The $u_i(t)$ (membrane potential) is obtained as:

$$\tau_m \frac{du_i(t)}{dt} = -u_i(t) + RI_i(t) \tag{8.1}$$

where $\tau_m = RC$ is the time constant of the membrane.

(i) Collecting spikes from the input neuron (j) of presynaptic. Assume that $I_{ji}(t)$ is a current from j to i. Here, j and i are neuron and its width 2ε and pulse mean I_e. Let $u_0 = RI_e$. The input neuron (i) membrane potential can be obtained as:

$$u_i(t) = \sum_{j \in \Gamma_i} u_0 \left[H\left(t - \left(t_{ji}^{pre} - \varepsilon\right)\right) H\left(\left(t_{ji}^{pre} + \varepsilon\right) - t\right) \left(1 - e^{\frac{\left(t - \left(t_{ji}^{pre} - \varepsilon\right)\right)}{\tau_m}}\right) \right. $$

$$\left. + H\left(t - \left(t_{ji}^{pre} + \varepsilon\right)\right) \left(e^{\frac{2\varepsilon}{\tau_m}} - 1\right) e^{-\frac{\left(t - \left(t_{ji}^{pre} - \varepsilon\right)\right)}{\tau_m}} \right] \tag{8.2}$$

where $H(.)$ is denoted as Heaviside step function, t_{ji}^{pre} peak current time, peak current denoted as $I_{ji}(t)$ hit at the I. Γ_i is a set of neurons j (j=1, 2,...m). $u_i(t)$ output neuron (i) increases when it collects presynaptic neuron spikes as input. When $u_i(t)$ hits a threshold (θ) at t_i^f (firing time of i), neuron i creates a spike.

From the STDP [6–9] (spike-timing-dependent plasticity) learning, the synapse efficiency [10–13] is increased if $t_i^f - t_{ji}^{pre} \geq 0$ and depressed means $t_i^f - t_{ji}^{pre} < 0$. Then,

$$t_j^{pre} = t_j^f + d_{ji},$$

$$\text{Here, } d_{ji} = t_i^f - t_j^f - \varepsilon. \tag{8.3}$$

where, d_{ji} denoted as latency of synapse and ε is the external current half duration of presynaptic neuron.

8.4 Rule Representation Based on Spiking Neural Network

Rule 1: *"If the human body temperature is equal to 37°C means normal otherwise abnormal".*

SNN holds two neurons. One is sensory neuron denoted as j and other one is integrate-and-fire neuron denoted as i. These two neurons are linked by the synapse. The synapse holds with some delay [14–17] and it's denoted as d_{ji}. Let ε=30 ms and assume that input neuron (j) revamps a temperature to the spike by utilizing the following formulae,

$$t_i^f = \text{round}\left(\frac{(x_j - x_{j\,min})}{(x_{j\,max} - x_{j\,min})} \times T\right)$$

where encoding period is denoted as t and its value as T=100 ms; the minimum and maximum input temperatures are denoted as $x_{j\,min}$ and $x_{j\,max}$ and their values are $x_{j\,min}$=34°C and $x_{j\,max}$=44°C. Then, $t_i^f = \text{round}(((37 - 34)/(44 - 34)) \times 30) = 30$ ms. Assume that the firing time target of output neuron (i) is 160 ($t_i^f = 160$), which means "normal", otherwise "abnormal". Abnormal means no neurons are firing. The threshold value is put to a maximum value of $u_i(t)$. As stated in spike-timing-dependent learning rule in Equation 8.3, we get

$$d_{ji} = 160 - 30 - 30 = 100.$$

TABLE 8.1

Value List of Neuron Potential ($\tau_m = 60$ ms)

$T^\circ(C)$	35.0	36.0	36.5	37.0	37.5	38.0	39.0	40.0	41.0
$u_i(t)$	0.71	0.84	0.92	1.00	0.95	0.89	0.76	0.62	0.45

From Equation 8.2, the membrane potential for trained output neuron (i) is obtained as:

$$u_i(t) = u_0 \left[H\left(t - \left(t_j^f + 70\right)\right) H\left(\left(t_j^f + 130\right) - t\right) \left(1 - e^{-\frac{\left(t - \left(t_j^f + 70\right)\right)}{\tau_m}}\right) \right.$$

$$\left. + H\left(t - \left(t_j^f + 130\right)\right) \left(e^{\frac{2 \times 30}{\tau_m}} - 1\right) e^{-\frac{\left(t - \left(t_j^f + 70\right)\right)}{\tau_m}} \right]$$

Changing the input temperature values to $\{35, 36, 36.5, 37, 37.5, 38, 39, 40, 41\}$ to firing time and computing the compatible values of membrane potential $u_i(t)$, the values are listed in Table 8.1. Let $u_0 = 1$ (i.e., maximal potential of u_0). If the threshold value is 1, the output neuron (i) fires only at an input temperature of 37°C. Additionally, the SNN can be utilized to uncertain or fuzzy rules.

> Rule 2: *"If human body temperature is around 37°C then 'normal', otherwise 'abnormal'".*

It is simple to say this imprecise explanation for a neuron in virtue of position the threshold (θ) value is 0.92 rather than 1. Next, the input temperature values (from 36.5°C to 37.8°C) are considered normal. It therefore describes the Rule 2 of SNN representations. By adjusting τ_m and ε, the input range is changed.

8.5 WML-SNN (Waveform Matching Learning-Spiking Neural Network) Model

SNNs [18–22] are efficient to be a fuzzy or logic rule. The difficulty now is a way to sketch their learning mechanisms and architecture. In this topic, a unique waveform matching learning-SNN (WML-SNN) model supported by the spiking neuron model has been proposed. The learning mechanism is a method of waveform matching, known as the WML-SNN model. To clarify this model, Table 8.2 is taken as an associate example to indicate that a WML-SNN model will learn from the information in it.

Afterward learning, the WML-SNN model [23–26] will determine the animal kind by taking up three real numbers for height, weight, and age.

The neural network includes three layers. An input layer holds sensory neurons that change data or stimuli to spikes. Hidden layer neurons were self-organized in virtue of training patterns. The amount of hidden neurons is decided by the training set and algorithm. Hidden neurons are joined to output neurons as per the training patterns of target values. The quantity of output cells is an adequate variety of target values. For example, three input neurons are put for height, weight, and age for sets of training shown in Table 8.2. Every hidden neuron joins to three input neurons via three synapses by latencies d_{ji} (for $j = 1,2,3$). Every output neuron represents the decision while it fires.

Example: The firing of neurons is denoted as K. If K=1 for "goat", K=2 means "cow", and K=3 means "fox". Whether hidden neurons fire (i) or assist the result of output neuron (k), a link is produced amidst the two neurons. Therefore, let $w_{ik} = 1$, otherwise $w_{ik} = 0$. In accordance with the data in Table 8.2, rules can be acquired as follows:

"R1: If age=0 and height=40 and weight=9 then it is a goat".
"R2: If age=0 and height=43 and weight=18 then it is a cow".
"R3: If age=0 and height=16 and weight=6 then it is a fox".

For depicting such rules, let $\tau_m = 5$ ms and $\varepsilon = 5$ ms. The three inputs are encrypted through three input neurons. Values are changed to spiking times in virtue of the following formula, $t_i^f = \text{round}\left(\left(x_j - x_{j\ min}\right) / \left(x_{j\ max} - x_{j\ min}\right) \times T\right)$. Let $T = 30$ ms. Based on R1 (Rule 1), a spiking time of neurons is shown as follows:

$$\text{Age: } t_1 = \text{round}\left(\frac{(0-0)}{(10-0)} \times 30\right) = 0$$

$$\text{Height: } t_2 = \text{round}\left(\frac{(40-16)}{(106-16)} \times 30\right) = 8$$

$$\text{Weight: } t_3 = \text{round}\left(\frac{(9-6)}{(106-6)} \times 30\right) = 1$$

where t_1, t_2, and t_3 are denoted as input neuron spikes. In the beginning stage, the hidden layers don't have any neurons. The WML-SNN model includes a new neuron to that hidden layer. Assume that such neurons firing at a time $t_i^f = 30 + \tau_m = 35$ ms.

TABLE 8.2

Record of Animal Growth

Age (Month)	Height (cm)	Weight (kg)	Animal Name	Age (Month)	Height (cm)	Weight (kg)	Animal Name	Age (Month)	Height (cm)	Weight (kg)	Animal Name
0	40	9	Goat	0	43	18	Cow	0	16	6	Fox
1	45	12	Goat	1	52	28	Cow	1	18	16	Fox
2	47	18	Goat	2	57	38	Cow	2	21	24	Fox
3	50	22	Goat	3	67	48	Cow	3	24	34	Fox
4	55	28	Goat	4	73	58	Cow	4	28	46	Fox
5	58	36	Goat	5	78	68	Cow	5	31	57	Fox
6	60	41	Goat	6	81	78	Cow	6	34	64	Fox
7	63	46	Goat	7	86	88	Cow	7	36	73	Fox
8	68	52	Goat	8	92	98	Cow	8	38	83	Fox
9	68	52	Goat	9	97	108	Cow	9	41	92	Fox
10	68	52	Goat	10	106	118	Cow	10	46	106	Fox

Based on learning Rule 3, a group of time delays is acquired. The time delays are $d_{11} = 30, d_{21} = 25$, and $d_{31} = 29$. After this, put a suitable threshold value, then neurons will fire, while it observes examples with spiking time related to t_1, t_2, and t_3. Whether the threshold value is disputing a maximum potential, a neuron fires at 35 ms just for inputs ($t_1 = 0$, $t_2 = 5$, and $t_3 = 1$). Though a threshold value is put to lower than a maximum potential, neurons portray an R1 rule, i.e., fuzzy rule. As stated, the example of target value is goat, associated between the output and hidden neurons. When $K=1$ is established, $w_{11} = 1$. When a fresh instance is joined, the entire former neurons provide their own potential waveform. Any one of the neuron waveforms is well suited, it means that an instance is possible to be covered via those neurons. No waveforms are matched to the instance; the fresh neuron is formed through analogy. The remaining neurons relevant to R2 and R3 are demonstrated as follows:

The synapse latencies and connectivity of the second neuron is ($d_{11} = 30$, $d_{21} = 21$, and $d_{31} = 27$) and $w_{22} = 1$ for R2.

The synapse latencies and connectivity of the third neuron is ($d_{11} = 30$, $d_{21} = 30$, and $d_{31} = 30$) and $w_{33} = 1$ for R3.

While fresh instances are accessible, a novel neuron is possible to be added similarly. On balance, instances within the training set were utilized. In the group of hidden layer neurons, the connectivity matrix is denoted as W and the delay matrix is denoted as D being acquired. Later, verifying for excess neurons may be led through the axiom on waveform matching. While two neurons have the identical range of input means one neuron is eliminated.

Every output neuron incorporates its own potential within the hidden layer fired neurons. Let $u_k(t)$ denote the output (k) neuron potential. We get

$$u_k(t) = \sum_i w_{ik} u_i(t). \qquad (8.4)$$

An output neuron is rival; a neuron of maximum potential produces a spike, so it suggests the result of output, and the remaining neurons don't fire.

The waveform matching, assume an animal about height=40.1 cm, weight=20.6 kg, and age=0.3 month. Indicate that those ranges never arise in Table 8.2. Which kind of animal is it in line with this information in Table 8.2? Through the model of WML-SNN constructed over, it is quite simple to obtain an answer. An input neuron transfers the ranges to spikes ($t_1 = 0$, $t_2 = 16$, and $t_3 = 8$), after that the hidden neurons in the model of WML-SNN obtain the responsive potential waveform displayed in Figure 8.3.

The second neuron potential waveform is much closer to the well-suited waveform, i.e., well-matched, which made the entire input spikes effectively delivering to the firing time $t_i^f = 35$ ms.

Nearer to the potential maximum value at 35-ms time, an enhancement of the three input waveforms is suited. By examining a potential value at 35-ms

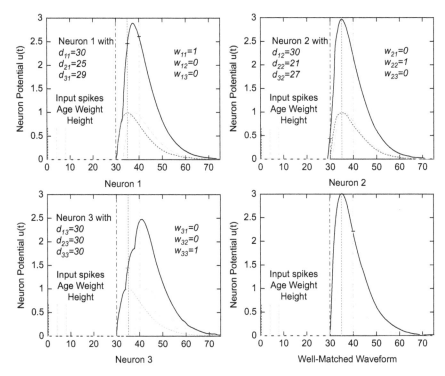

FIGURE 8.3
Waveforms on the three hidden neurons as reactions to the three-input neuron. Solid curve denotes the input neuron potential waveform and dashed curve denotes a potential effect apart by three (Source: Ref. [24])

time, neurons can assess in what way the input waveforms suit a memory synapse latency.

Algorithm:

1. Define the input neuron number as m and pattern range as p_m. Parameterize u_0, T, ε, and τ_m. Let targeting fire time be denoted as $t_i^f = T + \varepsilon$, and parameter of hidden layer neuron be set as $\Phi = \emptyset$.

2. For pattern of training, set as $p=1$ to p_m.

3. Change the input value (x_j^p) to the pattern of spiking as t_j^{fp}.

4. Compute the output $u_i^p\left(t_i^f\right)$ for $i \in \Phi$.

5. Whether it is not $u_i^p\left(t_i^f\right) = m\,u_0$ for $i \in \Phi$, after, make a fresh hidden neuron developing a list of d_{ij} as per (3) and a list of w_{ik} on the basis of target value and also include it to the hidden layer Φ.

6. End if.

7. End for.

8.6 Conclusions

In this chapter, we discussed the SNN and their learning mechanism of STDP and addressed the rule representations based on SNNs. This chapter analyzes the approach of WML-SNN. Various datasets are analyzed using this approach. In this chapter, we also gave an analysis of the animal growth data

References

[1] http://medicalxpress.com/news/2018-07-neuron-axons-spindly-theyre-optimizing.html

[2] J. Dethier, P. Nuyujukian, S. I. Ryu, K. V. Shenoy, and K. Boahen, "Design and validation of a real-time spiking-neural-network decoder for brain–machine interfaces," *J. Neural Eng.* 10, 036008, 2013. doi: 10.1088/1741-2560/10/3/036008

[3] S. A. Aamir, Y. Stradmann, P. Müller, C. Pehle, A. Hartel, A. Grübl, et al. An accelerated LIF neuronal network array for a large scale mixed-signal neuromorphic architecture. *IEEE Transactions on Circuits and Systems I: Regular Papers*, 65(12), 4299–4312, 2018.

[4] A. N. Burkitt, "A review of the integrate-and-fire neuron model: I. Homogeneous synaptic input," *Biol. Cybern.* 95, 1–19, 2006. doi: 10.1007/s00422-006-0068-6

[5] https://neuronaldynamics.epfl.ch/online/Ch1.S3.html

[6] Y. Bengio, T. Mesnard, A. Fischer, S. Zhang, and Y. Wu. STDP as presynaptic activity times rate of change of postsynaptic activity. *arXiv [Preprint].* 2015. arXiv:1509.05936.

[7] Y. Bengio, T. Mesnard, A. Fischer, S. Zhang, and Y. Wu, "STDP-compatible approximation of backpropagation in an energy-based model," *Neural Comput.* 29, 555–577, 2017. doi: 10.1162/NECO_a_00934

[8] Y. Cao, Y. Chen, and D. Khosla, "Spiking deep convolutional neural networks for energy-efficient object recognition," *Int. J. Comput. Vis.* 113, 54–66, 2015. doi: 10.1007/s11263-014-0788-3

[9] A. Delorme, J. Gautrais, R. VanRullen, and S. J. Thorpe, "SpikeNET: A simulator for modeling large networks of integrate and fire neurons," *Neurocomputing* 26–27, 989–996, 1999.

[10] H. Markram, J. Lubke, M. Frotscher, and B. Sakmann, "Regulation of synaptic efficacy by coincidence of postsynaptic APs and EPSPs," *Science* 275, 213–215, 1997.

[11] S. Song and L. F. Abbott, "Column and map development and cortical re-mapping through spike-timing dependent plasticity," *Neuron* 32, 339–350, 2001.

[12] S. M. Bohte, J. N. Kok, and H. L. Poutré, "SpikeProp: Error-backpropagation for networks of spiking neurons," *Neurocomputing* 48, 1–4, 17–37, 2002.

[13] Q. X. Wu, T. M. McGinnity, D. A. Bell, and G. Prasad, "A self-organising computing network for decision-making in data sets with diversity of data types," *IEEE Trans. Knowl. Data Eng.* 18, 7, 941–953, 2006.

[14] M. C. W. Rossum, G. Q. Bi, and G. G. Turrigiano, "Stable Hebbian learning from spike timing-dependent plasticity," *J. Neurosci.* 20, 23, 8812–8821, 2000.

[15] J. W. Sohn, B. T. Zhang, and B. K. Kaang, "Temporal Pattern Recognition Using a Spiking Neural Network with Delays," *Proceedings of the International Joint Conference on Neural Networks* (IJCNN'99), vol. 4, pp. 2590–2593, 1999.

[16] A. L. Hodgkin and A. F. Huxley, "A quantitative description of membrane current and its application to conduction and excitation in nerve," *J. Physiol.* 117, 500–544, 1952.

[17] R. P. N. Rao and T. J. Sejnowski, "Spike-timing-dependent Hebbian plasticity as temporal difference learning," *Neural Comput.* 13, 2221–2237, 2001.

[18] W. Gerstner and W. Kistler, *Spiking Neuron Models. Single Neurons, Populations, Plasticity*, Cambridge University Press, 2002.

[19] S. Thorpe, A. Delorme, and R. V. Rullen, "Spike-based strategies for rapid processing," *Neural Netw.* 14, 6–7, 715–725, 2001.

[20] D. O. Hebbe, *The Organization of Behavior*, John Wiley and Sons, New York, NY, 1949.

[21] C. W. Eurich, M. C. Mackey, and H. Schwegler, "Recurrent inhibitory dynamics: The role of state-dependent distributions of conduction delay times," *J. Theor. Biol.* 216, 31–50, 2002.

[22] G. Q. Bi and M. M. Poo, "Synaptic modifications in cultured hippocampal neurons: Dependence on spike timing, synaptic strength, and postsynaptic cell type," *J. Neurosci.* 18, 10464–10472, 1998.

[23] P. D. Roberts and C. C. Bell, "Spike timing dependent synaptic plasticity in biological systems," *Biol. Cybern.* 87, 392–403, 2002.

[24] W. Maass, "Networks of spiking neurons: The third generation of neural network models," *Neural Netw.* 10, 9, 1659–1671, 1997.

[25] Y. Bao, X. Du, and N. Ishii, "Improving performance of the K-nearest neighbor classification by GA and tolerant rough sets," *Int. J. Knowl.-Based Intell. Eng. Syst.* 7, 2, 54–61, 2003.

[26] Q. Wu, D. Bell, G. Qi, and J. Cai, "Knowledge Representation and Learning Mechanism Based on Networks of Spiking Neurons," *2006 IEEE International Conference on Systems, Man and Cybernetics, Taipei*, pp. 2796–2801, 2006, doi: 10.1109/ICSMC.2006.385297

9

Multi-View Representation Learning

G. Muthu Lakshmi and N. Krishnammal

9.1 Introduction

Multi-view data produced from multiple viewpoints or sensors is common in real-world applications. The well-known commercial depth sensor Kinect, for example, estimates depth using both visible light and near-infrared sensors. Using both visual and radar sensors, Autopilot produces real-time 3D information on the lane. Face recognition algorithms prefer face images from different angles for high-fidelity reconstruction and identification. Various points of views are often regarded as separate domains from various distributions. When faced with a dilemma, it's crucial to minimize a viewpoint divergence by combining information from various viewpoints or adapting knowledge from one perspective to another. Assume we have a set of data A=A1, A2, and Av from v views, such as face poses, camera views, and feature types (multi-view data). Data communication can be shown by the following two examples: first, in multi-view data [1], the samples from v views are equal, making multi-view learning traditional; second, no data correspondence exists between samples from different perspectives, which comes under the domain adaptation scenario, in which discriminant information is transferred. To begin, multi-view learning combines information from different viewpoints in order to either expose common knowledge or employ complementary knowledge in specific views to assist learning tasks. In recognition tasks, multiple features extracted from the same object by different visual descriptors, such as LBP, SIFT, and HOG, for example, are highly discriminant. Another example is multimodal data that is captured, interpreted, and stored in different formats, such as near-infrared and visible face, and image and text. Second, in order to reduce the learning burden, domain adaptation attempts to transfer information from labeled source domains to target domains with sparse or no labeled samples. Multi-view data representation using a single learning method includes multi-view learning as well as domain adaptation. Multi-view learning and domain adaptation are separated into two parts as a single goal: word for multi-view alignment and regularizer for feature learning. This formulation would cover most

DOI: 10.1201/9781003126898-9

multi-view representation learning algorithms in the fields of multi-view learning and domain adaptation. Second, multi-view learning and domain adaptation are based on a single perspective, especially for their multiple problem environments.

In real-world applications where examples are defined by different feature sets or views, multi-view data, such as image + text, audio + video, and web-page + click-through data, has become increasingly accessible. Multi-view learning will be able to use this additional information to learn more descriptive representations than single-view learning methods.

The process of constructing a prediction model from a variety of data features and extracting useful information is known as multi-view representation learning. This multi-view representation learning has received a lot of attention, and it's gaining traction in real-world applications (Figure 9.1). The data from various perspectives contains complementary information, by which one uses multi-view representation learning method to show more robust representations than single-view representation learning methods. Since data representation is so important in machine learning algorithms [2], multi-view representation learning is extremely useful. Canonical correlation analysis (CCA) [3, 4] and its kernel extensions are representative techniques in multi-view representation learning. When it comes to capturing high-level correlations between multi-view data, CCA and its kernel versions demonstrate their ability to model the relationship between two or more sets of variables, but they have limitations. The output of deep neural networks [5] gives a joint representation that is coupled between multiple views at a higher level after learning several layers of view-specific features in lower layers motivated by deep CCAs.

The issue of how to know about a successful multi-view data association is still open. Multi-view representation learning enables a better understanding of different approaches as well as the resolution of a variety of problems

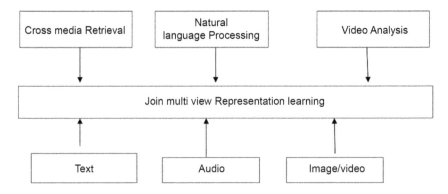

FIGURE 9.1
Multi-view data and several related applications based on joint multi-view representation learning

in specific applications. Based on the fundamental theories of CCAs and the advancement of deep neural networks, a large number of multi-view representation learning algorithms have been presented. Multimodal topic learning, multi-view sparse coding, and multi-view latent space Markov networks, as well as multimodal deep auto encoders and multimodal recurrent neural networks (RNNs), are all discussed. There are many types of multi-view representation learning: (1) feature alignment is used to capture the relationships between many different views in multi-view representation alignment; (2) multi-view representation fusion is the fusion of separate features learned from many different views into a single representation. Both approaches attempt to represent the data in a comprehensive way by combining the complementary details contained in different views.

In Figure 9.2, on the left, the architecture of multi-view representation learning methods based on alignment is shown, and on the right, the structure of multi-view embedding models based on fusion is shown.

Range, similarity, and correlation are used to investigate the alignment of multi-view representations. The basic idea is that a mapping function processes the data from each view, and then the learned separate representations

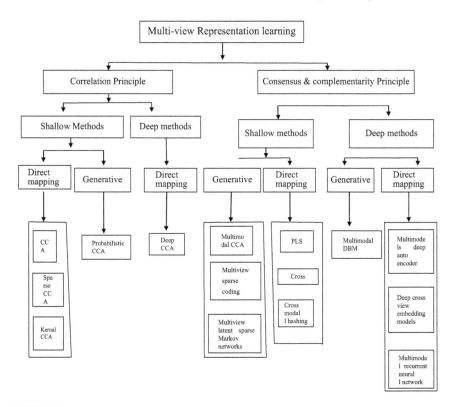

FIGURE 9.2
Multi-view Representation Learning with Different Methods

are regularized using constraints to form a multi-view aligned space. In multi-view representation fusion, probabilistic graphical and neural network perspectives are used. This chapter examines multi-view representation learning and gives a general overview of this active path.

9.2 Multi-View Representation Learning

9.2.1 A Taxonomy on Multi-View Representation Learning

Multi-view representation learning, which offers the relating information of multiple views of the data, is used for the best learning outcomes. Audio and visual data are used to recognize expression. Raw pixels, for example, are difficult to relate to audio waveforms, while the data in the two views resembles mid-level representations such as phonemes and visemes. It focuses on multi-view joint learning of mid-level representations, in which one embedding is used to model one view, and then all of the embeddings are combined to take advantage of the abundant information from multiple views. The characteristics of the most common multi-view representation learning strategies currently available were thoroughly examined. Multi-view representation learning approaches can be divided into two categories: alignment of multi-view representations and merger of multi-view representations. The diagram in Figure 9.3 depicts the two cases.

9.3 Multi-View Representation Alignment

9.3.1 Correlation-Based Alignment

Multi-view representation alignment approaches are methods for aligning representations learned from several viewpoints. Two aspects of representative examples may be investigated: (1) correlation-based coordination

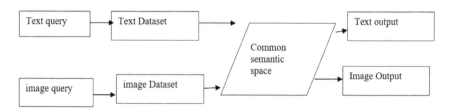

FIGURE 9.3
An illustrative application of CCA in cross-modal retrieval

and (2) alignment based on similarity and distance. We start by looking at correlation-based alignment techniques like CCA and its extensions, which range from traditional modeling [6] to nonlinear deep embedding. After that, standard examples of distance- and similarity-based alignment are provided to illustrate the benefits of multi-view representation learning.

Assume that A and B are two view datasets. The alignment of multi-view representations is represented as follows:

$$f(A; W_f) \leftrightarrow g(B; W_g) \tag{9.1}$$

The embedding function for g for each view converts the original space into a multi-view aligned space with some constraints and denotes the alignment $\leftrightarrow$ operator.

9.3.1.1 Canonical Correlation Analysis

Because of its ability to accurately model the relationship between two or more sets of variables, CCA [7] has increased in popularity. From the perspective of multi-view representation learning, CCA helps compute a mutual embedding of both or more sets of variables by maximizing the similarities within the variables among these sets. In multi-view learning tasks, CCA is widely used to construct low-dimensional representations. Improved generalization efficiency has been observed in areas such as dimensionality reduction and clustering. Figure 9.3 shows an interesting cross-modal use of CCA in cross-media retrieval.

Given a pair of datasets $A = [a_1, ..., a_n]$ and $B = [b_1, ..., b_n]$, CCA tends to find linear projections W_a and W_b.

At the top, you can see an example of retrieving text in response to an image query using a popular semantic space. Figure 9.3 shows how CCA [8] was used to make the corresponding examples in the two datasets maximally associated in the projected room in response to a text question. The correlation coefficient between the two datasets in projected space is given by

$$\rho = \text{corr } (w_a^T A, w_b^T B) = \frac{w_a^T C_{ab} W_b}{\sqrt{(w_a^T C_{aa} W_a)(w_b^T C_{bb} W_b)}} \tag{9.2}$$

where C_{ab} denotes the covariance matrix:

$$C_{ab} = \frac{1}{n} \sum_{i=1}^{n} (a_i - \mu_a)(b_i - \mu_b) T \tag{9.3}$$

where $\mu_a = \frac{1}{n} \sum_{i=1}^{n} a_i$ and $\mu_b = \frac{1}{n} \sum_{i=1}^{n} b_i$ and are the means of the two views, respectively. Similarly, the definitions of C_{xx} and C_{yy} can be found. CCA can be presented as a constrained optimization problem since the association is invariant to the scaling of W_a and W_b.

$$\text{Max } w_a{}^T c_{ab} \ w_b$$

$$\text{s.t. } w_a{}^T c_{aa} \ w_a = 1; \ w_b{}^T \ c_{bb} \ w_b = 1 \tag{9.4}$$

The Lagrangian dual of Equation 9.4 can be used to prove that solving a pair of generalized eigenvalue problems is equal to solving Equation 9.4 [3]:

$$c_{ab} \ c_{bb}{}^{-1} c_{ba} \ w_a = \lambda^2 \ c_{aa} \ w_a$$

$$c_{ba} c_{aa}{}^{-1} c_{ab} w_b = \lambda^2 \ c_{bb} \ w_b \tag{9.5}$$

There are several other ways to describe the canonical correlations of a pair of matrices; however, all of which are shown to be equal, apart from the definition of CCA given earlier. A constrained least squares optimization problem in CCA is the same as an unconstrained least squares optimization problem. Furthermore, Golub and Zha [9] present a classic CCA algorithm that involves performing a QR decomposition of the data matrices to whiten the data, then an SVD of the whitened covariance matrix, and colossal data matrices. This technique causes a significant slowdown. For CCA with a pair of tall-and-thin matrices, Avron et al. [10] proposed a subsampled randomized Walsh-Hadamard transform [11] that only subsamples a small proportion of the training data points to estimate the matrix product. Lu and Foster [12] use sparse design matrices and an efficient iterative regression algorithm for large-scale CCA. The help of CCA one is capable of multi-view function learning and is commonly used in a variety of fields, it does have some limitations in some applications. It, for example, ignores the nonlinearities of multi-view results. As a result, several CCA-based algorithms build on the original CCA in real-world applications have been proposed. In the pages that follow, look over its many widely used extensions, such as sparse CCA, kernel CCA, and deep CCA.

9.3.1.2 Sparse CCA

There has been an increase of interest in sparse data representations in recent years. Similarly, in the multi-view representation learning group, the topic of sparse CCA has gotten a lot of attention. A variety of factors can motivate the pursuit of sparsity. The first is the ability to account for predicted outcomes. In certain cases, the big picture is built on a small number of main variables, with details left to chance. The second explanation for sparsity is regularization and continuity. Reasonable regularization is important for lowering CCA's sensitivity to a small number of observations and reducing the impact of noisy data. Sparse CCA is a subset selection scheme that reduces the dimensionality of the vectors and allows for a stable solution. The problem of sparse CCA is to find a pair of linear combinations of w_a and w_b with a given cardinality that maximizes the relation. The solution to the sparse CCA problem is as follows:

$$\rho = \begin{array}{c} \max \\ w_a w_b \end{array} \frac{w_a^T C_{ab} w_b}{\sqrt{w_a C_{aa} w_a w_y C_y w_y}}$$

$$\text{s.t } \|w_a\|_0 <= s_a, \|w_b\|_0 <= s_b \tag{9.6}$$

In the majority of sparse CCA methods, the LASSO trick [13] is used as a shrinkage and selection technique for linear regression. Hardoon and Shawe-Taylor [14] suggested formulating CCA as two constrained simultaneous regression problems [15] to approximate non-convex constraints with 1-norm. Setting each index of the optimized vector to 1 and constraining the remaining coefficients to the 1-norm achieve this. Elastic net-type regression has been suggested by Waaijenborg et al. [16]. Sun et al. [32] suggested a sparse CCA by recasting CCA as a multi-label least squares problem and computing it directly with the Least Angle Regression algorithm (LARS) [17]. Furthermore, using the least squares formulation makes it simpler to integrate unlabeled data into the CCA system, allowing the data's local geometry to be captured. To deal with unlabeled data, the graph Laplacian, for example, can be used in this framework. In fact, the advancement of sparse CCA is inextricably linked to the advancement of sparse PCA [18, 19]. The generalized eigenvalue problem's classical sparse PCA solutions can easily be extended to sparse CCA [20, 21]. Torres et al. [34] extend a DC programming method for solving sparse eigenvalue problems to create a sparse CCA algorithm. Witten et al. [22] proposed applying a penalized matrix decomposition to the covariance matrix Cab, resulting in a penalized sparse CCA method. As a consequence, structured sparse CCA has been proposed, which adds a structured sparsity inducing penalty to penalized CCA [40].

9.3.2 Distance- and Similarity-Based Alignment

A standard distance-based alignment between the jth pair representations of x_j and y_j can be calculated using the formula given next:

$$\begin{array}{c} \min \\ \theta \end{array} \left\| f(a_i; w_f) - g(b_i, w_g) \right\|_2^2 \tag{9.7}$$

This alignment constraint was extended to solve various multi-view representation learning methods. Li et al. [23] suggested a cross-modal factor analysis as a simple example of multi-view embedding learning based on the alignment theorem.

It aims to find the orthogonal transformation matrices W_a and W_b that minimize the following expression, given a pair (x_a, y_b):

$$\left\| a_i^T w_a - b_i^T w_b \right\|_2^2 + r_a(w_a) + r_b(w_b) \tag{9.8}$$

where $r_a(\cdot)$ and $r_b(\cdot)$ are regularization terms. The principle of distance-based alignment is often used in multi-view deep representation learning. Exchange of letters is done in order to establish correspondence between two views' representations; the auto encoder imposes a distance-based restriction on selected code layers, and its loss function for any pair of inputs is defined as follows [19]:

$$L = \lambda_a \left\| a_i - \widehat{a}_i \right\|_2^2 + \lambda_b \left\| b_i - \widehat{b}_i \right\|_2^2 + \left\| f^c(a_i; w_f - g^c(b_i; w_g)) \right\|_2^2 \tag{9.9}$$

The same code layers are denoted by f^c (a_i; W_f) and g^c (b_i; W_g). Similarity-based alignment has also become a common method of learning-matched spaces [24]. A deep visual semantic embedding model with higher dot product similarity between the visual embedding output and the right label representation than between the visual embedding output and other randomly selected text concepts is shown as:

$$\sum_{j \neq 1} max\left(0, m - S(tl, vimg1) + S(tj, vimg1)\right) \tag{9.10}$$

where vimg1 is a deep embedding vector for the given image, tl is the learned embedding vector for the provided text label, tj is the embedding of the other text terms, and $S(\cdot)$ measures the similarity between the two vectors.

Karpathy and Fei-Fei [25] established a deep cross-modal alignment model that associates the segments of sentences and the region of an image that they represent using a multimodal embedding space and similarity-based organized intent.

Correlation-based alignment is another common form of multi-view representation alignment, which uses CCA to optimize the correlations of variables across multiple views. Hotelling [26] proposed CCA to find linear projections w_a and w_b that maximize the correlation between the corresponding examples in the two datasets in the predicted room, given a pair of datasets $A = [a_1,..., a_n]$ and $B = [b_1,..., b_n]$:

$$P = \max_{w_a, w_b} \; corr\left(w_a^T A, w_b^T B\right) \tag{9.11}$$

where correlation $(\cdot)$ denotes the sample correlation function between $w > aA$ and $w < bB$. Thus, by maximizing the correlations between the projections of the instances, the basis vectors for the two sets of variables can be computed and applied to two-view data to obtain the requisite embedding. Furthermore, multi-view neural networks can be used to learn deep and abstract multi-view representations using association learning. Andrew et al. [27] propose using deep CCA to obtain maximally correlated deep nonlinear mappings between two views, A and B.

9.3.2.1 Partial Least Squares

Partial least squares (PLS) refers to a group of techniques for predicting relationships between sets of observed variables. It is a commonly used method in the field of chemometrics for regression, classification, and dimensionality reduction. The underlying assumption of all PLS methods is that the observed data is produced by a process driven by a small number of latent variables. By maximizing the covariance between different sets of variables, PLS generates orthogonal latent vectors. Given a pair of datasets $A = [a_1,...,a_n] \in R^{d_a} \times n$ and $Y = [y_1,..., y_n] \in R^{d_b} \times n$ a, k-dimensional PLS solution can be parameterized by a pair of matrices, $w_a \in R^{d_a} \times k$ and $w_b \in R^{d_a} \times k$. The PLS problem can now be expressed as:

$$\text{Max tr}\left(w_a^T c_{ab} w_b\right)$$

$$\text{s.t. } w_a^T w_a = I, w_b^T w_b = I \tag{9.12}$$

The singular vectors of the covariance matrix correspond to the columns of the ideal W_a and W_b, as shown $c_{ab} = E_{ab}{}^T$. The LS target, like the CCA target, is an expectation optimization with fixed constraints. The highest correlation directions are found by CCA, while the maximum covariance directions are found by PLS. The statistical methods of covariance and correlation are used to explain how variables interact. In a variety of ways, PLS and CCA have been shown to be closely linked. Guo and Mu [28] compare PLS models to CCA-based methods for solving the joint estimation problem, such as linear CCA, regularized CCA, and kernel CCA. They provide a simple ranking of the aforementioned methods for estimating age, gender, and ethnicity. Cross-modal factor analysis (CFA), a least square form of PLS, was also introduced by Li et al. [25]. CFA's aim is to find orthogonal transformation matrices W_x and W_y by reducing the number of orthogonal transformation matrices W_x and W_y.

Following expression: $\left\|a^T w_a - b^T w_b\right\|_F^2$

$$\text{subject to: } w_a^T w_a = I, w_b^T w_b = I \tag{9.13}$$

where $\|.\|_F$ denotes the Frobenius norm. The solution to the previous optimization problem in Equation 9.13 is the same as PLS, which can be easily checked. By integrating nonlinearity and supervised knowledge, several extensions of CFA are provided.

9.3.2.2 Cross-Modal Ranking

Cross-modal ranking has received a lot of attention in the correlation-based alignment, rating insight into multimodal embedding learning. Bai et al. [29] suggest a supervised semantic indexing (SSI) model, which is a nonlinear model that has been discriminatively trained to convert multimodal input pairs into ranking scores. SSI tries to learn a similarity function f(q; d) between a text query q and an image d using a pre-defined ranking loss. Using the learned function f, each text-image pair is directly mapped to a ranking score based on their semantic significance. SSI aims to find a linear scoring function to calculate the significance of d, given a text question q 2 Rm and an image d 2 Rn.

$$q:\ f(q,d) = q^T\ w\ d = \sum_{i=1}^{m}\sum_{j=1}^{n} q_i w_{ij} d_j \tag{9.14}$$

where the parameter f(q; d) is the score between the query q and the image d, and the parameter f(q; d) is the score between the query q and the image d. $W \in R^{MXN}$ encapsulates the correspondence between the data's two separate modalities: the connection between the ith dimension of the text space and the jth dimension of the image space is described by W_{ij}. Since W_{ij} allows both positive and negative values, the embedding approach can accommodate both positive and negative associations between different modalities. Given the similarity function in Equation 9.14 and a set of tuples, each of which contains a query q, a relevant image d⁺, and an irrelevant image d⁺, SSI tries to choose the scoring function f(q; d) in such a way that f(q; d⁺)> f(q; d⁻), expressing the belief that d⁺ should be prioritized over d⁻. SSI accomplishes this by reducing the margin rating loss, a technique that is already widely used in information retrieval:

$$\sum_{(q,d^+d^-)} \max\left(0, 1 - q^T w d^T + q^T w d^-\right) \tag{9.15}$$

Stochastic gradient descent can be used to solve this optimization problem:

$$w < -+\lambda \left(q\left(d^+\right)^T - q\left(d^-\right)^T \right)$$

$$\text{if } (1 - q^T w d^+ + q^T w d^- > 0) \tag{9.16}$$

This method is a special margin rating perceptron, which has been shown to be comparable to SVM. In comparison to classical SVM, stochastic training is highly scalable and easy to implement for millions of training instances. Computationally, the models for all pairs of multimodalities input features are still difficult. As a result, in order to solve this issue, SSI proposes low-rank representation, sparsification, and correlated feature hashing as improvements to the earlier basic model. Grangier and Bengio [30] propose the passive-aggressive model for image retrieval, a discriminative cross-modal ranking model (PAMIR), which not only considers different image kernels but also adopts a learning criterion relevant to the final retrieval performance to take advantage of the online learning of kernel-based classifiers.

9.4 Multi-View Representation Fusion

For multi-view representations, fusion methods typically incorporate multiple inputs into a single compact representation. The examining representative cases can be done from two perspectives: (1) graphical models and (2) neural network-based models. Normal examples of neural network-based fusion approaches are then used to show the expressive potential of the deep multi-view joint representation.

9.4.1 Graphical Models

For the two-view datasets A and B, multi-view representation fusion is represented as follows:

$$h = \varphi(a, b) \tag{9.17}$$

where data from multiple views is merged into a single representation h that completely represents the data by using the complementary details contained in multiple views.

Multi-view function learning is all about learning a small collection of latent random variables to define a distribution over observed multi-view data. $p(a, b, c)$ is a probabilistic model [31] over the joint space of mutual latent variables c and observed two-view data a, b. The representation values $p(c|a, b)$ are determined by the posterior probability. In the Multimodal subject learning, multi-view sparse coding, multi-view latent space Markov networks, and multimodal deep Boltzmann machines are all examples of multimodal deep Boltzmann machines [32]. For example, a simple type of PCMF considers the data matrices of two-view $\{A \in R^{nXd_a}, B \in R R^{nXd_b}\}$ dimensionality in the same line and factorizes them all at the same time using the probabilistic approach described next:

$$P\left(A \mid \sigma_a^2\right) = \prod_{i=1}^{n} N\left(a_i \mid U_i V_a^T, \sigma_a^2\ I\right)$$

$$P\left(B \mid \sigma_b^2\right) = \prod_{i=1}^{n} N\left(b_i \mid U_i V_b^T, \sigma_b^2\ I\right) \tag{9.18}$$

where N $(a, |\mu, \sigma^2)$ indicates a Gaussian distribution with a mean μ and variance of σ^2, and the data in both views has the same lower dimensional factor matrix $U \in R\ R^{n \times k}$, which can be regarded as a standard representation. $v_a \in R^{d_a \times k}$ and $v_b \in R^{d_b \times k}$ are the loading matrices for the two views, which are usually expressed as zero-mean spherical Gaussian priors.

9.4.1.1 Multi-View Sparse Coding

In multi-view sparse coding, the dictionaries are a collection of linear mappings that link a shared latent representation to multi-view data. Its property is that it can locate a shared representation h^* that chooses the most appropriate bases while zeroing the rest, resulting in a high level of correlation with the multi-view input. Because of the explaining away effect, this property occurs naturally in directed graphical models [33]. A non-probabilistic model is one that is not based on probability. Learning the representation or code vector with respect to a multi-view sample, given a pair of datasets, can be formulated as a multi-view sparse coding scheme f A; B$_g$:

$$h^* = \arg\ \min \|a - w_a\ h\|_2^2 + \|b - w_b\ h\|_2^2 + \lambda\ \|h\|_1 \qquad (9.19)$$

To optimize the following target with respect to w_a and w_b f W_a; W_{bg}:

$$Jw_a,\ w_b = \sum_i^h \left(\left\| a_i - w_a h_i^* \right\|_2^2 + \left\| b_i - w_b h_i^* \right\|_2^2 \right) \qquad (9.20)$$

where the modal inputs are a_i and b_i, and h^* is the mutual sparse representation computed with Equation 9.20. W_a and W_b, the necessity of having unit-norm columns, in particular, helps to keep things in order. The previously regularized form of multi-view sparse coding can be generalized to a probabilistic model. In probabilistic multi-view sparse coding, assume the following generative distributions:

$$P(h) = \Pi_j^{(dh)} \frac{\lambda}{2} \exp\left(-\lambda |h_j|\right)$$

$$\forall_{(i=1)}^n: P(a_i\ |\ h) = N\left(a_i; w_a h + \mu_{a_i} \sigma_{a_i}^2 I\right)$$

$$P(b_i\ |\ h) = N\left(b_i; w_b h + \mu_{b_i} \sigma_{b_i}^2 I\right) \qquad (9.21)$$

In this case of multi-view probabilistic sparse coding, we try to get a sparse multi-view representation by computing the MAP (maximum a posteriori) value of h: $h^* = \arg\ \max_h p(h\,|\,a,b)$ rather than the predicted value $E(h\,|\,a,b)$. By maximising the likelihood of the data, given the joint MAP values of W_a and W_b, it is possible to learn the parameters W_a and W_b, $h^* = \arg$ $\max w_a, w_b \prod_i p(a_i \mid h^*)$.

In general, expectation-maximization and reciprocal representation can be used to learn dictionaries (W_a; W_b) (h^*). Multi-view sparse representation can improve performance, particularly when features from different views complement each other, which appears to be the case. As a multi-view feature learning scheme, it has a wide range of applications, including human pose estimation, image recognition, web data mining, and cross-media retrieval. For example, Liu et al. [34] propose multi-view Hessian discriminative sparse coding (mHDSC), which combines multi-view discriminative sparse coding with Hessian regularization. To improve learning performance, mHDSC uses Hessian regularization to exploit the local geometry of the data distribution and fully utilizes the complementary knowledge of multi-view data.

9.4.1.2 Multi-View Latent Space Markov Networks

Two special cases of undirected graphical models, also known as Markov random fields, are the exponential family Harmonium and the restricted Boltzmann machine. In the context of unsupervised multi-view feature learning, Xing et al. [35] introduce a multi-wing Harmonium model, which is a kind of multi-view latent space Markov network model. This model can be thought of as the undirected counterpart to the earlier mentioned driven aspect models, such as multimodal. LDA [36] has the advantages of being easy to infer thanks to the conditional independence of the hidden units and the ability to achieve topic mixing by integrating aspects from various documents and features. Begin with a dual-wing Harmonium model, which has two input unit modalities for ease of use, $A = \{a_i\}_{i=1}^n$, $B = \{b_j\}_{j=1}^n$, and a set of hidden units $H = \{h_k\}_{k=1}^n$. In this dual-wing Harmonium, any modality of input units and hidden units generates a complete bipartite graph in which units in one set have no relations but are absolutely connected to units in the other set. In addition, there are no relationships between two input modalities. Consider all scenarios in which all observed and hidden variables are members of the exponential family:

$$p(a_i) = \exp \{\theta_i^T \varnothing(a_i) - A(\theta_i)\}$$

$$p(b_j) = \exp \{n_j^T \varphi(a_i) - B(n_j)\}$$

$$p(h_k) = \exp \{\lambda_k^T \varphi(a_i) - C(\lambda_k)\} \tag{9.22}$$

where $\varnothing(.), \varphi(.)$, and $\varphi(.)$ are potentials generated by individual nodes over cliques, θ_i, n_j, and λ_k, which are the weights of possible functions that are correlated with them, and A(.), B(.), and C(.) are log partition functions.

By coupling the random variables in the log domain and adding other words [37], the joint distribution is formed.
$p(A; B; H)$ is as follows:

$$
P(A,B,H) \propto \exp \left\{
\begin{array}{l}
\sum_i \theta_i^T \; \varphi\,(a_i) + \sum_j n_j^T \; \varphi\,(b_i) + \sum_k \lambda_j^T \varphi\,(h_k) + \\[2ex]
\sum_{ik} \varphi(a_i)^T\, w_{ik}\; \varphi(h_k) + \sum_{jk} \varphi(b_i)^T\, U_{jk}\; \varphi(h_k)
\end{array}
\right\}
\tag{9.23}
$$

where $\varnothing(a_i)\varphi(h_k)$, $\varphi(b_{j,})$, and $\varphi(h_{k,})$ are potentials over cliques made up of pairwise connected nodes, and w_{ik}, w_{jk} are the weights of possible functions that are correlated with them. It is possible to derive conditional distributions from the joint distribution.

$$
P(a_i \mid H) \propto \exp \left\{ \tilde{\theta}_i^T \varphi\,(a_i) - A\!\left(\tilde{\theta}_i\right) \right\}
$$

$$
P(b_j \mid H) \propto \exp \left\{ \tilde{n}_j^T \varphi\,(b_j) - B\!\left(\tilde{n}_j\right) \right\}
$$

$$
P\!\left(h_k \mid A,B\right) \propto \exp \left\{ \tilde{\lambda}_k^T \varphi\,(h_k) - C\!\left(\tilde{n}_k\right) \right\}
\tag{9.24}
$$

where the shifted parameters $\tilde{\theta}_i = \theta_i + \Sigma_k w_{ik}\, \varnothing(h_k)$, $\tilde{n}_j = n_j + \Sigma_k U_{jk}\; \varphi(h_k)$, and $\lambda_k = \lambda_k + \Sigma_i W_{ik}\varnothing(x_i) + \Sigma_j U_{ik}\varphi(y_i))$

During training, the parameters of probabilistic models are typically changed to increase the likelihood of the training data. The updating laws are obtained by taking the derivative of the sample's log-likelihood specified in Equation 9.23 with respect to the model parameters. The multi-wing model can be directly obtained by extending the dual-wing model when multimodal input data is detected.

Chen et al. [11] define a multi-view latent space Markov network and its large-margin extension that satisfy the weak conditional independence assumption that data from different views and response variables is conditionally independent, given a set of latent variables, according to authors. Centered on the multi-wing Harmonium model and metric learning method proposed by Xie and Xing [38] propose a multimodal distance metric learning (MMDML) framework. Using distance supervision, this MMDML describes a principled method for embedding data from various modalities into a single latent room.

9.4.2 Neural Network Models

Neural network-based models have been commonly used for data representation learning, such as visual and textual data. When trained on large datasets, deep networks have demonstrated their superiority for a number of tasks, including object recognition, text classification, and speech recognition. Deep architectures can be adapted to specific domains, like multi-view signal measurements, video processing, and cross-media retrieval. From the neural network modeling perspective, multi-view representation learning first learns the respective mid-level features for each view and then integrates them into a single and compact representation. Some examples include a multimodal auto encoder, a multi-view convolutional neural network (CNN), and a multimodal RNN. Instead of fusing the network at the softmax layer, a multi-view CNN fuses the network at the convolution layer to learn multi-view correspondence feature maps. Assume that x_a and x_b are two function maps for views a and b learned by tied convolution, with weights shared between the two views. The following are some simple examples of two-view convolutional function fusion:

- Sum fusion: h sum = $x_a + x_b$.
- Max fusion: h max = max $\{x_a, x_b\}$.
- Concatenation fusion: h cat = $[x_a, x_b]$.

Fusion techniques are also used in other neural network-based representation fusion methods. Kiela and Bottou [39] combine a skip-gram linguistic representation vector with a visual concept representation trained with a deep CNN to construct multimodal concept representations. The most popular use of max fusion is in circumstances involving synthetic views of unimodal quantities, such as multiple time stamps in a time sequence. McLaughlin et al. [40] combine the visual features from all time stamps to achieve a precise appearance role for the entire sequence of video-based person re recognition. Karpathy and Fei-Fei [23] used a multimodal RNN to generate image descriptions. This method represents common multimodal embeddings for language and visual data and then uses its complementary information to predict variable-sized text from an image.

9.4.2.1 Multi-View Convolutional Neural Network

CNNs have had a lot of success in the field of visual recognition [35], and they've recently been applied to speech recognition and natural language processing [36]. The views in many directions in comparison to single-view networks, CNN has a multi-view network. In situations where multiple views of data are available, such as 3D object recognition, video action recognition, and multi-camera person reidentification, CNN shows convolutional representations (features) of learning. Its aim is to combine useful information from different perspectives in order to learn more detailed representations for later predictor learning. Consider 3D object recognition, which makes use of a multi-view CNN architecture that considers data from several 2D views of an object into a single and compact representation.

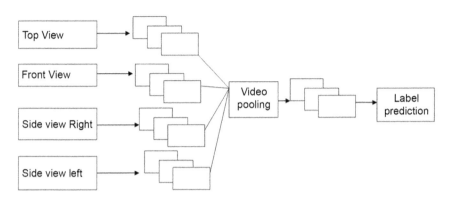

FIGURE 9.4
The multi-view CNN architecture

Multi-view images of a bus with 3D rotations are sent through a shared CNN (CNN1) separately, fused at a view-pooling layer and then sent through the rest of the network, as shown in Figure 9.4 (CNN2). Across all views, the view-pooling layer performs an element-by-element maximum operation. This multi-view mechanism functions in a similar way to "data augmentation," in which modified copies of data are used during training to learn invariance to changes such as flips, transformations, and rotations. In this multi-viewing system instead of averaging final scores from various perspectives, one learns from CNN a fused multi-view representation of 3D object recognition. Investigate various ways of integrating CNN representations both spatially and temporally to fully exploit the informative spatiotemporal information for human behavior recognition in videos [41]. It demonstrates that fusing a spatial and temporal network at a convolutional layer is superior to fusing at a softmax layer in terms of parameter savings and performance. Take spatial fusion, for example, to show its superiority in capturing spatial correspondence.

Suppose that $x^a \in R^{HXWXD}$ and $x^b \in R^{HXWXD}$ are two CNN-learned function maps, respectively, from two separate views a and b. As a first step, the proposed conv fusion joins the two feature maps at the same spatial positions i j across the feature channels d.

$y^{cat} = f^{cat}\left(x^a, x^b\right)$ where y^{cat} is spatial fusion.

The concatenated representation is then convolved using a bank of filters f and biases b:

$$y^{conv} = y^{cat} * f + b \tag{9.25}$$

where f is a one-dimensional convolution kernel that represents the weighted combination of the two feature maps x^a, x^b at the same spatial location. As a consequence, in order to better classify behavior, the correspondence

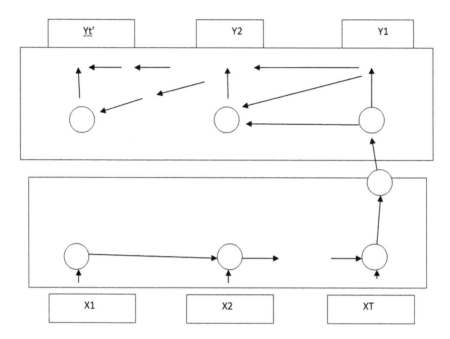

FIGURE 9.5
RNN encoder-decoder

between the networks of different points of view is studied. Views from various angles in CNN are often used in the reidentification of individuals. When given a pair of images from different views as input, this task returns a similarity value indicating whether the two input images represent the same person. In order to capture local relationships between two input images, Ahmed et al. [1] propose a multi-view mid-level feature fusion layer that computes cross-input neighborhood differences. Multi-view convolutional representation fusion is classified as cross-image representation learning by Wang et al. [42], who suggest a joint learning method for person reidentification that combines single-image and cross-image representations (Figure 9.5).

9.4.2.2 *Multimodal Recurrent Neural Network*

A RNN is a form of neural network that processes varying-length sequences $x = (x_1, ..., x_t)$ via the representation of secret states h. At each time step t, the RNN's secret state h_t is determined:

$$h_t = f(h_{t-1}, x_t) \tag{9.26}$$

where f is a nonlinear activation function chosen based on the data modeling needs. A simple case is a standard element-wise logistic sigmoid function, while a complex case is a long short-term memory (LSTM) unit. It is well known that an RNN can learn a probability distribution over a sequence by being trained to predict the next symbol in the sequence. In this planning, the conditional distribution decides the prediction at each time step t, $p(x_t \mid x_{t-1}, \dots x_1)$. To learn a multinomial distribution as an output, for example, a softmax activation function can be used:

$$P\left(x_t, j = 1 \mid x_{t-1}, \dots x_1\right) = \frac{\exp\left(w_i h_t\right)}{\sum_{j=1}^{k} \exp\left(w_g h_t\right)} \qquad (9.27)$$

w_j are the corresponding rows of a weight matrix w, where $j = 1, \dots, k$. The following probabilities can be used to measure the likelihood of the sequence x:

$$p(x) = \prod_{t=1}^{T} p\left(x_t \mid x_{t-1}, \dots x_1\right) \qquad (9.28)$$

By iteratively creating a symbol at each time point, it is easy to create a new sequence using this learned distribution. In an RNN encoder-decoder model, RNN is used to bind multimodal sequences. A neural network decodes a variable-length source sequence into a fixed-length vector representation, which it then transforms back to a variable-length target sequence. In fact, it's a general method for learning the conditional distribution over an output sequence that's conditioned on another input sequence, like $p(y_1; \dots; y_{T'} \mid x_1; \dots; x_T)$, T and T0 are the input and output sequence lengths, respectively. The encoder in the proposed model is an RNN that sequentially encodes each symbol of an input sequence x into the corresponding hidden state, according to Equation 9.28. After reading the end of the input sequence, a summary hidden state of the entire source sequence c is obtained. The proposed model's decoder is a second RNN that predicts the next symbol y_t with the secret state h_t to generate the target sequence.

Based on the recurrent property, both y_t and h_t are also conditioned on $y_{(t-1)}$ and the input sequence's definition c. As a consequence, the hidden state of the decoder at time t is computed as:

$$h_t = f\left(h_{t-1}, y_{t-1}, c\right) \qquad (9.29)$$

and the conditional distribution of the next symbol is

$$p\left(y_t \mid y_{t-1}, y_{t-2}, \dots y_1, c\right) = g\left(h_t, y_{t-1}, c\right) \qquad (9.30)$$

where g is a real probability-generating softmax activation function. The main idea behind the RNN-based encoder-decoder architecture is to train two RNNs together to optimize conditional log-likelihood:

$$\max_{\theta} \frac{1}{N} \sum_{n=1}^{N} \log p_{\theta}\left(y_n \mid x_n\right) \tag{9.31}$$

where θ is the set of model parameters and each pair (x_n, y_n) is an input and output sequence from the training set. To estimate model parameters, a gradient-based algorithm can be used. A general end-to-end approach for multimodal sequence-to-sequence learning is based on deep LSTM networks, which is particularly useful for learning problems with long-term temporal dependencies. The conditional probability is also calculated using this method: $p(y_{1,...}y_{T'} \mid x_n,...x_{T'})$. The conditional probability is determined by first obtaining the fixed dimensional representation of the input series v $(x_1,..., x_T)$; the probability of occurrence is computed after LSTM-based networks are encoded $(y_1,..., y_{T'})$. LSTM-based networks, the hidden state of which is initially set to the representation, are difficult to decode v of $(x_1,..., x_T)$:

$$P\left(y_1,...y_t \mid x_1,...x_t\right) = \prod_{t=1}^{T'} \left(p\left(y_t \mid v, y_1,...y_{t-1}\right)\right) \tag{9.32}$$

where each $py_t \mid v, y_1,...y_{t-1}$ is conditional probability. A softmax is used to represent the distribution of vocabulary words. Multimodal RNNs have also aided image captioning, video captioning, visual question answering, and information retrieval. Karpathy and Fei-Fei [23] suggest a multimodal RNN architecture to generate new image region concepts. To construct a bidirectional mapping between images and their sentence-based explanations, RNNs are used. A RNN model used for making video captions that works from beginning to end. Xu et al. [44] present an attention-based multimodal RNN model that uses the standard back-propagation approach to train the multimodal RNN in a deterministic manner. It contains two types of attention mechanisms: a "rock" attention mechanism and a "soft" attention mechanism. When making a caption for an image, the proposed model has the advantage of concentrating on the most important aspects of the image.

9.5 Challenges for Multi-View Representation Learning

Learning multi-view representations has been difficult due to a variety of factors, including but not limited to (1) unacceptable multi-view embedding modeling goals; (2) input data of poor quality (e.g., noisy and missing values);

(3) the presence of divergent points of view; and (4) the need for scalability in processing. As a result of these difficulties, the efficiency of multi-view representation learning can suffer.

A number of multi-view embedding methods have been suggested to solve these issues. These approaches are typically based on various aspects of multi-view representation learning and thus have distinct characteristics. In general, they plan to respond to the following questions:

- What are the most important objectives to achieve when studying successful multi-view representation?
- What are the best deep learning architectures for learning multi-view representations?
- How should the embedding function be modeled in multi-view representation learning with hierarchical inputs/outputs?
- What are the theoretical similarities and differences between various multi-view representation learning paradigms?

The essence of the multi-view learning tasks and the multi-view skills available determine the answers to these questions. As a consequence, it's critical to dig into the current literature's underlying theoretical principles and investigate in detail each theory's representative multi-view embedding models. We developed a survey to help researchers understand some basic principles of multi-view representation learning and choose the best models for their particular tasks based on this consideration (Figure 9.6).

9.6 Conclusion

Multi-view representation learning [43] has received a lot of attention in the fields of machine learning [44] and data mining. This chapter introduces the two major types of multi-view representation learning: multi-view representations that must be aligned and multi-view representations that must be merged. As a result, the representative approaches and hypotheses of multi-view representation learning are focused on the alignment perspective. Look at multi-view representation learning developments that involve generative approaches from a fusion perspective, such as multimodal topic learning, multi-view sparse coding, and multi-view latent space Markov networks, as well as neural network models, such as multimodal auto encoders, multi-view CNN, and multimodal RNN. There are a variety of applications for multi-view representation learning. The aim of this chapter is to provide a clear picture of the theoretical foundations and current developments in the field of multi-view representation learning, as well as to aid in the selection of the best methodologies for specific applications.

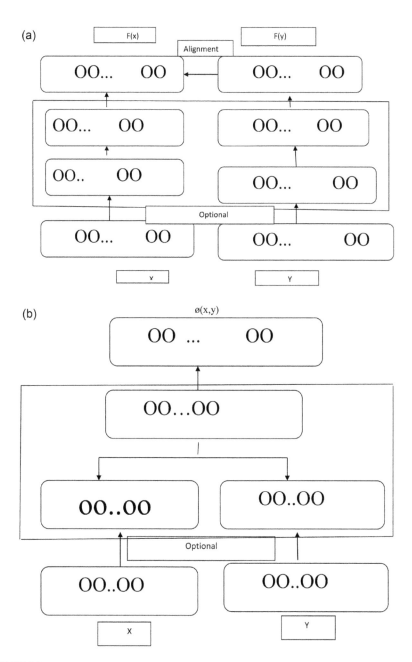

FIGURE 9.6
Multi-view representation learning schemes. The multi-view representation alignment scheme is shown in (a) where the representations from different views are enforced by the alignment through certain metrics, such as similarity and distance measurement. The multi-view representation fusion scheme (b) aims to integrate the multi-view inputs into a single and compact representation.

References

[1] Xing, E. P., Yan, R., & Hauptmann, A. G. (2012). Mining associated text and images with dual-wing harmoniums. *arXiv preprint, arXiv:1207.1423*

[2] Sun, S. (2013). A survey of multi-view machine learning. *Neural Computing and Applications, 23*(7), 2031–2038.

[3] Hardoon, D. R., Szedmak, S., & Shawe-Taylor, J. (2004). Canonical correlation analysis: An overview with application to learning methods. *Neural Computation, 16*(12), 2639–2664.

[4] Wiesel, A., Kliger, M., & Hero III, A. O. (2008). A greedy approach to sparse canonical correlation analysis. *arXiv preprint, arXiv:0801.2748.*

[5] Zhang, Y., & Wallace, B. (2015). A sensitivity analysis of (and practitioners' guide to) convolutional neural networks for sentence classification. *arXiv preprint, arXiv:1510.03820.*

[6] Blei, D. M., & Jordan, M. I. (2003). Modeling annotated data. In Proceedings of the 26th annual international ACM SIGIR conference on research and development in information retrieval (pp. 127–134).

[7] Ahmed, E., Jones, M., & Marks, T. K. (2015). An improved deep learning architecture for person re-identification. In Proceedings of the IEEE conference on computer vision and pattern recognition (pp. 3908–3916).

[8] Feng, F., Wang, X., & Li, R. (2014). Cross-modal retrieval with correspondence autoencoder. In Proceedings of the 22nd ACM international conference on multimedia (pp. 7–16).

[9] Golub, G. H., & Zha, H. (1995). The canonical correlations of matrix pairs and their numerical computation. In *Linear algebra for signal processing* (pp. 27–49). Springer, New York, NY.

[10] Avron, H., Boutsidis, C., Toledo, S., & Zouzias, A. (2013). Efficient dimensionality reduction for canonical correlation analysis. In *International conference on machine learning* (pp. 347–355). PMLR.

[11] Ngiam, J., Khosla, A., Kim, M., Nam, J., Lee, H., & Ng, A. Y. (2011). Multimodal deep learning. In ICML.

[12] Lu, Y., & Foster, D. P. (2014). Large scale canonical correlation analysis with iterative least squares. *arXiv preprint, arXiv:1407.4508* (pp. 91–99).

[13] Sun, L., Ji, S., & Ye, J. (2008). A least squares formulation for canonical correlation analysis. In Proceedings of the 25th international conference on machine learning (pp. 1024–1031).

[14] Hardoon, D. R., & Shawe-Taylor, J. (2011). Sparse canonical correlation analysis. *Machine Learning, 83*(3), 331–353.

[15] Li, Y., Mark, B., Raskutti, G., & Willett, R. (2018). Graph-based regularization for regression problems with highly-correlated designs. In *2018 IEEE global conference on signal and information processing (GlobalSIP)* (pp. 740–742). IEEE.

[16] Waaijenborg, S., de Witt Hamer, P. V., & Zwinderman, A. H. (2008). Quantifying the association between gene expressions and DNA-markers by penalized canonical correlation analysis. *Statistical Applications in Genetics and Molecular Biology, 7*(1), 3.

[17] Efron, B., Hastie, T., Johnstone, I., & Tibshirani, R. (2004). Least angle regression. *Annals of Statistics, 32*(2), 407–499.

[18] Bach, F. R., & Jordan, M. I. (2002). Kernel independent component analysis. *Journal of Machine Learning Research, 3*(Jul), 1–48.

[19] d'Aspremont, A., Bach, F. R., & Ghaoui, L. E. (2007). Full regularization path for sparse principal component analysis. In Proceedings of the 24th international conference on machine learning (pp. 177–184).

[20] Torres, D. A., Turnbull, D., Sriperumbudur, B. K., Barrington, L., & Lanckriet, G. R. (2007). Finding musically meaningful words by sparse CCA. In Neural information processing systems (nips) workshop on music, the brain and cognition.

[21] Vincent, P., Larochelle, H., Bengio, Y., & Manzagol, P. A. (2008). Extracting and composing robust features with denoising autoencoders. In Proceedings of the 25th international conference on machine learning (pp. 1096–1103).

[22] Witten, D. M., Tibshirani, R., & Hastie, T. (2009). A penalized matrix decomposition, with applications to sparse principal components and canonical correlation analysis. *Biostatistics, 10*(3), 515–534.

[23] Li, D., Dimitrova, N., Li, M., & Sethi, I. K. (2003). Multimedia content processing through cross-modal association. In Proceedings of the eleventh ACM international conference on multimedia (pp. 604–611).

[24] Jia, Y., Salzmann, M., & Darrell, T. (2010). Factorized latent spaces with structured sparsity. In NIPS (Vol. 10, pp. 982–990).

[25] Karpathy, A., & Fei-Fei, L. (2015). Deep visual-semantic alignments for generating image descriptions. In Proceedings of the IEEE conference on computer vision and pattern recognition (pp. 3128–3137).

[26] Hotelling, H. (1992). Relations between two sets of variates. In *Breakthroughs in statistics* (pp. 162–190). Springer, New York, NY.

[27] Andrew, G., Arora, R., Bilmes, J., & Livescu, K. (2013). Deep canonical correlation analysis. In *International conference on machine learning* (pp. 1247–1255). PMLR.

[28] Guo, G., & Mu, G. (2013). Joint estimation of age, gender and ethnicity: CCA vs. PLS. In 2013 10th IEEE *international conference and workshops on automatic face and gesture recognition* (FG) (pp. 1–6). IEEE.

[29] Bai, B., Weston, J., Grangier, D., Collobert, R., Sadamasa, K., Qi, Y., ... & Weinberger, K. (2010). Learning to rank with (a lot of) word features. *Information Retrieval, 13*(3), 291–314.

[30] Grangier, D., & Bengio, S. (2008). A discriminative kernel-based approach to rank images from text queries. *IEEE Transactions on Pattern Analysis and Machine Intelligence, 30*(8), 1371–1384.

[31] Cohn, D., & Hofmann, T. (2001). The missing link – a probabilistic model of document content and hypertext connectivity. *Advances in Neural Information Processing Systems*, 430–436.

[32] Srivastava, N., & Salakhutdinov, R. (2012). Multimodal learning with deep Boltzmann machines. In NIPS (Vol. 1, p. 2).

[33] Xu, K., Ba, J., Kiros, R., Cho, K., Courville, A., Salakhudinov, R., ... & Bengio, Y. (2015). Show, attend and tell: Neural image caption generation with visual attention. In *International conference on machine learning* (pp. 2048–2057). PMLR.

[34] Liu, W., Tao, D., Cheng, J., & Tang, Y. (2014). Multiview Hessian discriminative sparse coding for image annotation. *Computer Vision and Image Understanding, 118*, 50–60.

[35] Xing, E. P., Ng, A. Y., Jordan, M. I., & Russell, S. (2002). Distance metric learning with application to clustering with side-information. In NIPS (Vol. 15, No. 505–512, p. 12).

[36] Chen, J., Bushman, F. D., Lewis, J. D., Wu, G. D., & Li, H. (2013). Structure-constrained sparse canonical correlation analysis with an application to microbiome data analysis. *Biostatistics, 14*(2), 244–258.

[37] Barnard, K., Duygulu, P., Forsyth, D., De Freitas, N., Blei, D. M., & Jordan, M. I. (2003). Matching words and pictures. *Journal of Machine Learning Research, 3*(1107–1135), 3.

[38] Xie, P., & Xing, E. P. (2013). *Multi-modal distance metric learning.* In Twenty-Third International Joint Conference on Artificial Intelligence.

[39] Kiela, D., & Bottou, L. (2014). Learning image embeddings using convolutional neural networks for improved multi-modal semantics. In Proceedings of the 2014 conference on empirical methods in natural language processing (EMNLP) (pp. 36–45).

[40] McLaughlin, N., Del Rincon, J. M., & Miller, P. (2016). Recurrent convolutional network for video-based person re-identification. In Proceedings of the IEEE conference on computer vision and pattern recognition (pp. 1325–1334).

[41] Wang, W., Arora, R., Livescu, K., & Bilmes, J. (2015). On deep multi-view representation learning. In *International conference on machine learning* (pp. 1083–1092). PMLR.

[42] Wang, F., Zuo, W., Lin, L., Zhang, D., & Zhang, L. (2016). Joint learning of single-image and cross-image representations for person re-identification. In Proceedings of the IEEE conference on computer vision and pattern recognition (pp. 1288–1296).

[43] Bengio, Y., Courville, A., & Vincent, P. (2013). Representation learning: A review and new perspectives. *IEEE Transactions on Pattern Analysis and Machine Intelligence, 35*(8), 1798–1828.

[44] Svensén, M., & Bishop, C. M. (2006). *Pattern recognition and machine learning.* Springer.

10

COVID-19 Applications

R. Manimala and G. Muthulakshmi

10.1 Introduction

In the year 2020, the worldwide pandemic caused by Severe Acute Respiratory Syndrome Coronavirus 2 (SARS-CoV-2) a.k.a. COVID-19 will be remembered. COVID-19 was declared a Public Health Emergency of International Concern (PHEIC) by the World Health Organization (WHO) on January 30, 2020, as the virus spread across the world [1]. Governments around the world have implemented lockdowns, recommended self-isolation, mandated work-from-home policies, imposed stringent social distancing standards, and deployed emergency health responses, the latter of which involves substantial new facilities for treatment and mass testing for the general public. Both of these steps are being taken to stop the virus from spreading. COVID-19 carriers can be infectious even though they don't show any symptoms. When a carrier tests positive, it's possible that they've already transmitted the virus to a large number of people who have come into contact with them. This necessitates a procedure known as "touch tracing," which identifies individuals who came into close contact with the positive carrier and may now be infected. Because of person-to-person touch, it spreads all over the world.

The Symptoms of COVID-19 are fever, coughing, shortness of breath, difficulty breathing, fatigue, chills, body aches, headache, sore throat, congestion/runny nose, loss of smell or taste, nausea, diarrhea and others [2]. It often affects the upper respiratory tract (sinuses, nose, and throat) or the lower respiratory tract (bronchitis, pneumonia, and bronchitis) (windpipe and lungs). Pneumonia, respiratory failure, cardiac attacks, liver problems, septic shock, and death are all symptoms of the infection. Many COVID-19 complications are caused by a cytokine storm or cytokine release syndrome. When an infection causes the immune system to release inflammatory proteins known as cytokines into the bloodstream, it destroys tissues and causes organ damage. The signs will appear in 2 days or 14 days. It differs from one individual to the next. Blood clots have been found in the legs, lungs, and arteries of certain individuals. To prevent the pandemic epidemic from spreading, the people have self-quarantined themselves.

DOI: 10.1201/9781003126898-10

The variant virus may cause some severity because of virus circulation [3]. The more viruses circulate, the more it will mutate therefore the algorithm has to be improved automatically according to the changes, to diagnose the disease. The second wave of the pandemic has some other symptoms such as body ache, fatigue, dizziness (neurological symptoms), and lack of saliva production, while the remote consultation has to be transformed according to it.

Artificial intelligence (AI) is a technology to predict the pandemic regions, risk modeling (who will get infected and develop symptoms), testing strategy optimization, vaccine development, and others. A massive amount of data is the source for intelligent machine or smart applications that solve real-world problems in the field of bioinformatics, finance, agriculture etc. The sensitive information is handled by smart applications, it raises security issues. To handle these issues, blockchain technology can be used, which has a distributed database network to ensure security. Machine learning makes smart applications or an intelligent machine to learn, think, and act like a human without their intervention. It is considered to be one of the applications of AI. Its basic idea is to build a model by analyzing the large dataset to make predictions.

The blockchain [4] is a distributed data system made up of serially connected blocks. A block is made up of a number of transactions, the current block's hash value, the previous block's hash, the timestamp (indicating when the block was created), and so on. The chain is formed by each block containing a hash of the previous block. The blockchain is replicated on any node in the network. It is a growing distributed ledger that is replicated and shared among the nodes in a network. This network uses peer to peer system. It is a decentralized system so there is no central authority but there are standard rules for adding only the valid transactions. Every node has a copy of the blockchain where the data is updated too. The new record contains the history of the chain. So we can track the previous transaction. For example, the patient medical history can be tracked with this technology.

Blockchain is immutable while a simple change made in the data changes the hash code. The hash value is a unique id of the block that depends on the block's content. For example, Bitcoin uses the SHA256 algorithm, while Ethereum uses the hash algorithm. So data tampering is impossible in the blockchain.

Smart contracts are programs with specific conditions. When the particular condition is met, the transaction will be processed automatically. It reduces the intervention of middlemen. Ethereum is the world's first programmable blockchain. It is used to develop innovative applications.

Types of blockchain:

1. Public blockchain: Open to everyone for access. The consensus algorithm is used to validate the transactions.

2. Private blockchain: It can be accessed by only a certain group such as an organization and bank. It needs permissions from the administrator.

3. Hybrid blockchain: It is a combination of public and private blockchains [5].

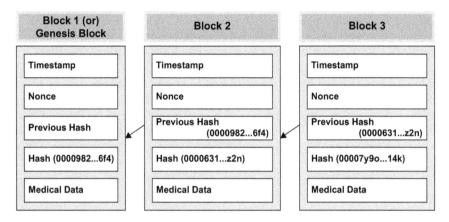

FIGURE 10.1
Blockchain structure

Stuart Haber and W. Scott Stornetta, two research scientists, suggested blockchain technology in 1991. To store the time-stamped digital document, they create a stable blockchain. Blockchain is a database that is open-source. Merkle trees were later incorporated into the design in 1992 to allow for the storage of several documents in a single block. The documents are organized in a chronological order. The most recent record in the chain includes the entire chain's history (Figure 10.1).

As a prototype for digital currency, Hal Finney developed a method called reusable proof of work (RPoW) in 2004. The double-spending issue was solved by RPoW by registering the ownership of tokens on a trustworthy server. This server was created so that users all over the world could check its accuracy and credibility in real time.

Satoshi Nakamoto first proposed distributed blockchains in 2008. He changed the design so that new blocks could be added to the existing chain without the need for signatures from trusted parties. It solves the double-spending problem by using a peer-to-peer network to time-stamp and checks each exchange. The architecture now serves as the public ledger for all cryptocurrency transactions. He launched bitcoin, a digital currency that is governed by cryptographic rules and generates units of currency. It's also known as decentralized digital currency. It can be purchased, sold, and transferred securely between the two parties through the internet. Bitcoin may also be used to purchase goods and services, make purchases, and trade value electronically. In recent years, the file size of cryptocurrency blockchains containing records of all network transactions has increased dramatically.

In recent days, distributed applications or DApps are developed like a traditional application for storing and distributing secured documents in various fields such as finance, insurance, banking sector, entertainment, healthcare, and government.

Working of blockchain:

The block contains block number, nonce (number used once), data, the current block's hash value, and the previous block's hash value (this links the blocks and creates the chain) [6].

A nonce is a number that is generated at random. The miner usually starts with a nonce value of 1 and increases it until the created hash meets the required criterion. As a result, it may take several iterations to produce the desired hash with four leading zeros. The time it takes to generate a block in the bitcoin system is estimated to be 10 minutes. If the miner has successfully mined the block, he releases it into the scheme, making it the chain's final block.

The hash algorithm generates one-of-a-kind results (or hash). A cryptographic hash is a digital signature that represents a specific amount of data. The transactions are taken as input and run through a hashing algorithm that produces a fixed-size output in cryptographic hash functions. It's a one-way operation, which means that unlike conventional encryption, we can't get the original text from the hash value using a key. The hash value with the leading four zeros is contained in a valid block. If someone attempts to alter the data, the hash value's first four zeros are converted to other characters, resulting in no signature.

To put it another way, if the ledger is changed or updated, each node generates a new transaction, and then the nodes use a consensus algorithm to vote on which copy is correct. If a consensus algorithm has been developed, all other nodes are updated with the latest and most accurate copy of the ledger. If a consensus algorithm is created, all other nodes are modified with the most recent and accurate version of the ledger.

In a blockchain network, PoW is the first consensus algorithm. Solving the mathematical problem that produces the new block is the central working concept of PoW. PoW is when the machine that solves the puzzle shares the solution with all of the other nodes in the network. The PoW is verified by the entire network. The new block will be added to the chain if it is right. As a result, the algorithm accepts the transaction and adds a new block to the chain of transactions. Mining is the term for the method of validating a transaction.

10.2 Literature Review

COVID applications are developed in a number of ways. Natural language processing (NLP) techniques can be used to analyze information derived from unstructured data such as clinical records and medical journals using machine learning algorithms. A machine learning algorithm model is designed to predict the disease by analyzing structured data. Unsupervised learning and supervised learning are two types of machine learning algorithms. Unsupervised learning is known for feature extraction, while supervised learning is well-suited to predictive modeling by defining relationships between patient data (as input) and the desired outcome (as output). Semisupervised learning combines unsupervised and guided learning to help with missing grades [7].

Supervised algorithms: To make predictions, a model is created via a training phase [8]. The training process continues until the model achieves accuracy. Classification and regression trees, random forest, and gradient boosted trees (XGBoost) are supervised algorithms that use decision trees to repeatedly divide data into categories using attributes and outcomes. The Encouragement of data is presented in a multidimensional format by vector machine, which uses a "hyperplane" to isolate data based on outcomes. Support vector machine (SVM) applications are used to detect faces, identify images, and classify proteins, genes, and cancers.

The k-nearest neighbor (KNN) algorithm predicts the outcome of a new dataset using a model constructed from the observations closest to it. Using the distance function, it determines the distance between all inputs in the data. After event B has occurred, the naive Bayes algorithm aids in determining the likelihood of event A. It is mostly used in recommendation systems and other similar applications.

Regression created a model based on the relationship between variables and iteratively refined the outcome by testing the error. Linear regression is a technique for determining the relationship between two variables, the values of which are dependent on one another. For prediction, one variable is independent, while the other is dependent on the independent variable. The logistic regression [9] algorithm is used in binary classification problems where events occur as a function of one of two values, such as true or false and qualified or ineligible.

Unsupervised algorithms: This type of algorithm creates clusters based on shared characteristics. There is no need to build a model in the manner of a supervised algorithm. It's used to find a previously unknown or concealed pattern [10]. The k-means clustering is an unsupervised learning algorithm that divides a collection of n observations into k clusters, with each observation belonging to the cluster mean closest to it. The unsupervised algorithm creates patterns in electronic medical records (EMRs) for disease diagnosis as well as new patterns in disease symptoms. For preventing controversies, the SIMON [11] algorithm is being used to help predict immune response to influenza vaccine, which can also be used in COVID vaccination.

By selecting or extracting features, dimensionality reduction algorithms reduce the dimension. These algorithms are primarily used to preprocess data and eliminate redundant features before training the optimized model. Linear discriminant analysis, principal component analysis, multidimensional scaling, and locally linear embedding are some of the dimensionality reduction algorithms. For constructing accurate predictive models, principal component analysis is used to reduce the dimensions of feature space by using either feature exclusion or feature extraction. The algorithm is used for image processing, recommendation system etc.

Random forest implements decision trees and uses a variety of algorithms to classify and predict data. It generates a large number of decision trees from random datasets and iteratively trains the model until the result is correct. The outcomes of all the decision trees are combined to find the most appropriate outcome. The outcomes of all the decision trees are combined to find the most appropriate outcome.

Boosting is a strategy for turning weak learners into strong learners in ensemble machine learning algorithms [12]. When dealing with large amounts of data, boosting algorithms are needed to minimize bias and variance in supervised learning. For classification and regression problems, the gradient boosting algorithm is used to iteratively construct the prediction model. It helps slow learners to become more accurate learners by educating them on the mistakes of strong learners. When the poor learners fail, AdaBoost improves the model. It modifies the weights assigned to the instances in the sample, and the weak learners' output is combined to form a weighted total to generate the final boosted output.

Reinforcement learning: The algorithms learn the best outcome by choosing an action and observing the consequences. This process is repeated again and again until the algorithm chooses the right strategy. It's also used in robotics, where the computer picks up information from its surroundings. The robots determine how to travel and serve the patient based on the circumstances. It also decides on drug dosing adjustments, among other things.

The deep learning algorithm is used to refine the result by minimizing errors over a number of iterations. Deep neural networks, also known as artificial neural networks (ANNs), are made up of multiple layers of "neurons," each of which is linked to the next layer above it in an iterative process. It functions similarly to a human brain, with interconnected nodes passing data to and from other nodes in an iterative process to produce an accurate result. It was primarily used to identify trends. Using deep neural networks and chest radiographs, the algorithm diagnoses COVID-19 [13]. Google DeepMind Structure's AlphaFold [14] deep learning algorithm predicts the structure of the protein associated with SARS-CoV-2, the virus that causes COVID-19. It helps researchers figure out how viruses infect cells and how immune cells identify viral invaders. It enhances protein structure predictions, which are crucial for the development of the COVID-19 vaccine [15].

Icolung (Icometrix) is a tool for assessing the severity of disease in COVID-19 patients. InferRead CT Pneumonia (InferVision) is a warning device for COVID-19 positive cases. Lung Density Analysis (Imbio) creates visualizations and measurements of lung regions of abnormal tissue density, as well as mapping normal lung, air-trapping, and areas with persistent low density.

Convolutional neural networks (CNNs) are deep learning algorithms that process input images and analyze various aspects to distinguish one image from another. CNNs adopt a hierarchical model that creates a structure to provide a completely connected layer where all the neurons are connected and output is processed, similar to the communication pattern of neurons in the human brain. It ensures that the pattern of COVID-19 patients' lung scan reports is accurate.

Based on travel data provided by the International Air Transport Association, the BlueDot algorithm predicted the early spread of COVID-19 outside of Wuhan.

10.3 Materials and Methods

In recent years, governments are adopting blockchain technology in many fields such as land registration, supply chain traceability, corporate registration, healthcare, voting system etc. Data reliability is essential in machine learning to improve the accuracy of results. The integration of these two technologies put forward the precise result in predictions. So the machine can think and act similar to human.

Blockchain is ideal for the storage of highly sensitive personal data like personalized recommendations or medical notes etc. Using machine learning, supply chain solutions can be improved by reducing wastage and enabling transparency, security, and compliance checks.

Nowadays, US healthcare [16] depends on the patient. They decide when they need to see their doctor if visible symptoms have appeared, or an accident has occurred. The patient's virtual assistant can cross-reference their calendar with their doctor's and schedule an appointment automatically. They offer the relevant details of their medical history. When the patient arrives, blockchain will ensure that they have a secure, accurate, digital medical history for the doctor's reference. Internet of Things (IoT), sensors, wearable, smart devices, medical devices produce the patient's current health-related issues. Machine learning algorithm builds models from the medical dataset and electronic health records (EHRs) in blockchain for future predictions and diagnosis of diseases. The proposed method is an agglomerative machine learning method that combines many models to produce the optimized prediction result. The framework contains agglomerative machine learning models to diagnose disease with the help of various symptoms, which changes over a while. The second wave has some different symptoms than the first wave. The symptoms are analyzed with EHR updated by blockchain technology. By analyzing the EHR, the new pattern of symptoms can be detected easily. A decision tree determines the prediction based on series of questions and conditions of patients. SVM algorithm is used to identify the face to suspects the corona positive. It also is used to classify the protein and gene of the virus to identify the mutation and its severeness. Naive Bayes algorithm is used to predict the future suspects in a particular region after a while. The reinforcement learning model is used to insist on the drug dosing according to the mutation of the virus and its severity. ANN is used to repeatedly analyze the EHR to identify the new pattern of protein structure which is used for researchers to develop the vaccination according to it. These multiple models generated by multiple learners can be combined using the bagging technique in the form of voting. The prediction result is used to detect the corona suspects with the symptoms and the severeness monitored by the framework with the help of sensors and smart devices. It displays the drug details before injecting the vaccine. It also displays the virus mutation details over the period that helps the researchers to develop the vaccine. Moreover, it displays the most corona-affected region and also predicts the region going to be affected most and mortality rate in the near future. Remote monitoring globally is possible to get better assistance and treatment (Figure 10.2).

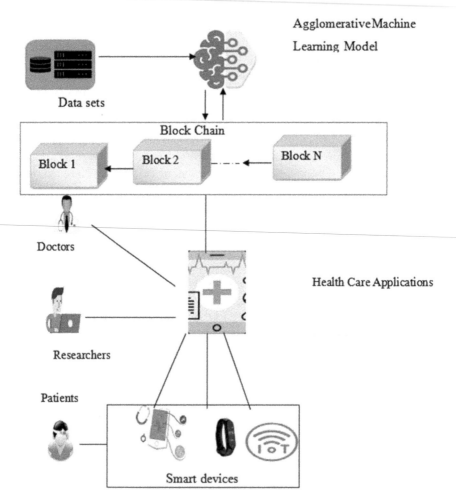

FIGURE 10.2
COVID-19 application framework using ML, BT, and IoT

When sharing health-related data, privacy is the main concern where blockchain provides solutions to vulnerabilities such as hacking and data theft. Blockchain technology in healthcare offers interoperability, which enables the exchange of medical data securely among the different systems and offers an effective communication system, time reduction, and enhanced operational efficiency.

Moreover, fake drug supply is eliminated because of blockchain technology. The use of blockchain technology for claims mediation and billing management application is predicted to register 66.5 percent growth by the year 2025 [17], owing to several issues such as errors, duplications, and incorrect billing. These are overcome by blockchain technology.

To prevent the distribution of counterfeit or illegal products, safe supply chain monitoring is needed in drug traceability. When drugs' ingredients are modified or added in unauthorized quantities, they run the risk of serious side effects, some of which could be fatal. Pharmaceutical companies may use the blockchain to register their goods and monitor their movement from the point of origin to the end customer, ensuring protection and transparency. It can prevent vaccine controversies, and people may be more willing to inject the vaccine without fear if they are aware of the drug's specifics (Figure 10.3).

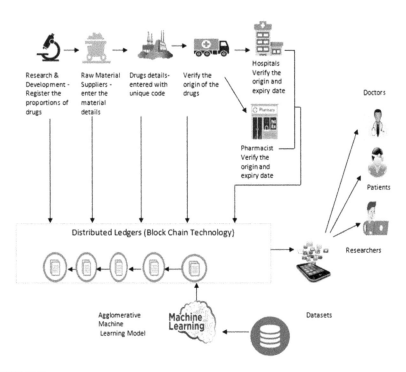

FIGURE 10.3
Supply chain management of COVID-19 drugs using ML and BT

10.4 Case Study and Applications

There are a variety of contact-tracing applications available to help you find the infected person. To prevent the spread of infection, the app will alert users to a nearby infected individual.

Many studies have been conducted to determine the utility of blockchains in the medical sector, with a focus on the personal health record (PHR) in a private blockchain. Yu Rang Park et al. [18] built a private blockchain network on top of the Ethereum platform and used 300 PHRs for verification. One hospital node and 300 patient nodes made up the private blockchain network. PHRs is loaded in a transaction between the hospital and patient nodes and propagated to the entire network to test the efficacy of blockchain-based PHR management. This research shows that PHR data can be exchanged in a private blockchain network.

Xiaobao Zhu, Jing Shi, and Cuiyuan Lu [19] created a simulation study on breast tumor diagnosis and proposed a cloud health resource-sharing model based on consensus-oriented blockchain technology. As the consensus algorithm for block generation, proof of authority is chosen. Even if the patient is in another country, he or she can easily send a hospital service request, often with a low-cost cap, and wait for notification since their health information is safely stored in blockchain. The patient will pay the fee in virtual currency, i.e. without having to think about currency conversion. Ethereum is used to construct the structure. Smart contracts are written in the solidity programming language. A recommendation algorithm is used to locate the most appropriate care providers for a patient's needs. 9893 Service requests from 100 users are generated and fulfilled by 22 providers during the 500-hour simulated period of generated service requests. All requests are met by service providers based on the weighted KNN algorithm's recommendations. KNN weights greatly improve the system's efficiency.

Ariel Ekblaw et al. [20] suggested "MedRec," a distributed ledger for keeping patient EHRs in a safe and immutable format. The ability to share EHRs is a benefit of open Application Programming Interfaces (APIs). Patients can access their medical records from any place. On the Ethereum blockchain, smart contracts keep track of patient-provider relationships, as well as the medical record, with viewing permissions and data retrieval instructions that can be executed on external databases. Researchers, public health officials, and others will participate as "miners" in the blockchain network. To prevent material tampering, the PoW algorithm was used. They also suggested a data mining system to enable medical researchers to access the MedRec network for a vast number of health records. It enables patients to forecast their own futures based on their family history and previous health-related data. Machine learning and data analysis layers can be used in these open APIs to build an "automatic learning health framework."

Most countries around the world are adopting blockchain technology in a variety of fields due to its safe decentralized nature. The Estonian government has teamed up with the start-up Guard time to deploy blockchain-based technology throughout the country to protect public and internal data. When Estonia revealed and used blockchain technology to protect the health-care data of over a million people in 2016, it once again became the world pioneer in blockchain technology [21]. To enhance care management, the technology distributes data to approved parties. Health costs are reduced as a result of improved insurance claim coordination for treatment. The capacity of the Estonian medical record blockchain project to keep medical records private while still making them freely accessible to medical professionals and insurance firms will determine its effectiveness. Their eHealth initiative's overall success or failure would be determined by their ability to increase the average citizen's life expectancy from the present 77.6 years. They converted 99 percent of prescriptions to digital format. To improve health-care efficiency, they use decision support algorithms that identify drug reactions at the point of prescribing. The e-ambulance system, which provides emergency teams with all specific medical information about the patients, is also a complement to emergency health-care allergies, already prescribed medications, health condition, and so on before they arrive at the hospital [22]. Family doctors can consult with specialists about their complicated cases through e-consultations from anywhere in Estonia. This is beneficial for patients who are unable to visit the hospital. Estonia has e-health data going back 12 years [23]. These facilities help to prevent diseases like cardiac arrest from occurring. In September 2018, Estonia launched a project to assist disabled people and senior citizens, in collaboration with the International Foundation of Integrated Care (IFIC) and with funding from the European Commission's Structural Reform Support Programme (SRSS). They also train algorithms to identify people who need medical assistance. Patients may seek advice from physicians from anywhere in the world, which cuts down on hospital wait times and relieves doctors' workload. The EHR is a national system that integrates data from Estonia's various health-care facilities into a single, online-accessible record for all patients. Patient site on the internet [23] is a versatile tool that allows doctors to view a patient's records, lab test reports, X-rays, and scan results from distant hospitals. To ensure the accuracy of EMRs, KSI blockchain technology is used. In that country, 99 percent of patients have an EHR, which allows a doctor to access information such as blood group, allergies, recent procedures, current prescription or pregnancy, and sugar complaints using the patient's ID code in an emergency. The documents are used by the government to monitor epidemics, assess health patterns, and so on. The patient can review medical visits and current prescriptions, as well as see which doctors have access to their files, using an electronic ID card. Health-care e-solutions are provided by Estonian companies such as Nortal, Helmes, Guard time, INTELSYS, Stacc, Queretec, and Industry. e-Prescription is a software program that is used to manage medical prescriptions.

With an ID card, the patient receives the prescription from the doctor and goes directly to the pharmacy. The pharmacists use the device to access the patient's details and then issue the medication. It is not necessary to return to the hospital for repeat prescriptions. Their decision-making software for medication interactions and contraindications [24] linked to an e-prescription database, so every time a doctor wants to prescribe something that could interact with a patient's medications, the device warns them. This reduces the likelihood of unwelcome drug side effects or adverse events. After these alerts are displayed, the majority of prescriptions are updated.

In 2019, the COVID-19 pandemic will begin in Wuhan, China. It spread from the city to neighboring towns, nearby nations, and eventually the entire planet. The country takes the requisite steps to contain the outbreak in a variety of ways, including lockdowns and technology. It also creates software that prevents people from coming into contact with one another.

A WeChat system and Hospital EMRs are needed for the Digital China Health Integrated System [25], daily case reports are used to create the data model for prediction, and the victims, inpatients, discharged patients, and long-term follow-up are all monitored. However, blockchain technology can easily replace these.

Beijing ZhuYi Technology Co., Ltd. has created Zuo Shou Yi Sheng (ZSYS, or Left-Hand Doctor). Deep learning, big data analytics, NLP, and medical interactive dialogues are among the tools used to introduce smart medical technologies to the health-care industry. Smart self-diagnosis, smart consultation, smart prediagnosis, smart pharmaceutical Q&A, and smart Q&A are the five key services offered by the app. With the personalized questions, the application creates an EMR and answers about personal history, allergies, and family medical history, as well as the explanation for hospital visits, etc. The program uses deep learning and machine learning algorithms to create prediction models from these EMR in order to diagnose diseases. It is used to track changes in COVID patients' symptoms by collecting and generating records on a regular basis.

Hanwen (Hava) Zhang is China's first platform to merge the IoT, big data, and AI to provide smart, personalized services. It allows for remote monitoring via sensors, machine-assisted identifications, and predictions, reducing the risk of virus transmission via person-to-person communication. Since COVID-19 has a long incubation period, it is critical to contain the source of infection and eliminate all potential transmission routes as soon as possible. The most critical methods for detecting COVID-19 are temperature and symptom control. There are two control systems: Cheetah, a remote surveillance system, and Dolphin, a smart system. The source of infection is identified using camera surveillance and a cheetah remote monitoring device. The data is uploaded to the Dolphin smart machine, which generates body temperature graphs and verifies the accuracy of the temperature data obtained. In a crucial situation, IZhaohu has an alarm solution. It sends a warning to a family member as well as emergency services. Based on the data collected,

IZhaohu smart cameras were able to identify symptoms and issue alerts. Nonemergency teleconsultations with doctors from top-tier medical hospitals are available via the app. This lowered the number of visits to the hospital, lowering the risk of infection and transmission. Furthermore, IZhaohu has developed a contactless medication dispensing system by connecting a consumer app to smart pillboxes. People can place orders for medication and deposit it in the pillbox. Employees from IZhaohu clean the smart pillbox and deliver the drug to the elderly person.

The National Informatics Centre of the Ministry of Electronics and Information Technology established Aarogya Setu, an Indian COVID-19 contact-tracing application. The app tracks people's movements using GPS and Bluetooth proximity features, and alerts users to the number of corona positive cases within 5 km, 10 km, and up to 500 km. Aarogya Setu is divided into four sections: User status, self-assessment, COVID-19 updates, e-pass integration [26]. This app has nearly 17.08 crore users as of March 14, 2021. With the aid of this app, the government will quickly identify hotspots. It also includes information on the disease's symptoms and precautions. This app also provides information on local hospitals. Furthermore, this software can be used to schedule CoWIN vaccination registration.

A team from the Indian Institute of Science created the "GoCoronaGo" app, which alerts people who have crossed paths with COVID-19 suspects [27]. In the backend, it uses temporal network analytics to detect high-risk people who spread the virus. It also sends out isolation warnings and aids in social distancing. It also has a geofencing feature that allows those under quarantine to have symptoms that are included in the risk assessment.

The ZOE COVID-19 Symptoms Study app helped to identify "COVID tongue," which may be a new disorder linked to COVID-19. Several participants reported their symptoms to this app on a regular basis, assisting in the identification of this rare disease symptom.

Gainify is a health-care application that uses AI, IoT devices, and blockchain to perform a variety of medical tasks. This application allows monetization of anonymous clinical data via a crypto payment system, which is useful for medical research, as well as appointment scheduling, digital payments, identity verification, and medical records management. GainfyCare (consumer platform), GainfyDoc (ID and credentials), GainfyPay (crypto and digital wallet platform), Gainfy Marketplace (product and service marketplace), and GainfyEnterprise (digital solutions) are the digital solutions (health data management) [28].

Medicoin [29] is a blockchain-based software application that provides pharmaceutical firms, insurers, and researchers with immutable data for medication management. They used Hyperledger technology to create smart contracts. The tokens in this example are used to improve the initiation/confirmation process for healthcare data.

Medicalchain [30] is a blockchain-based platform that allows users to share their health information with medical professionals. In the distributed ledger, Medicalchain records are transparent and stable. Since blockchain technology prevents current records in the blockchain from being changed, it eliminates health insurance fraud. Hyperledger fabric is a forum for maintaining the required level of privacy in medical records. It supports several authorization layers, allowing the owner of a collection of data to monitor which sections of their data are accessed. By collecting and validating clinical records directly from patients with their consent, third-party interference is prevented. Researchers can read permission EHRs both dynamically and internationally for their research purposes (Figure 10.4).

Fitchain is a blockchain-based machine learning factory that enables researchers to train machine learning models from user data in real time. The use of real-time health data in the fight against modern disease gives

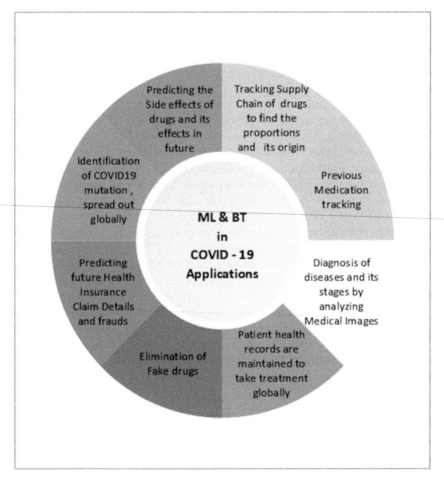

FIGURE 10.4
Advantages of ML and BT in COVID-19 applications

them control of their health and also the information gathered by monitoring exercise, diet, sleep, and other health-related activities. More data provided by the user is stored in the blockchain in 256 kb encrypted format if the user's health app is connected to the Fitchain network. Researchers can choose which health data they want based on their needs. Fitchain eliminates the need for a middleman by using a blockchain network and smart contracts.

Danku is a public blockchain-based protocol for testing and buying machine learning models. Cyber is a decentralized search engine that can learn from information graphs and forecast future outcomes.

doc.ai: doc.ai uses AI to decentralize precision medicine on the blockchain. Vytalyx: Vytalyx is a health technology company that aims to store and analyze medical data using AI and blockchain.

10.5 Conclusions with Future Research Scopes

In this pandemic situation, the e-health system helps to take treatment and prescriptions at their home so that spreading out of COVID-19 can be avoided. There is no need to wait for the specialists at the hospital. The doctors can predict the spreading of COVID-19 using the machine learning algorithm with the help of EHRs in a distributed ledger. The technologies reduce the mortal rate due to COVID-19 because any specialist from anywhere can analyze the previous health-related data about the patient and provide the necessary consultation in these critical situations.

Remote patient monitoring (RPM) [31, 32] is a rapidly growing health-care segment. A key component of RPM is wearable device that allows medical professionals to monitor and diagnose patients in their home or any other countries. After undergoing successful COVID-19 treatment, a patient is discharged. These devices can remotely monitor patient vitals as well as other symptoms. It transmits medically accurate data to a doctor or nurse at a nearby location. If doctors were able to see patterns over an extended period, a more rapid and accurate diagnosis can be performed with agglomerative machine learning models.

Sensors and smart devices are also used to track the patient's current status. The ability for doctors to monitor the disease in the home reduces the cost and redundant visits to the hospitals in this pandemic situation. It improves preventive measures as well as the diagnosis results. Shortly, a doctor's visit may happen completely from the comfort of patient's home in any country for any complicated disease with affordable virtual currencies. This is because of the integration of blockchain technology and machine learning. The future research scope will be in the integration of emerging technologies such as IoT, AI, blockchain technology to provide better service globally and to reduce the mortality rate with real-time inputs from sensors and wearables. For example, COVID-19 patient status and symptoms can be nearly observed by medical wearable as well as from their historical medical records in blockchain to predict whether they are in critical condition. If they are in an emergency or having a breathing problem, the smart devices have to pass the alert messages to nearby hospitals for providing the ambulance service. These integrated technologies can be used in pandemic to save the life. Moreover, in the future, people from any country can get a consultation from global experts without traveling to other countries for medical treatment with more improving technologies.

References

[1] Satoshi Nakamoto (2008). Bitcoin: A Peer-to-Peer Electronic Cash System. *Decentralized Business Review*, 21260.

[2] John Jumper, Kathryn Tunyasuvunakool, Pushmeet Kohli, et al. "Computational Predictions of Protein Structures Associated with COVID-19", 2020. www.deepmind.com/research/open-source/computational-predictions-of-protein-structuresassociated-with-COVID-19

[3] "Coronavirus Disease (COVID-19): Virus Evolution", December 2020 [online], Available: www.who.int/news-room/q-a-detail/sars-cov-2-evolution

[4] Toshendra K. Sharma, "How to Leverage Blockchain for Making Machine Learning Models More Accessible?", 2019 [online], Available: www.blockchain-council.org/blockchain/how-to-leverage-blockchain-for-making-machine-learning-models-more-accessible/

[5] Rim B. Fekih, Mariam Lahami, "Application of Blockchain Technology in Healthcare: A Comprehensive Study", International Conference on Smart Homes and Health Telematics, June 2020.

[6] "What is Blockchain Technology and How Does It Work?", April 1, 2021 [online], Available: www.simplilearn.com/tutorials/blockchain-tutorial/blockchain-technology

[7] Fei Jiang, Yong Jiang, Hui Zhi, Yi Dong, Hao Li, Sufeng Ma, Yilong Wang, Qiang Dong, Haipeng Shen, Yongjun Wang, "Artificial Intelligence in Healthcare: Past, Present and Future", Stroke Vasc Neurol 2017, doi:10.1136/svn-2017-000101.

[8] Jason Brownlee, "A Tour of Machine Learning Algorithms", in Machine Learning Algorithms, August 12, 2019 [online], Available: https://machinelearningmastery.com/a-tour-of-machine-learning-algorithms/

[9] Claire D. Costa, "A Tour of Machine Learning Algorithms", May 11, 2020 [online], Available: https://towardsdatascience.com/a-tour-of-machine-learning-algorithms-466b8bf75c0a

[10] Danai Khemasuwan, Jeffrey S. Sorensen, Henri G. Colt, "Artificial Intelligence in Pulmonary Medicine: Computer Vision, Predictive Model and COVID-19", Eur Respir Rev 2020, *29*: 200181, https://doi.org/10.1183/16000617.0181-2020

[11] Adriana Tomic, Ivan Tomic, Yael Rosenberg-Hasson, et al. SIMON, "An Automated Machine Learning System, Reveals Immune Signatures of Influenza Vaccine Responses", J Immunol 2019, *203*: 749–759.

[12] Sudeep Tanwar, Qasim Bhatia, Pruthvi Patel, Aparna Kumari, Pradeep K. Singh, Wei-Chiang Hong, "Machine Learning Adoption in Blockchain-Based Smart Applications: The Challenges, and a way Forward", IEEE Access, Special Section on Artificial Intelligence (AI)-Empowered Intelligent Transportation Systems, 2020.

[13] Tulin Ozturk, Muhammed Talo, Eylul A. Yildirim, et al. "Automated Detection of COVID-19 Cases Using Deep Neural Networks with X-Ray Images", Comput Biol Med 2020, *121*: 103792.

[14] Andrew W. Senior, Richard Evans, John Jumper, et al. "Improved Protein Structure Prediction Using Potentials from Deep Learning", Nature 2020, *577*: 706–710.

[15] Ahmad Alimadadi, Sachin Aryal, Ishan Manandhar, et al. "Artificial Intelligence and Machine Learning to Fight COVID-19", Physiol Genomics 2020, *52*: 200–202.

[16] "Blockchain in Healthcare and the Life Sciences" [online], Available: https://consensys.net/blockchain-use-cases/healthcare-and-the-life-sciences/

[17] "AI, Machine Learning, and Blockchain are Key for Healthcare Innovation", May 15, 2020 [online], Available: www.healtheuropa.eu/ai-machine-learning-and-blockchain-are-key-for-healthcare-innovation/99990/

[18] Yu R. Park, Eunsol Lee, Sungjun Park, Yura Lee, Jae-Ho Lee, "Is Blockchain Technology Suitable for Managing Personal Health Records? Mixed-Methods Study to Test Feasibility", J Med Internet Res 2019, *21*(2): e12533.

[19] Xiaobao Zhu, Jing Shi, Cuiyuan Lu, "Cloud Health Resource Sharing Based on Consensus-Oriented Blockchain Technology: Case Study on a Breast Tumor Diagnosis Service", J Med Internet Res 2019, *21*(7): e13767.

[20] Ariel Ekblaw, Asaph Azaria, John D. Halamka, Andrew Lippman, "A Case Study for Blockchain in Healthcare: "MedRec" Prototype for Electronic Health Records and Medical Research Data", published by IEEE, August 2016.

[21] Thomas F. Heston, "A Case Study in Blockchain Healthcare Innovation", April 28, 2020. Posted on Authorea November 13, 2017, [online], Available: https://doi.org/10.22541/au.151060471.1075595

[22] Federico Plantera, "Estonia's Minister of Health and Labour Explains Why the Future of Care is Digital", November 2018 [online], Available: https://e-estonia.com/minister-health-explains-future-care-digital/

[23] "e-Estonia Healthcare" [online], Available: https://e-estonia.com/solutions/healthcare/

[24] "Learning from the Estonian e-Health System", January 11, 2019 [online], Available: www.healtheuropa.eu/estonian-e-health-system/89750/

[25] Hanwen (Hava) Zhang, Zhe Yu, Sheng (Shawn) Gu, Ta Ting (Tina) JA, "Tackling COVID-19 Pandemic through Integrating Digital Technology and Public Health: Linking Experiences in China to the World", Rockefellerfoundation.org, accessh.org, August 2020.

[26] "Aarogya Setu" [online], Available: www.aarogyasetu.gov.in

[27] "From 'GoCoronaGo' to 'Sampark-o-Meter': IISc, IITs Develop Mobile Apps to Aid Covid-19 Fight" [online], Available: www.indiatoday.in/education-today/news/story/4-iits-iisc-create-mobile-apps-to-fight-covid-19-coronavirus-1665097-2020-04-09

[28] "Gainfy Healthcare Applications" [online], Available: https://tracxn.com/d/companies/gainfy.com

[29] Medicoin [online], Available: www.devteam.space/project/medicoin/

[30] Abdullah Albeyatti, Mo Tayeb, "Medicalchain", 2018 [online], Available: https://medicalchain.com/Medicalchain-Whitepaper-EN.pdf

[31] Jiang Li, "Three Challenges to Remote Patient Monitoring", June 11, 2018 [online], Available: www.healthcarebusinesstoday.com/three-challenges-to-remote-patient-monitoring/

[32] Gautam Srivastava, Ashutosh D. Dwivedi, Rajani Singh, "Automated Remote Patient Monitoring: Data Sharing and Privacy Using Blockchain", arXiv: 1811. 03417v1, October 30, 2018.

Index

A

Agglomerative 205, 213
Artificial bee colony 65, 78, 79
Artificial Intelligence 61, 91, 111, 200
Artificial neural network (ANN) 99, 102, 148, 163, 164, 206
Auto encoders 12, 121, 177, 182, 189, 194
Axon 164

B

Bacterial foraging 65, 66
Bayesian networks 114
Bias 204
Big Data Analytics 144, 145, 152, 154, 210
BlueDot 205
Boltzmann machine 118–120
Brain 143, 151, 163
Brain-computer interface 94, 163

C

Canonical correlation analysis 179
Classification 5, 16, 21, 36, 64, 183, 204
Classifier 5, 18, 59, 89, 94, 134, 139
Clustering 2, 81, 97, 149, 179, 203,
convolutional neural network 126, 133, 145, 146, 165, 189
Convolutional neural network (CNN) 126, 133, 145, 146, 165, 189
Correlation 8–12, 14, 92, 100
Correlation-based alignment 178, 179
Covariance matrix 91, 105, 106, 179
COVID-19 199, 201, 203, 204
Cross media retrieval 179, 187, 189, 190
Crossover networks 50, 51

D

DApps 201
Data representation 55, 82, 94, 143, 144
Declarative 37
Deep belief networks 149, 152

Deep learning 5, 6, 12, 16
Deep learning architectures 145, 194
Denoising 65–67, 72, 73
Dictionary learning 81, 86–89, 97, 108

E

Entity description 127, 133, 134

H

Hammersley-Clifford Theorem 118
Handcrafted features 5
Heuristic knowledge 38
Histogram of Oriented Gradient (HOG) 5

I

International Foundation of Integrated Care (IFIC) 209
Implicational networks 49
Independent component analysis 81, 94, 96
Inference algorithms 115
Internet of Things (IoT) 125–127, 131, 139

K

k-means 81, 89, 90, 97, 108, 203
Knowledge base 37, 138
Knowledge representation 113, 122

L

Latency 166, 171
Latent variable 114, 183, 185, 188
Leaky integrate-and-fire neuron 165
Learning networks 49, 50
Learning rule 100, 101
Linear embedding 92, 108, 204
Local binary pattern 5
Logic rule 167
Long-term memory (LSTM) 145

Milton Keynes UK
Ingram Content Group UK Ltd.
UKHW031532071024
449327UK00005B/119